Maid to
Order in
Hong Kong

Maid to Order in Hong Kong

Stories of Migrant Workers

SECOND EDITION

NICOLE CONSTABLE

Cornell University Press

Ithaca and London

First edition published 1997 by Cornell University Press
Second edition published 2007 by Cornell University Press
First printing, Cornell Paperbacks, 2007

Printed in the United States of America

Library of Congress Cataloging-in-Publication Data
Maid to order in Hong Kong: stories of migrant workers / Nicole Constable.—2nd ed.
  p. cm.
 Includes bibliographical references and index.
 ISBN-13: 978-0-8014-4647-4 (cloth : alk. paper)
 ISBN-13: 978-0-8014-7323-4 (pbk.: alk. paper)
  1. Women domestics—China—Hong Kong. 2. Alien labor, Philippine—China—Hong
Kong. 3. Alien labor, Indonesian—China—Hong Kong. 4. Filipinos—Employ-
ment—China—Hong Kong. 5. Indonesians—Employment—China—Hong
Kong. 6. Women alien labor—China—Hong Kong. I. Title.
 HD6072.2.H78C66 2007
 331.4'816404609599—dc22   2007013550

Cornell University Press strives to use environmentally
responsible suppliers and materials to the fullest extent
possible in the publishing of its books. Such materials include
vegetable-based, low-VOC inks and acid-free papers that are
recycled, totally chlorine-free, or partly composed of nonwood
fibers. For further information, visit our website at
www.cornellpress.cornell.edu.

Cloth printing   10 9 8 7 6 5 4 3 2 1
Paperback printing   10 9 8 7 6 5 4 3 2 1

CONTENTS

PREFACE TO THE SECOND EDITION

Since the publication of the first edition of this book I have been asked many times about the impact of 1997 on foreign domestic workers in Hong Kong, and about what has changed since I first conducted research on the topic in the mid-1990s. These questions prompted me to return to Hong Kong in 2005 and 2006 to see what had changed and to update my research.

This edition conveys some of the key changes that have taken place since July 1, 1997, when Hong Kong became a Special Administrative Region (SAR) of the People's Republic of China (PRC), since the Asian financial crisis of 1997–1998, and since the outbreak of Severe Acquired Respiratory Syndrome (SARS) in 2003. Although Hong Kong's change in political status is not the sole or even the primary cause of major changes that have taken place among domestic workers (i.e., some changes would have occurred even without the changeover), the year 1997 stands out in many people's minds and provides a significant point from which to ask "What has changed and why?"

The single most important and visible change among foreign domestic workers is the entry of tens of thousands of Indonesian women. In the early 1990s there were but a few thousand Indonesian domestic workers and well over 100,000 Filipinas. By 2006 there were close to 100,000 Indonesians, about 125,000 Filipinas, and several thousand more domestic workers from Thailand, India, Sri Lanka, and elsewhere. Whereas Filipinas congregate in Central District, especially in Statue Square and Chater Garden on their Sundays off, Indonesians now congregate in the thousands at Victoria Park in Causeway Bay. Every week they can be seen in small clusters chatting, singing, praying, eating, talking on cell phones—some wearing Muslim modest dress of headscarves and long gowns, and others dressed in baggy blue jeans and revealing tank tops dancing to hip hop music.

Another change involves migrant worker activism. Although it is still true that only a small minority of domestic workers are politically active in Hong Kong, they have become much more visible and more active since 1997. Whereas concerns with policies that impact domestic workers have prompted organized responses including marches and rallies from politically active domestic worker groups since at least the 1980s, by 2005 the scope and range of issues has grown to include much broader human rights and international development concerns. New coalitions that crosscut different nationalities of domestic workers have been established and alliances between migrant workers and locals are more in evidence.

What has not changed so drastically in recent years are the day-to-day experiences of foreign domestic workers in Hong Kong. Although the names and the nationalities of domestic workers have changed, the minimum allowable wage has gone down, and some specific employment policies have been altered, the individual experiences and the challenges that they face in their working lives—whether they are Filipina or Indonesian, Thai, Sri Lankan, or Indian—remain in many ways the same as a decade earlier. My main argument about the multiplicity of power and the various forms of discipline, pleasure, resistance, and accommodation among domestic workers therefore still holds. What is clearer to me today, however, is how the situation in Hong Kong is but one small part of the wider picture of globalization and the inequalities of worldwide gendered labor migration.

Since the publication of the first edition of this book in 1997, gender and globalization has become an increasingly hot topic in anthropology and in the social sciences. Scholars have also produced a rich and burgeoning multidisciplinary literature on domestic workers in and beyond Asia. Although I do not attempt to provide an exhaustive review of the new literature, I have added new references, especially those that expand or elaborate on my findings or point in new important and comparative directions.

Field research and interviews for this new edition were conducted in Hong Kong in May and June of 2005, December 2005, and in June and July of 2006. During those visits I became reacquainted with staff members from the Mission for Filipino Migrant Workers and other nongovernmental organizations (NGOs), and with Filipino activists. I met only a few of the domestic workers I had known a decade earlier, but learned about several who had returned permanently to the Philippines, others who had gone on to work as care providers in Canada, and a few who had gone to Taiwan and Macao. I talked with many domestic workers I had not known before, but whose mothers, aunts, or sisters had worked there during my earlier visits.

In 1993 and 1994 I volunteered at the Mission for Filipino Migrant Workers. At the time the vast majority of its clients were Filipinas. By 2005 most clients were from Indonesia, and the process had begun to officially drop "Filipino" from the name to become the Mission for Migrant Workers. In the summer of 2005, I volunteered at the Asian Migrant Centre, which had grown from a small grassroots Hong Kong–focused organization in the early 1990s, to a much more globally oriented migrant worker organization. Staff at the Mission, the Asia Pacific Mission for Migrants (formerly the Asia Pacific Mission for Migrant Filipinos), and the Asian Migrant Centre helped to put me in touch with domestic workers and migrant worker activists of various nationalities, especially from the Philippines and Indonesia. I visited Sunday classes and group activities for Indonesian migrant workers that took place in a small flat in Causeway Bay run by members of the Hong Kong Coalition of Indonesian Migrant Workers Organization (KOT-KIHO). In Victoria Park I visited four groups belonging to the Association of Indonesian Migrant Workers (ATKI)—the mobile counseling group, the cultural group, the religious group, and the lesbian group. I attended a play performed by Filipina domestic workers who took Sunday classes at the Philippine Women's University, and visited a Filipino arts festival that included a small display of illustrations by domestic workers. I attended the first Filipino Women Migrant Workers Summit; was a participant-observer at numerous protests, marches, candlelight vigils, concerts, religious rallies, and public performances; and visited two domestic shelters for laid-off workers.

The stories that the Filipina and Indonesian residents of the shelters told me about their conflicts with employers, physical abuse and unemployment, and homesickness and loneliness were strikingly similar to the stories I had heard a decade earlier. Staff at the shelters suggested that the greater number of shelters (now close to twenty) and the regular stream of residents were not necessarily indicative of increasing abuses by employers but of the growing awareness and assertiveness on the part of domestic workers—especially among Indonesians. Whereas the vast majority of the women I had encountered in the shelters or seeking assistance from volunteers and NGOs in the 1990s were Filipino, now they were mostly Indonesian. These women readily availed themselves of the growing support structures, and many of them expressed a strong commitment to asserting their own rights, to raising the consciousness of fellow migrant workers in Hong Kong, and to carrying on the struggle for workers' rights when they returned home.

In December 2005, during the People's Action Week organized by the Hong Kong People's Alliance (HKPA) against the World Trade Organization (WTO), I visited Hong Kong with my eldest son, Peter, a budding photojournalist of fifteen. Many migrant worker groups joined the HKPA and participated in the eight days of protest against the WTO's Sixth Ministerial Conference. They constituted the vast majority of the protestors, especially during the two Sunday marches and rallies. This weeklong protest, like many other rallies and protest actions, was indicative of some very important political shifts in the concerns and rhetoric of domestic worker activism and also of the new ethnic and international alliances that developed in recent years within and beyond the migrant worker community.

The new material in this edition comes from participant observation, archival research, published sources, and from interviews and informal conversations with Filipina, Indonesian, and other foreign domestic workers, activists, employers, and NGO and government staff. Although I draw attention to the phenomenal growth in numbers of Indonesian domestic workers in Hong Kong, and to the burgeoning research on Indonesian domestic workers and workers of other nationalities, the bulk of the stories in this book are still about Filipinas.[1] Nevertheless, Indonesian and other foreign and local domestic workers provide an important point of comparison with Filipinas, not only in the imagination of employers but also because of some broad cultural differences among them.

Whereas most Filipinas are Roman Catholic (some are Protestant and a small minority are Muslim), most Indonesians are Muslim. On the whole Filipinas are also older, more likely to be married, and more highly educated than Indonesian domestic workers. Filipinas have also been in Hong Kong longer and have had more opportunity to develop support networks. Such differences are no doubt related to the greater problems

---

1. Amy Sim has conducted important extensive dissertation research on Indonesian domestic workers in Hong Kong. See Sim 2007; see also Sim 2003; Wee and Sim 2004, 2005. For detailed research on Indian domestic workers in Hong Kong, see James Keezhangatte 2004 and 2005.

faced by Indonesian domestic workers, including much higher rates of underpayment than among Filipinas and much higher rates of overcharging by employment recruitment agencies. The differences in the problems they face, however, are more in degree and frequency than in kind, with the exception of problems relating to Muslim dress, prayer, or food. Filipinas do encounter conflicts with their employers relating to dress codes and food, but Indonesians face unique problems when their employers prohibit them from wearing modest dress *(hijab)* while at home, forbid them from participating in the daily rituals of Muslim prayer, or require them to cook pork. Such issues and others relating to recruitment, public protest and activism, and pleasure are alluded to but warrant further study.

Small changes, citations, and updates have been incorporated in most of the chapters. New material pertaining to recent patterns of labor migration is incorporated into Chapter 2, "Global Themes and Local Patterns." Chapter 4, "The Trade in Workers," includes a new discussion of the recruitment of Indonesian workers; Chapter 6, "Disciplined Migrants, Docile Workers," includes an update on some rules and policies; Chapter 7, "Resistance and Protest," provides new examples of Indonesian protests and demonstrations after 1997; and Chapter 9, "Pleasure and Power," discusses new worker coalitions and post-1997 continuity and change.

I AM AGAIN deeply grateful to many of the same people who helped me with this project over a decade ago and to many new people whom I have met and learned from in the interim years. My admiration for migrant workers and activists (and especially those who are both) has multiplied as I have seen the energy they devote and the scarce resources they mobilize to fight for their vision of a just world. In the face of scholars and researchers such as myself who have repeatedly taken up their time, asking naive questions and mining for information and knowledge that will fuel academic books and papers, many individuals have exhibited remarkable patience, wisdom, and generosity. It is gratifying to know that my work has helped to motivate people to visit the mission and other migrant worker organizations and to donate their time and other resources. I hope this will continue. My own intermittent volunteer work, minor financial contributions, expressions of solidarity, and the small degree of publicity that my work might generate cannot begin to repay my debt to them.

In particular Cynthia Tellez, Corazon Cañete, and Rodolfo (Jun) Cañete have continued to offer great insight, inspiration, and friendship. Eni Lestari, Dolores Baladares, Eman Villanueva, and Sumiati, migrant workers who are also admirable leaders, and Ramon Bultron, Norman Carnay,

Christina Defalco, Peggy Lee, Nurul Qoiriah, Edwina Santoyo, and Rex Varona, were most helpful, sharing information and providing invaluable contacts. Amy Sim, James Keezhangatte, and Sealing Cheng—a new generation of scholars—provided rich food for thought and good company. I am grateful to Elizabeth Tang and Ip Pui Yu of the Hong Kong Confederation of Trade Unions for information regarding labor organization and activism in Hong Kong, and to Do Pang Wai Yee and Heidi Chow of the Labour Department for providing me with updated government information and alerting me to diverse perspectives regarding foreign workers in Hong Kong.

At the University of Pittsburgh, I appreciate the generous support I have received from the Office of the Dean at the School of Arts and Sciences, the Women's Studies Program, and the Asian Studies Center at the University Center for International Studies; without it I could not have carried out the second phase of research and would not have had the time to write. Runette Brown and Philippa Carter provided much appreciated technical assistance. I am grateful to Peter Wissoker, editor at Cornell University Press, and to Pamela Myers Moro and Marc Moskowitz for their support, encouragement, and constructive critique.

Unknowingly, Nathaniel and Peter Constable Alter again provided much of the motivation for careful time management during both the research and writing phases of this project. Joe Alter, ever a pillar of strength and inspiration, no longer pushes the double stroller, but he still does more than pull his weight. Peter provided a number of the new photographs for this volume and has helped me to see migrant worker protests through fresh eyes.

NICOLE CONSTABLE

Pittsburgh, Pennsylvania, 2006

PREFACE TO THE FIRST EDITION

My interest in Filipina domestic workers began in 1987 when I was conducting research on Hakka Chinese Christian identity (Constable 1994). Su-lin, a friend who lived in the village where I was working, took me to visit her elder sister, Su-lan, who lived and worked on Hong Kong island.[1] As our double-decker bus wound its way along the hilly slopes, Su-lin explained to me that Su-lan and her husband employed a *banmui* ("Philippine girl") to care for their son and clean their flat while they both worked full time. "Filipinas," Su-lin stated bluntly and categorically, "are very stupid." She saw my shock but did not retract her statement. Instead, she defended it. Su-lin said these "maids" understood little Chinese, could not follow the simplest instructions, and were "dirty and lazy." She believed, moreover, that Filipinas' morals were questionable. "Why else," she asked rhetorically, "would they willingly leave children and husbands behind in the Philippines?"

The eventual course of my conversation with Su-lin is not as important as the superiority and racism she so blatantly and unselfconsciously expressed and the impression they made on me. I became interested in the attitudes of the Chinese toward foreign domestic workers and in the contrast that they so often evoked between the "superior" Chinese domestic workers of the past and the "inferior Foreign Domestic Helpers" of today. I began to

1. All names are pseudonyms.

wonder how typical Su-lin's attitude was and what life was like for the Filipina domestic worker who worked for Su-lan. I later learned that she had a master's degree, had once worked as a schoolteacher, and had three small children cared for by relatives and by the young "helper" she employed back in the Philippines.

EARLY IN the summer of 1993, accompanied by my husband, Joe, and my two children (both under three at the time), I began the field research for this book. During the first two months of our stay, we sublet a modern but minuscule 450-square-foot flat on Queen's Road West, in Sai Ying Pun, one of the oldest Chinese working-class neighborhoods on Hong Kong island. The flat was ideally located a half-hour walk or a fifteen-minute bus ride from Central District, where Filipina domestic workers congregate, especially on Sundays, in large numbers. It was just two blocks away from a shelter for Filipinas who had no place to live because their contracts had been terminated without notice or because they were waiting for their cases to appear before the Labour Tribunal.

Upon our arrival at the flat we were surprised to learn that our exorbitant rent (by U.S. standards) included the part-time services of Acosta, a Filipina domestic worker. Given the topic of my research, I felt uncomfortable at the idea that I had—even indirectly—hired a domestic worker. Gradually my guilt feelings were overcome by a sense of good fortune. I learned a lot from Acosta, and she served as an entree into this research.

Like tens of thousands of other foreign domestic workers in Hong Kong who are officially on full-time contracts with a single employer, Acosta illegally worked part-time, or in the popular parlance of the time, did "aerobics." She commuted from Lamma Island—almost an hour away by ferry—to Sai Ying Pun several times a week. On the first day we met, she was prepared to clean the flat twice a week for two hours each time, as she had for Ann, the woman from whom we sublet, and as she did for her many other employers.[2] At first Acosta seemed slightly suspicious of an employer—albeit a surrogate one—who wanted her to sit and talk rather than work, but she quickly adjusted to the situation. When I explained that I wanted to write a book about Filipina domestic workers, she flatly

2. Like many of the single professionals Acosta worked for, Ann lived alone in a small flat and did not need to hire a full-time worker. As we later surmised, Ann had arranged for Acosta to work for us to ensure that the flat would be kept in reasonable shape and that Acosta's valuable services would continue in the fall. Although many women do part-time household work, few are willing to work for as few hours a week, or for as low wages, as Acosta, who charged as little as HK$35 (about US$4.50) per hour.

informed me that she would be an excellent subject: She had worked in Hong Kong for almost fifteen years, for many different Chinese employers, and other domestic workers often sought her advice because she really knew "the ropes."

As long as the flat was reasonably tidy when she arrived, Acosta was extremely pleased to talk. So each Monday and Thursday morning before she came, Joe would cart Peter and Nathaniel off to a playground or an air-conditioned shopping mall in the double stroller, and I would quickly scrub the bathroom, wash the dishes, pick up the toys, sweep and mop the floor. Occasionally Acosta and I would spend fifteen or twenty minutes straightening up the flat together, and sometimes she would insist on ironing while we talked. Although in the United States Joe and I were not in the habit of ironing many of our clothes—particularly not the children's underwear—Acosta insisted that we do so. If we didn't, she explained, in Hong Kong's tropical climate, the children would get "the itchies." Usually we would sit down at ten o'clock with my tape recorder, a cup of coffee, and a pastry, and she would tell me her news, information, and gossip. She brought letters and photographs from home, of her children, the house she had built, and the jitney bought with her remittances. She told me about her husband's infidelity in her absence, her concerns about her son's education, and her reluctance to allow her teenage daughter to come to work as a "helper" in Hong Kong. She discussed her techniques for dealing with difficult employers, her concerns about her health and appearance, and her pleasure when she found a good bargain in Hong Kong and returned home once a year laden with gifts for her family. She also described her anxiety about going home "for good." She had been away so long that she had difficulty envisioning her permanent role there. Her yearly visits were "more like a honeymoon than real life."

On several Sundays in a row, Acosta and I met at "the square"—Statue Square, a small park in the heart of Central District. There, opposite the "black statue," across the small footbridge where Filipinas from the province of Nueva Vizcaya congregated, she introduced me to Linda, Rina, and other friends and relatives. In her early forties, somewhat older than the average domestic worker, Acosta was very outgoing and had no qualms about approaching people she did not know. She would initiate conversations with women by saying, "This is my friend, and she is writing a book about the problems of Filipinas in Hong Kong." Then she would ask them about their work, their relationships with their employers, and their lives back home. Although Acosta's was not the description of my work I would have proffered—and I always pointed out that I was not just interested in "problems"—this approach provided an opening for dozens of conversations and informal interviews.

Women I talked to in the square, along Chater Road, and in Chater Garden sometimes began our conversations with a barrage of complaints about their work. I was told sad, poignant, and funny stories about ugly, greedy, jealous, and mean employers who shouted and criticized too much, demanded eighteen hours of work a day, made workers sleep on the floor, or provided only leftovers for them to eat. Occasionally I was told of employers who were physically or sexually abusive. Tears and other displays of emotion were not uncommon, even with women I was meeting for the first time. I was often struck by their willingness to bring up topics that might be considered very personal: homesickness, financial difficulties, bad marriages, unfaithful lovers, and a variety of other personal tragedies. I was also impressed by their strength, friendliness, warmth, and humor. On several occasions I was told point-blank that Filipinos are "cheerful and happy people" and that "no matter how serious our problems may be, we still laugh." As I walked around in the humid heat of the summer, looking for Acosta or someone else I knew, I was sometimes approached by Filipinas who asked if I could hire them or who pleaded with me to introduce them to employers. Their desperation sometimes left me feeling quite helpless.

For several weeks I conducted informal interviews and conversations with women I had met in the square on my own or with Acosta's help. On weekdays I also began to visit domestic workers' organizations, including the Asian Migrant Centre, the Asian Domestic Workers Union, and United Filipinos in Hong Kong (UNIFIL). Several of these organizations ran shelters. At each shelter I visited I interviewed residents, and at each organization I conducted interviews with the director or chairperson and members. I also began to work as a volunteer at the Mission for Filipino Migrant Workers. The mission became a central focus of my research and the main site for my "participant observation." Some weeks I spent thirty or forty hours there, interviewing women, typing and editing their letters to the Immigration and Labour Departments, looking up rules and regulations, or just listening.

The mission office stayed open for long hours every day of the week, and the Filipino staff and volunteers who worked there were extremely welcoming. On weekends, crowds of women waiting their turn for advice and consultations overflowed out the doors of the small offices. Through the women I met there, including other volunteers (most of whom were Filipina domestic workers at the time), I developed a somewhat different sense of the Filipino community in Hong Kong than I had from Acosta and her friends. Not only did I meet women with extremely serious problems, but I also met women who were actively involved in local politics and devoted to improving the situation for domestic workers. Some of these women were quite different from Acosta's friends and acquaintances, whose attitudes seemed far more fatalistic and accommodating.

Acosta was different from most of the volunteers I got to know at the mission. As she said, she knew the ropes (without having studied legal and paralegal advice booklets). She was bright, experienced, and well aware of the dangers of domestic work and the risk she took doing illegal work and signing a "bogus" contract. Acosta believed that she had the "wits" to pull it all off. She did not tell her friends about her "aerobics." "You never know when someone will get angry or jealous and tell the wrong person," she said. Nor did she tell her part-time employers that she was not a permanent Hong Kong resident and was therefore working illegally. During her first five years in Hong Kong she worked for one full-time employer and did just a few odd jobs on the side. Then she decided to play the game by her own rules, to "get what I can, while I can, and then leave." She was an opportunist and an independent player. She never joined any Filipina organizations because she felt they were not necessary for those who took precautions and behaved prudently. She had been careful, but she knew she had also been very fortunate.

Other women I met in the square, many of them through Acosta's networks—such as Linda, Rina, and their "crowd"—were involved in church activities, in "native place" associations, and in escapist entertainment. In times of difficulty Linda and Rina were more likely to turn to prayer and religion for reassurance, and they urged their friends to do likewise. They spent some of their time off inviting other domestic workers to join in their Seventh Day Adventist activities. They claimed to have little use for unions and said that they felt put off by the plain looking T-shirts, blue jeans, and shorts and the "unadorned" look of many of the women who participate in union activities. Rina agreed with a woman I spoke to who was sitting on a bench in Chater Garden, who said she was "embarrassed" by a protest of about five hundred domestic workers going on nearby. When I asked what she thought about the demands for higher wages, her friend answered for her: "If you raise the minimum wage, we may have no more jobs, because Chinese employers will no longer be able to afford helpers. Then what will our own families do?"

Elsa and Belle, sisters who did factory work in Manila before they came to Hong Kong, were volunteers at the mission on their days off. Unlike Acosta, Rina, or Linda, they were politically active and involved in a variety of domestic worker organizations. They were critical of what they saw as the fatalistic apathy of the majority of their fellow domestic workers. They criticized Filipinas who "waste their time" gossiping and complaining in the square but "do nothing about it." Cathy and Dally, two other women I met at the mission, were initially drawn to mission and UNIFIL activities when they experienced crises with their employers. Others, like Belle, were already active in labor unions in the Philippines or, like Elsa and Jane, joined because they felt they had a social responsibility to improve the situation for other domestic workers: for their daughters, their cousins, and their younger sisters who were also coming to Hong Kong to work.

Acosta, Elsa, Belle, Rina, and others whose experiences are at the core of this study should not be reduced to fixed "types." The tendencies and attitudes they expressed were complex and contradictory. Their views might fluctuate in the course of a day, or shift over the years with their work conditions and experiences. Rina and her friends—who often appeared extremely passive and looked for religious activities or sports events and entertainment to get their minds "off work" and to make their time in Hong Kong "pass more quickly"—were not as innocent as they sometimes appeared. Acosta, who took such pride in her know-how and independence, made a final point of getting the names of several women I knew at the mission before I left Hong Kong "just in case" she ever needed them. Elsa and Belle were adamantly fighting for social change; yet their confidence sometimes wavered, and at times they wondered out loud about romantic fairy-tale endings.

As of December 1995, according to the Hong Kong Departments of Labour and Immigration, the number of "Foreign Domestic Helpers" in Hong Kong exceeded 150,000. This figure included about 20,000 workers from Thailand, Indonesia, India, Sri Lanka, and Nepal, and over 130,000 workers (nearly all women) from the Philippines. The number of Filipina "domestic workers" (as most of the politically active Filipinas in Hong Kong prefer to be called) increased exponentially from just a few hundred in the 1970s to well over 100,000 in the early 1990s. These women are part of a growing transnational labor force who have left their own families behind in order to earn money by cleaning, cooking, and caring for the children of their employers.

Filipina domestic workers in Hong Kong, unlike Chinese domestic workers in the past, are not differentiated from their employers simply by economic class and status; they are also distinguished by ethnic and national identity and by their legal status as temporary migrants. Their position as outsiders who are unfamiliar with local customs and generally speak no Chinese and as members of a minority group in a low-status occupation has a bearing on many of their experiences in Hong Kong. It severely restricts their ability to improve their circumstances. Local forms of xenophobia, occupational and gender stereotypes, attitudes about ethnic, racial, and cultural differences, as well as local laws and government policies, all contribute to the difficulties faced by foreign domestic workers in their day-to-day lives.

This book is an ethnographic and historical account of the lives of Filipina domestic workers in Hong Kong. It is about the forms of control or discipline that Filipina domestic workers experience in their dealings with recruitment and placement agencies in the Philippines and in Hong Kong, with employers, and with government bureaucracy, rules, and regulations. It is also about the multiplicity of ways that foreign domestic workers respond to such discipline. Although Chinese employers constitute an important part of this book, the primary focus is on the perspectives and experiences of domestic workers within the wider cultural, economic, and historical context. The behavior of employers is seen mainly through the eyes of domestic workers.

Much of the material presented in this book was gathered during the summer and fall of 1993 and the summer of 1994 from conversations and interviews with domestic workers, Chinese employers, employment agency staff, migrant association leaders and volunteers, and government personnel. In addition to oral sources, I draw on archival materials, popular literature, editorials, and articles in local magazines, newspapers, and newsletters—by and about foreign domestic workers. I am fortunate to have access to large-scale, comprehensive quantitative studies conducted among Filipina domestic workers in Hong Kong (e.g., AMC 1991; French 1986a, b). These provide important background and useful "facts and figures" to substantiate observations of social trends and patterns that might otherwise appear far more speculative or impressionistic.

Over the past several years, I have had opportunities to see domestic workers on the job; I have observed their interactions with their employers and visited "servant quarters." Although I made a point of interviewing Chinese employers (including members of the Hong Kong Employers of Overseas Domestic Helpers Association), the vast majority of my interviews have been with employees. Most of my interactions with domestic workers took place outside the homes where they work. Many of my interviews were conducted with Filipinas whom I met at the Mission for Filipino Migrant Workers (often called simply "the mission") and at the offices of unions and organizations that advocate for domestic workers.

Roughly half of the workers I came to know had recently experienced fairly serious problems with their employers. In this sense they might be considered atypical; yet their difficulties do not make them less important or worthy of study. On the contrary, the most extreme and tragic cases often yield the most important insights. Many foreign domestic workers in Hong Kong experience serious difficulties, and recent surveys suggest that cases of maltreatment and abuse are on the rise (MFMW 1993a, b; AMC 1991). Many of the severe and less severe problems that domestic workers face, moreover, are common enough to suggest underlying cultural patterns rather than idiosyncrasy. Some of them are the same ones Chinese domestic workers experienced in the past. Yet most Filipinas I spoke to, regardless of the difficulties they had personally experienced, still considered the work conditions and salaries in Hong Kong relatively good, especially compared to Singapore and other parts of Asia and the Middle East.

THE FIRST three chapters of this book provide theoretical and historical background and place Filipina domestic workers within the context of a wider political economy. Chapter 1 locates this book in relation to the literature on household workers, power, resistance, accommodation, and docility. Chapter 2 describes some of the factors that have created an "export market" in Filipino workers and the great demand for foreign workers in Hong Kong. Chapter 3 describes several types of Chinese domestic workers in Hong Kong's past—slaves, *muijai, amahs*—with whom foreign domestic workers are often implicitly or explicitly compared. It asks how different categories of household workers are culturally, historically, and discursively linked with their predecessors and how particular local, cultural, and historical factors have influenced attitudes toward Filipina domestic workers and their treatment in Hong Kong today.

The three core chapters turn to the issue of discipline and look at the variety of ways that domestic workers are controlled and their bodies disciplined by employment agencies and the recruitment process (Chapter 4), by employers and the members of their households (Chapter 5), and by state, government, and legal policies and regulations in Hong Kong (Chapter 6). Although these various "agents" share certain objectives, their goals and methods are not identical. They represent competing and coexisting modes of domination and illustrate the multifariousness of power. These three chapters focus mainly on pressures that create or compel women to become docile workers and migrants; yet they also show that domestic workers are not completely powerless passive subjects. Individual domestic workers may often feel helpless, or ill fated, or forced by economic need to become domestic workers in Hong Kong, but they are active—as individuals—in the process of migration and employment, and they respond to control and body discipline in a variety of ways.

The three final chapters focus on resistance and docility. In Chapter 7 I describe a number of ways that domestic workers can be said to resist oppression and contest the identity assigned to them. Resistance may take the form of legal action or political protests, or the means may be less overt and confrontational—for example, jokes and pranks. Analysis of domestic workers' use of household and public space illustrates not only the hierarchical nature of relationships between employers and workers but also important everyday forms of resistance. Domestic workers, however, do not consistently or continuously oppose domination. In many cases, probably most of the time, they accept the rules and behave as they are instructed. As I illustrate in Chapter 8, they may also willingly impose strict forms of discipline on themselves. Yet "quietness," deference, and self-discipline should not automatically be "taken to reflect consensus to their condition" (Gaventa 1980:252; Scott 1990); nor should docility, self-discipline, and apparent support of the existing system of power necessarily be read as a sign of "false consciousness" (Abu-Lughod 1990:47; Scott 1990). In the final chapter I discuss the relationship between resistance and docility. Self-discipline, I maintain, often undermines overt attempts to bring about social change, but self-discipline can also be a source of satisfaction and "pleasure" (Foucault 1978, 1985). Attention to the concept of self-discipline—and to the ways in which extreme forms of self-discipline coexist with both active and passive forms of resistance—complicates the image of domestic workers and enables us to avoid the pitfall of depicting them as either class conscious or unaware, either involved in active protest or passively acquiescent.

THERE are many individuals and organizations that I owe an enormous debt of thanks. Among the Filipinas and Filipinos in Hong Kong who not only made this project possible but also made it enjoyable and meaningful are Cynthia Tellez, Jun Tellez, Azon Cañete, Jun Cañete, Malou Paez, Irma Laguindam, Imelda Laguindam, and many "anonymous" volunteers and clients at the Mission for Filipino Migrant Workers. Marrz Balaoro and

Connie Regalado of United Filipinos in Hong Kong, Remy Borlongan and Sirinya Chernklang at the Asian Domestic Workers Union, Mayan Villalba at the Asian Migrant Centre, and Melville Boase deserve special thanks. These individuals, along with Nars, Jane, Sunny, Leony, Bella, and many others I got to know in the course of this project, have earned my heartfelt appreciation, admiration, and respect.

Once again I am grateful for my affiliation with the Chinese University of Hong Kong, which allowed me access to libraries, special records, and faculty members, including Richard Man-wui Ho and Cheung Tak-sing, who were most generous with their help. My research has also benefited from the assistance of Mimi Chan, Elizabeth Sinn, and Rita Mak at Hong Kong University; Maria Jaschok, George Edwards, and Andrew Byrnes of the Hong Kong University Foreign Domestic Helper Project; Diva de Vera arid Linda Layosa of *Tinig Filipino;* Alfred Wing Kit Chan of the Labour Department; Virginia Son, Labour Attache of the Philippine Consulate General; Carrie Man Yee Cheng at the Catholic Centre; Betty Yung and Joseph Law of the Hong Kong Employers of Overseas Domestic Helpers Association. Western Michigan University's Faculty Research and Creative Activities Support Fund provided funding for an early stage of this research; the Asian Studies Program and the China Council of the University of Pittsburgh helped offset costs associated with the preparation of the final manuscript. I appreciate their backing.

I thank Sage Publications for permission to reprint parts of my article "Jealousy, Chastity, and Abuse: Chinese Maids and Foreign Helpers in Hong Kong," which appeared in *Modern China* 22, no. 4 (1996): 448–79, copyright © 1996 by Sage Publications, reprinted by permission of Sage Publications.

Friends and colleagues including Nancy Abelmann, Jeanne Bergman, Marianne Constable, and Harry Sanabria have lent varieties of support. My debt to Rubie S. Watson and James L. "Woody" Watson for helpful critiques and moral support has increased exponentially over the years. Neil Bose provided valuable bibliographic assistance. Carl T. Smith, Sister Ann Grey, and James Hayes have provided a wealth of information and suggestions, and Preeta Law and Suresh Unny offered input and distraction during a formative stage of this project. Although this is not the book he would have written, I thank Roger Sanjek for his comments and suggestions. I am especially grateful to Peter Agree at Cornell University Press for his kind and unwavering support.

Finally, I thank Joseph Alter and Peter and Nathaniel Constable Alter for sharing the adventures of fieldwork and tolerating the mundane aspects of academic life in good spirits. Peter and Nathaniel have taught me how difficult it can be to leave children behind, even for a short time. Joe provided expert childcare, housework, and emotional and intellectual labor at the most crucial times.

NICOLE CONSTABLE

Pittsburgh, Pennsylvania, 1996

ABBREVIATIONS

ADWU	Asian Domestic Workers Union
AMC	Asian Migrant Centre
AMCB	Asian Migrant Coordinating Body
APMM	Asia Pacific Mission for Migrants
APMMF	Asia Pacific Mission for Migrant Filipinos
ATKI-HK	Association of Indonesian Migrant Workers, Hong Kong (*Asosiasi Tenaga Kerja Indonesia, Hong Kong*)
CIIR	Catholic Institute for International Relations
CMR	Coalition for Migrants' Rights
FDH	Foreign Domestic Helper
FEONA-HK	Far East Overseas Nepalese Association of Hong Kong
HK-CS	Hong Kong Census and Statistics Department
HKCTU	Hong Kong Confederation of Trade Unions
HKEODHA	Hong Kong Employers of Overseas Domestic Helpers Association
HKG	Hong Kong Government
HK-ID	Hong Kong Immigration Department
HKIHM	Hong Kong Institute of Household Management, Manila
HK-LD	Hong Kong Labour Department
HKLDWGU	Hong Kong Local Domestic Workers General Union
HKPA	Hong Kong People's Alliance against the World Trade Organization

HKS	*Hongkong Standard*
HK-SC	Hong Kong Supreme Court
HKU-FDH	Hong Kong University Foreign Domestic Helper Project
HK$	Hong Kong Dollar. (In 1983 the Hong Kong dollar was pegged to the U.S. dollar and the exchange rate has remained at approximately HK$7.8 equal to US$1.00 ever since.)
HSW	Household Service Worker
ILO	International Labor Organization
IMWU	Indonesian Migrant Workers Union
IOM	International Organization for Migration
KOTKIHO	Hong Kong Coalition of Indonesian Migrant Workers Organization
LDH	Local Domestic Helper
LegCo	Legislative Council
MFMW	Mission for Filipino Migrant Workers until 2006, then Mission for Migrant Workers
NGO	Nongovernmental Organization
OFW	Overseas Filipino Workers
PRC	People's Republic of China
POEA	Philippine Overseas Employment Administration
SARS	Severe Acquired Respiratory Syndrome
SAR	Special Administrative Region
SCMP	*South China Morning Post*
TF	*Tinig Filipino*
WTO	World Trade Organization
UNIFIL	United Filipinos in Hong Kong

Maid to
Order in
Hong Kong

1 | FOREIGN AND DOMESTIC IN HONG KONG

Sundays in Central District are a spectacular sight. There in Hong Kong's most celebrated financial district, amidst awesome high-rise structures, towering hotels, and dwarfed colonial government buildings, crowds of domestic workers, mainly from the Philippines, but also from other regions of South- and Southeast Asia, gather to socialize, to attend to personal matters, and to escape the confines of their employers' homes and their mundane weekly routines of domestic work.

On Sundays in Central the noise is louder, the colors brighter, and the crowds more overwhelmingly female than on other days of the week. Filipinas who gather in Statue Square on Sundays and public holidays have been described as "one of the most colourful and cheerful features of life in Hongkong" (Donnithorne 1992), "the vibrant colours of their plumage . . . as striking to the eye as their incessant chatter is to the ear" (Flage 1987). Foreign domestic workers line the sidewalks and elevated walkways that connect the Central Post Office to the Star Ferry and Blake's Pier, and they gather in groups under the shade of the Hong Kong and Shanghai Bank—one of Hong Kong's most famous capitalist monuments—across the road from the square. On hot and steamy summer days, scores of women cluster under the trees in Chater Garden, along Battery Path, and in the parking lots and roads leading up toward Saint John's Cathedral, Hong Kong Park, and Government

House. Along Chater Road, which is closed to traffic on Sundays, they sit in the shadow of five-star hotels and designer boutiques, picnicking on straw mats, blankets, or newspapers, contributing to the festive atmosphere.

The crowd, though it might look to outsiders like random clusters of disarray, has a clear logic to those who are familiar with it. Domestic workers of different nationalities regularly congregate in specific locations. Many women from South Asia—India, Bangladesh, and Sri Lanka for example—gather in parks and gardens along the edge of Tsim Sha Tsui and Tsim Sha Tsui East, across the harbor from Central District in Kowloon, the region where many of their South Asian employers live and work. Women from Southeast Asia—Thailand, Malaysia, or Indonesia—are more likely to be found in Central District along the waterfront parks near the Central Post Office and Blake's Pier. By the late 1990s, Victoria Park in Causeway Bay had become the main place for Indonesians to congregate and Muslim domestic workers of many different nationalities clustered near Kowloon Park and the Kowloon Mosque. Filipinas have long clustered mainly in Statue Square, along Chater Road, in Chater Garden and up the hill toward Hong Kong Park. Different Philippine regional and dialect groups occupy different parts of Central District. Ilocanos, for example, congregate under the pavilion behind the "black statue" and those from Nueva Vizcaya are under the northeastern pavilion. Increasingly, they also congregate in parks and public spaces that are closer to the places where they live and work, in Kowloon and in the New Territories (a 398-square-mile region that adjoins mainland China).

On other days of the week one also finds dozens or even hundreds of domestic workers in Central, and especially in the square, but only a fraction of the Sunday crowd. On weekdays there are those who are allowed to go out after they finish their work, others who are permitted to stop by the square on their way to or from an outing with their charges, and mainly those who have been assigned a day other than Sunday as their rest day. Although a domestic worker has little choice but to accept whatever rest day her employer assigns, a day off other than Sunday is considered unfortunate, a conscious ploy on the part of the employer to keep a worker "in the dark" and away from friends and relatives, most of whom have Sundays off. A different day off means a worker cannot meet friends as easily or attend church or other worship services. Nor can she participate in migrant organizations, such as regional "circles," clubs, or Philippine associations, or join in the rallies or informational drives organized by the Asian Domestic Workers Union, United Filipinos in Hong Kong, and other groups.

On Sundays there is an unmistakable tide of Filipinas on all forms of public transportation that heads toward Central from the far corners of Hong Kong and the New Territories. They create a festival atmosphere that transforms the place. On weekdays there is less going on in the square, and the domestic workers who go there are counterbalanced by tourists and by local Chinese and westerners who also work, shop, and eat in Central District. But on Sundays, as one Filipina described it with a sigh, Central becomes "a corner of the Philippines transplanted into Hong Kong." Teddy Arellano, a staff member at the Asia Pacific Mission for Migrant Filipinos, described it: "Statue Square has become a haven for migrant workers from the Philippines and other countries. Especially for Filipinos, it has become . . . their 'Home away from home.' As they congregate, it brings back a slice of life from our country, which in a way alleviates their loneliness and homesickness. It has become an emotional blanket for many as it fortifies and recharges them from the rigours of the week's work" (Arellano 1992). A Hong Kong Filipino newspaper advises those who feel lonely to go to the square. There, "you can feel you're right in Luneta, Quiapo or Divisoria. News, gossip, magazines, komiks, pirated audio tapes and even designer clothes, these and more are available there. If you want to eat adobo, pinapaitan, dinakdakan, paksiw, halo-halo and ginataan, it's there. . . . If you like to gamble, this is your place; pusoy, shohan, black jack, 41, Lucky 9 and—believe it or not—jueteng!" (Madamba 1993:56).

THE BATTLE OF CHATER ROAD

The weekly transformations of Statue Square point to some striking changes in Hong Kong's social demography over the past three decades. Since the late 1970s, few full-time, live-in domestic workers have been Chinese; the vast majority of them have come from outside the colony. Local Chinese women and recent legal and illegal immigrants from mainland China do such work, increasingly so in the late 1990s, but mostly part-time, and they tend to "live out" (i.e., they do not reside with their employers). The numbers of the informal local labor force are difficult to estimate and often go unreported. Yet it is safe to say that the vast majority of domestic workers in Hong Kong are foreign women. Of the over 150,000 foreign domestic workers in 1995, about 95 percent were

TABLE 1.1 Number of Foreign Domestic Workers in Hong Kong, 1993–2005

	Dec. 1993	Dec. 1995	Dec. 1997	Dec. 1999	Dec. 2001	Dec. 2003	Dec. 2005
Philippines	105,400	131,200	138,100	143,200	155,450	126,560	118,030
Indonesia	6,100	16,400	24,700	41,400	68,880	81,030	96,900
Thailand	7,000	6,700	5,100	5,760	7,000	5,500	4,510
Others	2,100	2,700	3,100	3,340	3,950	3,770	3,760
Total	120,600	157,000	171,000	193,700	235,280	216,860	223,200

Source: Hong Kong Immigration Department.

women, and over 130,000 were from the Philippines, making Filipinos the largest non-Chinese ethnic group in the colony.[1] In 1993 domestic workers from Thailand were the second largest group, numbering approximately 7,000, followed by 6,000 workers from Indonesia, and smaller numbers from Sri Lanka, India, Malaysia, Burma, Nepal, and Vietnam (Table 1.1). In the following decade, significant shifts occurred. By 2005, there were officially over 220,000 foreign domestic workers overall, up from over 120,000 in 1993. Hong Kong Immigration Department figures indicate that the number of Thai domestic workers decreased slightly over the next decade, while the number of Indonesian domestic workers continued to grow, reaching close to 100,000 in 2005, as the numbers of Filipinas briefly dropped to below 120,000 then rose to around 124,000 in 2006.

In the mid-1980s and early 1990s, as the number and visibility of Filipina domestic workers rapidly increased, so did complaints about their "takeover" of Central District, and critiques began to appear in the local newspapers (e.g., *South China Morning Post [SCMP]* 1986b, 1990; *Hongkong Standard [HKS]* 1986; Yeung 1991). A contentious public debate arose in the autumn of 1992 and early 1993 when Hongkong Land, Central District's leading landlord, suggested that the government reopen Chater Road to traffic on Sundays. This marked the beginning of what was dubbed the "Battle of Chater Road" (Tyrell 1992), fought in bellicose words. One editorial announced that Filipinos "are guest workers here with no 'divine right' to *commandeer* Central for their own use"

1. In 1991 Filipinos made up 84.5 percent of the migrant labor force in Hong Kong (AMC 1991:8–9). By August 1993 over 101,000 domestic workers (approximately 90 percent of all foreign domestic workers) came from the Philippines (HK-LD 1993, personal communication).

(Mercer 1992, emphasis added). Others accused foreign workers of having "invaded," "overrun," or "taken over" parts of Central, thus preventing others from using it.

Ironically, Hongkong Land had initiated the original petition to close the road to vehicular traffic ten years earlier on the grounds that a traffic ban would encourage pedestrian shopping. They had also cosponsored some of the concerts and competitions designed to attract people to the area. The reasons Hongkong Land spokespersons gave for their change of heart were the "environmental problems" posed by the influx of domestic workers to the area, "undesirable activities" such as gambling and hawking, and the "continual complaints" they received from their hundreds of tenants in the area about "restricted access," crowds, and noise (Wallis 1992a). According to Hongkong Land, reopening Chater Road on Sundays would allow tenants to load and unload trucks, discourage the crowds of foreign workers from congregating there, decrease the congestion in the area, and thus encourage another "class" of people to come.

The eighteen-page report Hongkong Land submitted to the Central and Western District Boards included complaints from tenants who said off-duty foreign workers were giving "one of Asia's most glamorous shopping areas the appearance of a slum" and described the area as "a nightmare with the atmosphere of a third-rate amusement park." Other tenants disapproved of the "littering and messy situation . . . created by the maids" who congregate outside Alexandra House and the Princes Building, and declared their preference for "yuppies" and "quality families" who might go to such posh places to spend money. Another tenant wanted "more business, not Filipinos loitering around and creating all kinds of nuisance" (Wan 1992; AMC 1992b:24).

Such statements were widely criticized for their implicit or explicit racism. Another common reaction—largely from Western expatriates—was that Hong Kong people should "clean up their own backyard" before pointing the finger at Filipinos and that the litter in Statue Square is no worse than that left at train stations at Chinese New Year or at country parks on weekends (Atkinson 1992; R. Chan 1992; Hardie 1992). Others criticized the government for "not providing adequate manpower and resources" to deal with the illegal hawking, gambling, and six tons of litter reportedly "left by off-duty Filipino domestic workers in and around Chater Road each Sunday" (Wallis 1992d).

Individuals and organizations had already been seeking alternative venues and ways to "lure" domestic workers from parts of Central well before the autumn of 1992.[2] But Hongkong Land's proposal set off a new tidal wave of complaints about domestic workers and their use of Central District, and an equally vehement barrage of letters by and in defense of Filipinos. Among the flood of opinions aired in the local newspapers, Arthur Tso Yeung's was fairly typical. Like many, he considered foreign domestic workers a public nuisance that deprived others of their right to spend Sundays in Central. Yeung "applaud[ed] Hongkong Land for taking such a bold step in recommending a halt to this ridiculous arrangement which the majority of us have had to put up with for the past ten years." Furthermore, Yeung asked, "has it been ten years now since we have been deprived of the use of Statue Square? I wonder what the British and Americans would say if Leicester Square or Times Square were sealed off every Sunday for converging crowds of Chinese to gather to gamble, hawk, and exchange black market foreign currencies and generally to deface the vicinity" (Yeung 1992).

P. K. Lee reiterated the view among many Hong Kong Chinese that "maids" deprive others of access to the "inner Central area." He wrote, "This small area in Central becomes effectively out of bounds on Sundays to the local Chinese, as it is virtually impossible to move about and the facilities such as toilets are impossible to enter. . . . Maids sitting on footpaths and roads should be asked to quickly complete whatever business they may have and move along so that others can use the facilities." Lee recommended a solution: "Most maids would welcome the opportunity to do part-time work on Sundays: the Government could solve this problem by simply allowing them [to] work" (Lee 1992; see also Mercer 1992).[3]

Some, such as A. R. Hunt (1992) and David Granger (1992), responded that the square is open to everyone and that no one was preventing Yeung or Lee from going there. Others pointed out that reopening Chater Road would not prevent domestic workers from going to Central and that the most constructive approach would be to provide other sites for domestic workers to use (Madamba 1992; T. Giles 1992). Some readers criticized

2. A *South China Morning Post* article (Tam 1992) describes attempts to "lure Filipino maids" away from Statue Square and to repel their "invasion" of Central on Sundays. See also Finlay 1994; *HKS* 1992a, b. Complaints about Filipina domestic workers were fairly common by the early 1980s. See, e.g., Chu 1982; Lim 1983; Mitchell 1981; *Star* 1979. For views supporting foreign workers, see Elliott 1981; Hicks 1981, 1983.

3. In another letter, Lee (1993a) recommends that Filipinas who visit the airport should be charged HK$10 and that "maids should be asked to compensate shopkeepers for loss of business on Sundays."

the proposal to create special sites, however, as giving Filipinos special treatment that permanent Hong Kong residents did not receive. Arthur Tso Yeung asked, "Why should any particular foreign minority group be granted any special favours in any particular area?" (1992).

Hongkong Land proposed as a "constructive" approach to the problem of congestion in Central District that underground car parks could be offered as gathering places for domestic workers on their days off. The leader of a Rotarian group who had been working on alternative sites for carnivals and other activities to attract domestic workers away from Central criticized the suggestion, declaring that the noise would disturb the neighborhood and that domestic workers would not be attracted to car parks (Wallis 1992b). Many letter writers expressed horror at the "car-park suggestion" and called it "inhuman" (e.g., Chugh 1992; Palaghicon 1992). Some went so far as to point out parallels between "ethnic cleansing" in Eastern Europe and "proposals to herd Filipinos into underground car parks to create leisure *lebensraum* for 'locals'" (Marshall 1992; Free 1993).

Filipinos saw the proposal as yet another attempt to keep domestic workers "out of sight," akin to rules that force them to use back entrances to buildings and confine them to certain waiting areas in elite clubs (AMC 1992b:24). Staff at the Asian Migrant Centre pointed out that such restrictions reflect the insulting way in which domestic workers are "persecuted, segregated and pushed out of visible social life."[4] In Hong Kong these workers are "needed, yet needed out of sight." The AMC asked, "Is it right for power to be wielded towards alienating sections of people in society and pushing them somewhere less conspicuous and more convenient, especially when these very people help the wheels of society run smoothly?" (AMC 1992b:24).

Given the number of letters that Filipinos sent to the local papers over other issues, it may seem surprising that relatively few Filipinos wrote on the issue of Chater Road (exceptions include Arellano 1992; Madamba 1992; Palaghicon 1992). Yet as several Filipinas pointed out to me, their verbal response was not nearly as significant as their actions. The domestic workers who came and sat in the square and along Chater Road, passing around copies of the letters and editorials that were printed in the local newspapers, expressed their sentiments in more embodied ways, and thousands of domestic workers continued to gather in Central on Sundays, laughing,

---

4. For a discussion of similar prohibitions against Chinese in Shanghai, see Bickers and Wasserstrom 1995.

talking, and eating en masse. They demanded to be seen, and they refused to be moved. By 2006 the Battle of Chater Road was long forgotten. The area surrounding Statue Square, still filled with Filipinas on their day off, had become, as Hongkong Land had first imagined, a tourist attraction and a well-accepted part of the urban landscape.

RESEARCH ON DOMESTIC WORKERS

Before returning to the situation in Hong Kong, it is important to place this book in relation to other work that has been done on paid "household workers."[5] In the late 1980s Henrietta Moore observed that household work "is an area of waged employment which is very much under-researched" (1988:85–86). Since the 1960s, however, in the wake of the civil rights and women's movements in the United States, the body of anthropological, sociological, and historical literature has grown steadily. Many of these studies are rich in historical and ethnographic detail, which illustrates the multiplicity of regional variations in the patterns of household work—the employer-worker relationship, work conditions, and the treatment of and attitudes toward the worker. Cumulatively, whatever the intentions of individual authors, they constitute an argument against "modernization" approaches that posit universal patterns of economic development (Boserup 1970; Chaplin 1978; Coser 1973).

Of the many studies of household workers in the United States (e.g., Colen 1986, 1989, 1990; Coley 1981; Dill 1980, 1988, 1994 [1979]; Dudden 1983; Glenn 1986; Hondagneu-Sotelo 2001; Katzman 1978; Palmer 1989; Rollins 1985; Romero 1992; Salzinger 1991; Sutherland 1981), Latin America and the Caribbean (Chaney and Garcia Castro 1989; Gill 1994; Laguerre 1990), Europe (e.g., Anderson 2000; Boon 1974; Drummond 1978; Fairchilds 1984; Horn 1975; Maza 1983; McBride 1976; Parreñas

---

5. Shellee Colen and Roger Sanjek (1990a:1–2) prefer the term "household worker" to more stigmatized terms such as "servant," "domestic worker," or "maid." Despite their compelling argument, I retain the term domestic worker to refer to paid household workers in Hong Kong because of its specific meaning and political connotations in that context. As noted in the preface, many Filipinas use *"domestic worker"* in conscious opposition to "foreign domestic helper," "FDH," "helper," and other terms used by employers and government officials. The term "household worker," moreover, is problematic because it does not sufficiently distinguish between paid and unpaid workers (i.e., household members who do reproductive labor for free and those who are paid to do so). See Dumont 2000 on the term "helper" in the Philippines. See Constable 2006 for further discussion of the political importance of labels.

2001), and Africa (Cock 1980; Hansen 1989, 1990, 1992; Sanjek 1990), several provide useful overviews of the literature.[6]

As of the early 1990s, according to Sanjek and Colen, the scholarly literature on domestic workers in Asia "was the most meager of all" (1990b:194; see also Rollins 1985:38). Since the first edition of this book was published, however, this is no longer the case. Hundreds of new and important studies of domestic workers in or from Asia have been published. This includes edited volumes that span many regions of Asia (Adams and Dickey 2000; Huang, Yeoh, and Rahman 2005). Numerous book-length studies or doctoral dissertations have also been written about Filipina domestic workers in Taiwan (Cheng 2006; Lan 2006) and in Rome and Los Angeles (Parreñas 2001), Indonesian domestic workers in Hong Kong (Sim 2007), Indian domestic workers in Hong Kong (Keezhangatte 2005), foreign domestic workers in Malaysia (Chin 1998), and Sri Lankan domestic workers in the Middle East (Gamburd 2000), to name but a few.[7]

What I am especially interested in here is how household worker studies up until the 1990s dealt with—or neglected to deal with—the issue of power. Since the mid-1980s, there was already a good deal of interest in the independent and combined importance of gender, class, and race in relation to household work (e.g., Cock 1980; Colen 1986, 1989, 1990; Coley 1981; Palmer 1989; Rollins 1985; Romero 1992; Ruiz 1987; Sanjek and Colen 1990a). Much of this literature examined the causes and manifestations of oppression in the workplace and the means by which employers dominate household workers. Deborah Gaitskell and her colleagues, for example, described black women workers in South Africa as oppressed in three ways: "oppressed as blacks, oppressed as women, and oppressed as workers" (1983:86). Colen and Sanjek suggest that "the structuring of work in homes not only provides reproductive labor to employing households"

6. See the bibliography in Sanjek and Colen 1990b, and their brief history and a thematic review of literature on household workers. For detailed early literature reviews see Chaney and Castro 1989; Romero 1992. On the history of household work in various regions of the world, see Rollins 1995, chap. 2.

7. For two exceptionally important articles on the politics of domestic work in Hong Kong, see Wee and Sim 2004 and 2005. On resistance, power, and submission among Filipina domestic workers in Hong Kong and the epistemological implications, see Chang and Groves 2000; Groves and Chang 2002. Recent studies of Indonesian domestic workers in the Middle East include Hugo 2005; Robinson 2000; Silvey 2006. On Filipinas in Canada, see McKay 2003, 2005; on foreign domestic workers in Singapore, see also Huang and Yeoh 1996; Rahman, Yeoh, and Huang 2005; Yeoh and Huang 1998, 1999, 2000; von der Borch 2006; on foreign domestic workers in Taiwan, see Cheng 2006, 2003; Lan 2006, 2005, 2003; Loveband 2004.

but also "reinforces relations of power and inequality within each local society where it is found" (1990a:1). As Colen writes, "Globally, household work emerges from, reflects, and reinforces some combination of hierarchical relationships of class, gender, race/ethnicity, migration and/or age" (1990:90; see also Ehrenreich and Hochschild 2003). While few pre-1990 studies recognized the influence of global factors on local patterns of domestic work, most were highly attuned to inequality and oppression and richly document how they are inherent in the employer-worker relationship and in the work itself (e.g., Cock 1980). Other studies focused on the social and psychological factors that underlay and helped to perpetuate patterns of inequality (e.g., Rollins 1985, 1990; Coley 1981).

Accommodation, understood as acquiescence or obedience, is implicit in most of these studies but was rarely a central theoretical concern. Authors explain why workers feel obligated—by economic need, family pressures, gender role, or class position—to work hard in an occupation that is often difficult, degrading, and highly stigmatized (W. Giles 1992). The underlying implication is that domestic workers are "forced" to work mainly because they are poor and oppressed. Studies that centrally or exclusively focus on oppression, however, often tend to overemphasize the passivity and powerlessness of the worker, as well as the dominating power of the employer. Power is viewed too unidimensionally. It is understood as emanating from the employer's superior class position, sometimes reinforced by issues of race or ethnicity, gender, or other factors. The worker is simply cast as a victim, perhaps an extremely hardworking victim, perhaps an insightful victim who "understands" the power structure, or even a class-conscious one opposed to the structures of inequality. Such an approach neglects and even conceals other coexisting and competing forms of power and agency.

RESISTANCE AND EMPOWERMENT

With the notable exception of Mary Romero (1992), as of the mid-1990s few researchers paid close attention to household workers' attempts to improve their work conditions. In her study of Chicana household workers in Colorado, Romero looks at the causes and manifestations of oppression but also at resistance. As Romero (1992) and Leslie Salzinger (1991) demonstrate, under certain circumstances, household workers do not simply resign themselves to poor working conditions and work relations or express only forms of "unaggressive aggressiveness." They may actively and successfully struggle to improve their work situations.

Romero's main point is that despite the stigma of their work and the difficulties they face, Chicana household workers choose this kind of employment over others because of the salary, autonomy, and flexibility it can provide. According to Romero, Chicana household workers actively attempt to transform the degrading and demeaning aspects of their work and their relationships with their employers (1992:16). They choose day work over live-in work and part-time work for several employers over full-time work for a single employer; they prefer employers who allow them greater autonomy, better working conditions, and flexibility. Chicana workers struggle "to control the work process and alter the employer-employee relationship to a client-tradesperson relationship in which labor services rather than labor power are sold" (1992:15).

The situation of foreign domestic workers in Hong Kong is considerably different from that of Chicanas in Colorado. In Hong Kong, contracts prohibit these women from working part-time or for more than one employer, and with few exceptions workers must live with their employers. At least initially, domestic workers have little say in selecting employers, and once a contract has been signed, it is extremely difficult to change employers without first returning home to the Philippines, Indonesia, or elsewhere and sacrificing a great deal of money. Although government officials and employers claim that it is as easy for domestic workers as for employers to "terminate" contracts, given the larger system of inequality, this is clearly not the case. Regulations that were allegedly designed to protect the rights of both workers and employers often appear to favor the employer. Unlike Chicanas, who are able to structure their work in order to devote time and energy to their own households and communities (an important means of "diffusing" the stigma and an important source of their identities), Filipinas, Indonesians, and other foreign domestic workers in Hong Kong are forced to leave their families behind.[8] As in the case of Caribbean domestic workers in the United States (Colen 1990), attempts to resist oppression or to improve their work conditions often place their income at risk.

THE ROMANCE OF RESISTANCE

One of the objectives of this book, following Rollins (1985), is to link the treatment of foreign domestic workers in Hong Kong to social, cultural, and

8. Recently several scholars have written about domestic workers' children and families who are left behind (see Asis et al. 2004; Parreñas 2005; Silvey 2006).

historical patterns and to document and analyze factors that contribute to their oppression. Like Romero (1992), however, I am also interested in how domestic workers actively attempt to improve their situations and express agency (see also Rahman 2005). As Lila Abu-Lughod warns, it is easy to romanticize resistance, viewing its forms as "signs of the ineffectiveness of systems of power and of the resilience and creativity of the human spirit in its refusal to be dominated" (1990:42). Romero's study, for example, might be considered overly optimistic in its evaluation of the transformative power of resistance. By focusing on "successful" forms of resistance and neglecting to consider accommodation, passivity, or acquiescence adequately, Romero produces the impression of a "rupture" in power, making it seem ineffective. To borrow Abu-Lughod's words, "The problem has been that those of us who have sensed that there is something admirable about resistance have tended to look to it for hopeful confirmation of the failure—or partial failure—of systems of oppression. Yet it seems to me that we respect everyday resistance not just by arguing for the dignity or heroism of the resistors but by letting their practices teach us about the complex inter-workings of historically changing structures of power" (1990:53). Heeding these warnings, I intend not only to document structures of inequality or modes of oppression, and not to overemphasize the success of resistance, but also to integrate the study of domestic workers into a broader ethnographic discussion of subtler forms of power, discipline, resistance, and accommodation (Ortner 1995).

POWER

My approach has been influenced by ideas about power that developed out of the shift in focus from violent social movements, peasant rebellions, and revolutions (Scott 1976; E. Wolf 1969) to less dramatic "everyday" modes of resistance (Scott 1985), and less confrontational discursive forms of resistance (e.g., Abu-Lughod 1986, 1990; Brandes 1980; Haynes and Prakash 1991; Scott 1990; R. Watson 1994). Notions of power have become more complex, variably influenced by the works of Pierre Bourdieu (1977), Michel Foucault (1978, 1979), and Antonio Gramsci (1971). No longer is power considered a unitary, constant force that emanates from a particular social class or institution; rather, it is seen as a complicated, more tenuous "fabric of hegemonic forms" (Haynes and Prakash 1991:1; see also Abu-Lughod 1990; Calagione et al. 1992; Ortner 1995). In other words, power does not exist as a monolithic, autonomous, "natural state" until the moment when it becomes "fractured" by particular acts of resistance (Haynes and

Prakash 1991:2). Nor do employers have a monopoly on power and workers a monopoly on resistance. Rather, power and resistance coexist and constantly reassert themselves against each other. In Foucault's words, "Where there is power, there is resistance, and yet, or rather consequently, this resistance is never in a position of exteriority in relation to power" (1978:95–96). One of the primary objectives of this book is to situate foreign domestic workers *within* the field of power, not as equal players but as participants. I aim to show how domestic workers, like their recruiters and their employers, wield certain forms of power even as they are dominated by others.

Unlike most studies of household workers, this one does not focus solely or even centrally on the worker-employer relationship or on the workplace. To avoid a simplistic opposition, I examine a variety of disciplining agents— employers, employment and recruitment agencies, governments, and the workers themselves (see Calagione et al. 1992). Although paid household work clearly involves class exploitation, workers are not simply oppressed by their employers, nor are employers essentially active and workers passive. The situation entails a complex set of ambiguities and contradictions. The class identities of Chinese employers and foreign domestic workers are not as clear-cut as they might first appear. Domestic workers resist oppression in certain ways but also simultaneously participate in their own subordination. Moreover, workers, employers, and employment agencies are implicated—albeit in different ways—in a wider system of domination, their power restricted by government policies and regulations. Workers are controlled in some ways by their employers, but other forms of domination also exist.

ACCOMMODATION

As Louise Lamphere warns, it is important to "distinguish between strategies of resistance and those of coping or accommodation" (1987:30). Domestic workers actively and passively, consciously and unconsciously, resist domination. They practice foot dragging, are insolent in ways their employers do not understand, and play tricks to avoid particular household rules (cf. Scott 1985, 1990). Some forms of resistance, particularly public protests, are explicitly aimed at creating social change and improving work conditions. Other, more discursive methods serve more as forms of cultural critique or commentary or as personal means of coping with stressful and difficult situations (cf. Humphrey 1994). But at the same time, domestic workers also support existing structures of power. Like Bedouin women who break rules and partake in "irreverent discourse" while also supporting the existing system of power through such practices as veiling (Abu-Lughod 1986, 1990), Filipinas, Indonesians, and other foreign domestic workers both contest and embrace power structures.

Like the working women described by Lamphere (1987) and like household workers in many other contexts, Filipinas obey their employers because they need to work to support themselves and their families. Yet the collaboration of Filipina and other foreign domestic workers in the project of discipline goes further. Like members of the nineteenth-century English working class who promoted Methodism and espoused "clean living," domestic workers actively discipline themselves and their coworkers (Thompson 1963). Proper etiquette, cleanliness, and ladylike comportment, ever more efficient organization of work, and displays of extreme politeness and subservience toward employers are but a few of the restrictions domestic workers impose on themselves. These and other embodied forms of self-discipline cannot simply be explained as signs of "false consciousness" or a lack of awareness of their class position. As Abu-Lughod points out, such an explanation would dismiss workers' own understandings of their situation or their behavior as "impression management," thus depicting them as "cynical manipulators" (1990:47).

Few studies of domestic work have looked at accommodation, or the reasons why and the conditions under which domestic workers do not resist or attempt to improve their work conditions, aside from attributing it to their relative powerlessness and inequality. This book suggests that domestic workers are not simply passive objects of oppression or active subjects who successfully control themselves and their labor. Foreign domestic workers in Hong Kong neither simply resist oppression nor accept it.

Under certain circumstances, domestic workers may passively acquiesce in their employer's every desire and view their work situation as their "fate." As one Filipina worker wrote to a local newspaper, many domestic workers tolerate abuse because they "practice" the Philippine traits of "*hiya, tiis,* and *bahala na*: shame, endurance, and 'God will take care of everything'" (Katarungan 1993). Rina, Linda, and others I knew expressed a similar attitude. Others, however, such as Elsa, Belle, and Acosta, were not fatalistic and had very different perceptions and reactions. They insisted that no one forced them to come to Hong Kong; it was their choice, and it was up to them to improve their situation. These apparent contradictions suggest that the question of resistance cannot be resolved by appealing to simple phenomenological logic.

Whether a domestic worker is politically active or class conscious, whether she is seeking remedies to individual and communal hardships or passively accepting whatever her employer demands and provides, she can nonetheless, in many regards, be viewed as a "docile" worker. As Foucault observed of prisoners, citizens, students, workers, and others who willingly conform to patterns of self-discipline, domestic workers also contribute to their own subordination in ways that throw into question the problematic dichotomy between active resistance and passive compliance. As I suggest in the following chapters, domestic workers both actively resist and willingly participate in their own "oppression," in different ways and to different degrees. Yet they are also subject to, and participate in, more covert and insidious forms of self-discipline that can undermine and restrict their ability to create fundamental social change.

DISCIPLINE AND DOCILITY

Foucault describes a particular form of discipline that began to develop in Europe during the seventeenth and eighteenth centuries that was more subtle, abstract, and indirect than the harsher and more directly brutal forms of discipline found in slavery or service. Slavery, according to Foucault, is based on "a relation of appropriation of bodies" that was inefficient, "costly," and "violent." Service involved "a constant, total, massive, non-analytical, unlimited relation of domination, established in the form of the individual will of the master" (1979:137). The new "modern" form of covert discipline—different from service or slavery—involved a larger "scale of control," a "subtle coercion" of the various parts of the "mechanism itself including such minutiae as "movements, gestures, attitudes, rapidity" (136–37). This modern, covert discipline also involved a different "object of control," no longer the end product but the "mechanism"—the body and bodily practices. The "modality" is also different, in the sense that this form of discipline involved uninterrupted, constant coercion (137). Discipline was aimed at creating not only the growth of skills but "the formation of a relation that in the mechanism itself makes it more obedient as it becomes more useful" (137–38).[9]

---

9. Foucault developed a "political anatomy" and "mechanics of power" that "defined how one may have hold over others' bodies, not only so that they may do what one wishes, but so that they may operate as one wishes, with the techniques, the speed and the efficiency that one determines. Thus discipline produces subjected and practised bodies, 'docile' bodies" (1979:138).

Although the cultural and historical situation of Hong Kong is significantly different from that of seventeenth- and eighteenth-century Europe, Foucault's ideas about "docile bodies" and "covert discipline" are useful. As we shall see, some forms of control experienced by foreign domestic workers, particularly those enforced by the employer within the household, are reminiscent of forms of slavery and service. Others, particularly forms of discipline introduced by agencies and governments in the course of job recruitment, can be viewed as the "modern" form of "total" bodily discipline.

Domestic workers often respond very negatively to the more overt and violent forms of bodily discipline characteristic of slavery or service relations. Modern covert discipline, however, is not perceived as nearly as problematic as scolding and beatings administered by capricious employers. In other words, domestic workers, especially those who are highly educated or who had office jobs in the Philippines, respond far more positively to lists of duties and work-related regulations than they do to more overt verbal and physical discipline. Domestic workers who are informed at the agency that their hair must be short and that they must not wear lipstick, for example, are more easily compelled to obey such rules than those whose employers forcibly take them to have their hair cut or who slap them and scream when they see them wearing lipstick. As we shall see, the "blending" of various forms of discipline suggests that modern means are employed to impose older rules. Domestic workers, in their desire to "professionalize" their image, often express a preference for more modern coercive methods.

In the early 1990s, employers and recruitment agency staff in Hong Kong often considered less-educated women from rural parts of the Philippines more desirable workers, not only because their lack of knowledge often made them more docile but because traditional gender roles and the Philippine version of the patron-client, landowner-tenant relationship made them more familiar with harsher forms of discipline. Urban educated and professional Filipinas were likely to be more aware of their rights and also far less familiar with and accepting of harsher forms of discipline. Throughout the 1990s, as Filipinas on the whole were perceived to be increasingly savvy and assertive, more employers were attracted to domestic workers from rural Indonesia. As one employment agency staff member told me in 2006, Indonesians are "less smart" (i.e., savvy about workers' rights) and therefore make "better" workers.

Employers vary greatly in their approaches to discipline. Some, as we shall see, treat foreign domestic workers as though they had bought them, albeit for a limited time, and can therefore do with them as they please, just as they might have done with *muijai*, the traditional Chinese bondservants described in Chapter 3. Others impose many of the same working conditions on foreign workers as were imposed on muijai—long working hours and harsh conditions—but they use modern disciplining methods: lists of rules, timetables, and regulations. Yet others, following a more Western "liberal" pattern of discipline, employ the seemingly benign metaphor of the domestic worker as a "family member," which is a subtle form of coercion.

Allowing a domestic worker to choose when and how to do her work does not mean that she is not being controlled, but it often gives her a comfortable illusion of freedom. It is in such cases that we see the most concentrated form of Foucault's modern discipline and docility. That is why, I maintain, the changes that many domestic workers desire are not "absolute." Often they would merely replace older forms of discipline and coercion with more ambiguous, elusive, and therefore perhaps more insidious forms that appear less harsh.

2 | GLOBAL THEMES AND LOCAL PATTERNS

In the 1980s, as the economy in the Philippines worsened, married and unmarried Filipinas, mainly between the ages of twenty and forty, with college degrees or high school diplomas, left their families to work in homes in Hong Kong and other parts of Asia and the Middle East. In the 1990s, as the Indonesian economy worsened, rural Indonesian women, who were mostly single and on the whole younger and less educated than Filipinas, began to echo a similar pattern. Since the 1980s, as the wealth of upper- and middle-class Hong Kong Chinese increased and the availability of local workers decreased, for reasons I shall explain, Filipinas, Indonesians, and other foreign domestic workers were permitted to enter the colony with short-term visas and two-year work contracts to meet the demand. Elsa and Belle, sisters who grew up in a semirural area outside of Manila, illustrate this pattern.

Both were in their mid- to late thirties in 1993 when I first met them at the Mission for Filipino Migrant Workers, and both were single. Elsa, the younger, had worked in Hong Kong since 1979 and Belle since 1982. When I met them, Elsa had had seven different full-time employers, and Belle had had five, all of whom were Chinese but one. Both women enjoyed life in Hong Kong and considered their experiences there exceptionally good. Over the years they had managed to remit home a significant portion of their incomes to support their elderly parents and their younger brother and three sisters.

When they lived in the Philippines, Belle and Elsa also contributed to the family income. During her last year of high school, Elsa worked as a "helper" for a family who lived at a military air base in Manila. After that, she worked in an electronics factory for two years, and Belle worked in a textile factory. Despite official opposition to unions under the regime of Ferdinand Marcos, Belle helped organize a union. In 1979, when Elsa was twenty-two and Belle a few years older, their father became concerned about Belle's union activities and arranged for her cousin Gina, then a domestic worker in Hong Kong, to help find her a job there. Belle had just been elected as union leader, however; so she was reluctant to leave and urged Elsa to go instead.

After six months of paper processing, in 1979, at twenty-three years old, Elsa set off for Hong Kong to work with Gina for a wealthy Chinese family who lived at Jardine's Lookout, a wealthy neighborhood. As we sat in the back room of the mission office on a hot slow weekday afternoon, the air conditioner hummed loudly, and Elsa recounted the conversation she had with her father just before she left home.

> "Elsa," he told me, "can you help your sisters in their schooling? Because they like to study and you know that I don't have any capability to send them to college." He said, "Elsa, can you help me? Your sisters, they like to go to school." And I think that they are bright, bright girls, my two younger sisters, and so I said, "OK. No problem. This is my opportunity to help. Don't worry, Tay." *Tatay* means father. "Don't worry, Tay, I will try my best to help you." And so in time my sister got into college, and my next sister got into college.

Elsa's monthly salary started out at HK$950 (about US$125). This amounted to little more than 1,000 pesos per month, not a great salary even by Philippine standards but more than her sister earned in the factory. During the 1980s and early 1990s the Hong Kong dollar remained stable, valued at approximately HK$7.8 to US$1, but the value of the peso, continued to drop steadily—from 17 pesos to US$1 in 1984, to 25–30 pesos to US$1 in 1993. Meanwhile, Elsa's income continued to grow. In the early 1980s, when she was working for her second full-time employer, she began to do part-time work on her day off. She worked for an American family from 10 A.M. until 5 or 6 P.M. on Sundays for HK$15 per hour, and earned an extra HK$200 in a day. By the mid-1980s, domestic workers' salaries had also increased so that including the earnings from her part-time work she was able to send home an impressive US$1,500 a year (about 30,000 pesos).

By 1982 the union leadership had changed, and Belle was ready to join Elsa in Hong Kong. Her salary in Manila was a meager eighteen pesos a day, "only enough for a sack of rice and transportation home from work each month." Elsa's second employer's sister wanted to hire a domestic worker. So Elsa helped arrange for Belle to get the job, thus saving her sister and the employer agency fees.

Over the years, the largest portion of Elsa and Belle's remittances went toward the university education of their two younger sisters and the high school education of their younger brother. Their three sisters have college degrees. The eldest returned from Australia in the mid-1990s to manage a department store in Manila; she contributes what she can to the family income. One younger sister worked for a nongovernmental organization that assists migrant workers; her income was extremely low. Their youngest sister, Sarah, went to Italy as a domestic worker in 1993. Elsa, Belle, and their eldest sister had saved the required US$5,000 to pay her recruitment fees. As Elsa explained, even though Sarah had high marks and a university degree in management, she could not find a well-paying job at home. In Italy in the mid-1990s she earned US$1,300 per month—far more than she could earn in the Philippines and more than twice what she would earn in Hong Kong.

Elsa and her sisters share a common goal: "We did not taste luxury when we were small. So we are thinking that one day we will . . . and that our parents can have money." Elsa remembered that when she was young, her father supported the family by working very hard as a full-time collector for a furniture shop and by cooking and selling *viand* (main courses) in their neighborhood. Their mother also worked hard, taking in laundry to help support the family.

> All of my sisters, we are dreaming that we will have something that we didn't have when we were small. Because when we were small we were really very poor. We just rented one small room and we didn't have any things like a table—we were eating on the floor because we didn't have a table! But we had food because my father said that food is important. . . . My father saw to it that we had an abundance of food. Because he said that it's good for our bodies and minds. He said that if you don't have food you cannot think. He said that in the near future maybe, if we are very good children, then maybe we can buy the things that we don't have. He's good. And we think that way, when we are grown up. . . . My father said that he could not afford to send me to college but only secondary [school]. "So if you want to change our life, our kind of living," he said, "it's up to you."

From Elsa and Belle's remittances, the family bought some land in the province of Laguna, where their parents and their brother raise pigs, chickens, and geese and grow fruit trees. They also bought a small lot in a subdivision near Manila. Their brother often talked about going to Saudi Arabia to work.

> And of course . . . we are really concerned because he is the only one brother we have. So we said, "You just take your time and help our parents here." We have lots of animals at home. . . . So he has to help my parents to feed the animals—pigs, chickens, geese, ducks. In that way he is able to help. We were able to sell the ducks, the chicken, the turkey, you know, and they have some income with the fruits that are growing in the land that I have bought. It's a popular fruit, and my mother is really earning! Nowadays [when] it's in season, she is able to earn 1,000 pesos a week—10–15,000 pesos during the season! For fruits! So my mother has a little income too. Every year.

In 1994 Elsa and Belle's parents qualified for a low-interest government loan to expand the "piggery." Meanwhile their father was renovating the small house he lived in.

> My father, little by little, is renewing that [house] into something new. My first contribution was the things like refrigerator, then the bathroom—because we didn't have anything like that before! . . . We didn't have a television before so we have a television now. Ahh, a stove! All that we dream of!
>
> Now our dream is to build a very nice house—because we don't have our own. So we already have television so—we are dreaming of a big house that we can call our own. That is what we are looking for—we are dreaming! Me and all of my sisters! . . . A big house that we can call our own.

GLOBAL THEMES AND LOCAL PATTERNS

By the mid-1980s there were over a million and a half Filipinos employed as contract workers in over 120 countries worldwide (Catholic Institute for International Relations [CIIR] 1987:18). For the Philippine government, faced with over two decades of economic crisis, domestic workers, seamen, construction workers, and other Filipino migrant workers are a valuable commodity. Through the fees that all applicants for overseas work pay to the Philippine Overseas Employment Administration for work papers, insurance, and other requirements; exit taxes; and above all their remittances, migrant workers bring in much-needed foreign currency. They also help relieve the high rate of unemployment, which increased after 1996 and in the early 2000s.

For the government and the people of Hong Kong, foreign domestic workers, recruited mostly by agencies in the Philippines and Indonesia and channeled into the colony through Hong Kong agencies, solve the labor shortage problem. They provide relief from domestic chores for many women from upper-class or double-income middle-class households. As in many parts of the world, foreign workers allow Hong Kong women to take on more prestigious supervisory roles in the household and permit them the freedom to participate in other activities that are considered more interesting, entertaining, or lucrative. In many cases domestic workers do household work and care for the young and the elderly, enabling local women to contribute additional income to their households. In some cases local women opt to work even if their income is only slightly higher than the cost of hiring a domestic worker.

Shellee Colen and Roger Sanjek echo an anthropological approach to other types of work (e.g., Nash 1979; A. Ong 1987; Taussig 1980) in insisting that household work must be "viewed historically, locally, and contextually within a capitalist world system" (1990b:177). As this chapter illustrates, shifts in the global economy, the development or underdevelopment of industrial capitalism, and political and economic changes in mainland China, the Philippines, and other regions of Asia all have a bearing on the pattern of household work in Hong Kong today. Colonialism, neo-colonialism, political corruption, and underdevelopment help explain why the Philippines continues to be the largest exporter of workers in the Asia-Pacific region (with Indonesia running a close second) and why Filipino and Indonesian workers have come to be viewed as "commodities" that can be "sold" or "traded" to solve economic problems in the Philippines and Indonesia and as "resources" that can be tapped as part of a "natural" scenario of capitalist development in Hong Kong.

NINETEENTH-CENTURY HONG KONG

Given Hong Kong's teeming population of close to seven million in 2006, it is hard to believe that before it became a British colony in 1841, Victoria (Hong Kong island) was sparsely populated. A census taken in 1841, after China's defeat in the Opium War and Hong Kong's annexation as a British colony, counted four thousand Chinese and six hundred Europeans (Endacott 1958:65). Most of the Chinese were "boat people" who spoke a Min (Fujianese) dialect and subsisted on fishing. There were only a few farmers. Europeans were mainly involved in shipping and trade. Early in the colonial period, Chinese immigrants began to arrive from adjoining regions of Guangdong Province in search of work, and by 1845 Hong Kong's population had quintupled (AMC 1991:5).

Both the Europeans who resided in Hong Kong and their servants were predominantly male (Sankar 1978a:51–52). It was common colonial practice to hire menservants (see Hansen 1990, 1989). Hong Kong was a rough place, its "frontier condition" considered unsuitable for women and children (Sankar 1978a:52). Chinese parents, furthermore, were reluctant to allow their sons to take their wives and children with them to Hong Kong for fear that they would not remit money or return home. Thus, as Andrea Sankar notes, "in the 1870's approximately seventy percent of the Chinese living in the colony were employed in some form of domestic service . . . but of this number only a small percentage were women" (1978a:52).

In 1898 after the second Opium War, China was forced to sign over the "New Territories"—approximately 350 square miles of land that adjoined the mainland—to the British for ninety-nine years. Among the Chinese residents of the New Territories at that time were members of older-lineage villages, most of whom depended in part on agriculture for their subsistence (see J. Watson 1983; Baker 1966, 1968). The territory was also home to large and powerful lineages, whose households included "concubines, slaves, indentured menials, and servants as well as three or four generations of family members" (R. Watson 1991:231; see also J. Watson 1975; Potter 1968; Baker 1968).

EARLY TWENTIETH-CENTURY EXPANSION

The turn of the century brought rapid social and economic change to Hong Kong. Several outbreaks of bubonic plague were met by improvements in sanitary and housing conditions, and the environment began to be considered more suitable for Chinese and European women and children (Sankar 1978a:53). The downfall of the Qing dynasty and the Nationalist revolution of 1911 brought refugees and new immigrants, including wealthy merchants and compradors, to the colony. Between 1898 and 1901, the colony's population expanded from 245,000 to 300,000, and to 878,000 by 1931 (AMC 1991:5).

The increase in the number of women and children had important implications. Chinese and European women preferred female domestic workers, especially as personal attendants and to look after their children. As it was considered inappropriate for respectable women of the higher classes to go out in public, female household workers were necessary to do the marketing and run errands (Jaschok 1993).

"As the economic climate of Hong Kong continued to improve," Sankar notes, "and its trading and commerce grew more prosperous, wages for coolie (manual) labor rose. Men found better paying employment as laborers than as servants. Women moved into the lower paying jobs vacated by the men" (1978a:53). Although employment opportunities existed for women in light industry as early as the 1920s, "the harsh conditions of coolie labor and the lack of housing accommodations in light industry made both these alternatives less appealing for women than domestic service" (53). Housing was a serious problem in Hong Kong, and prostitution was one of the few occupations, aside from domestic labor, that provided sleeping quarters (54).

During the early decades of the twentieth century, an important source of female household labor were the *muijai*, young girls under ten years old, who were sold into servitude. They were a common source of household labor until opposition to the practice heightened beginning in the 1920s (R. Watson 1991; Jaschok 1988). By the 1940s the demise of muijai, correlated with the growth of a pool of women workers from the silk-producing region of the Canton Delta in Guangdong Province—many of whom were "sworn spinsters" (*sohei*) (see Chapter 3; Stockard 1989; Sankar 1978a, b, 1984; Gaw 1991; also Ooi 1992; Ho 1958). This labor pool was augmented by post-1945 refugees (Sankar 1978a, b). Until the 1970s, sworn spinsters and postwar refugees were the most popular paid household workers in Hong Kong.

INDUSTRY, WOMEN, AND THE GROWTH OF THE SERVICE SECTOR

From early colonial times through the late 1940s, Hong Kong served as a center for shipping and trade. The British government supported a laissez-faire approach to economic development, and the policy in Hong Kong was generally nonintervention. In the early 1950s, following the communist revolution, Hong Kong experienced a massive influx of capital and entrepreneurs from China. The colony burgeoned as a manufacturing center specializing in light industry, and by the early 1960s it had established a booming industrial economy based on exports (see Salaff 1981). By 1964 locally manufactured goods constituted approximately 75 percent of Hong Kong's total exports, compared to about 10 percent in 1947

(HK-LD 1992a:1). As the demand for labor grew in the post–World War II decades, Hong Kong drew on the growing population, including refugees and immigrants from the mainland. Women's participation in the formal sector of the workforce also increased. In 1961 the rate of female participation in the labor force (defined as the proportion of labor force members among all women aged fifteen or over) was at 40 percent.[1] Until the late 1980s the participation rate for women continued to increase (HK-LD 1992a:5; HK-CS 1993). During the 1960s and 1970s, garment, textile, plastic, electronic, and wig manufacturing accounted for 85 percent of the jobs of working women (Salaff 1974:11).

In the early 1970s the economy began to undergo another major but subtle shift. While light industry continued to grow, the service sector—which included wholesale, retail, import, and export trade; restaurants and hotels; transportation, communication, finance, insurance, and real estate; community, social, and personal services—flourished (HK-LD 1992a:2). "With the relatively rapid growth of the services sector since the early 1970s," one Labour Department report noted, "employment has been shifting from the manufacturing sector towards the services sector. The former's percentage share of the employed work force dropped from 47% in 1971 to 41% in 1981 and further to 28% in 1991. On the other hand, the share of the services sector in total employment increased from 41% in 1971 to 47% in 1981, and further to 63% in 1991" (1992a:2). Despite the drop in the percentage of the workforce in manufacturing, the total number of people in the workforce increased.[2]

As in Japan, Taiwan, Singapore, and other Asian "economic dragons," manufacturing continued to decline in the 1980s and 1990s. China's leaders pushed for greater economic liberalization and an open-door policy with regard to export production and foreign investment, and products once manufactured in Hong Kong became much cheaper to produce in China. Thus, echoing a pattern found in the United States, factories were

1. This figure does not include female participation in the informal sector; e.g., those working as unregistered household workers or hawkers.

2. Between 1961 and 1971 male labor force participation decreased by 5.6 percent and female participation increased by 4.8 percent (Sankar 1978a:57). From the early to mid-1980s the number of women in the workforce continued to increase. The rate of female participation, which had grown fairly steadily since the 1960s, rose to a high of 48.7 percent in 1987, decreased to 46.8 percent in 1990, and rebounded to 47.8 in 1991 (HK-LD 1992a:5). The slight decrease after the mid-1980s is probably explained by the decline in the manufacturing segment of the economy.

moved across the border where the labor was cheaper. Nevertheless, as a gateway to China, Hong Kong maintained its primary role as a trade center, and the renewed emphasis on trade and export fueled the demand for people to work in the service sector. By the 1980s opportunities for women in the service sector—especially those with a secondary school education or some tertiary training—increased. Women who supplemented their high school education with secretarial or clerical training were especially well qualified for lower-level positions.

Despite the shift of much industrial production across the border, Hong Kong's official unemployment rate in the 1980s and early 1990s remained low, especially by U.S. standards. At that time it never rose above 2 percent, and according to the Labour Department, it was necessary to import labor, including skilled professionals, construction workers, and people to work in the hotel, catering, clothing, and tourism industries. In 1991, 12,867 "professionals"—people with administrative, technical, or managerial skills—were admitted to work in the colony. Under another government scheme the same year, 4,418 "skilled workers" and 9,400 "experienced operatives"—the majority of whom worked in the "clothing, hotel, catering, tourism and construction industries"—were also brought in, and 2,000 additional workers were admitted to work specifically on the new airport project (HK-LD 1992a:11). As long as local workers could find work, foreign workers were viewed as more of a necessity than a problem.

A Growing Labor Shortage

Hong Kong's shift toward a service economy in the 1970s and 1980s changed the female composition of the workforce. Middle-class "housewives" who had worked in their own homes for no income and would not have dreamed of doing factory work entered the paid workforce. As educated women increasingly found jobs, provisions had to be made for childcare and housework. By the 1960s and 1970s, the household structure in urban Hong Kong was already quite different from the "ideal" extended family described in the literature on rural China, Taiwan, and Hong Kong (M. Cohen 1976; Freedman 1970; M. Wolf 1968, 1972), and during the 1980s the average size of Hong Kong households continued to drop.[3] One 1988 estimate was that "forty percent of mothers in Hong

---

3. According to the Department of Census and Statistics, "The average size of domestic households has experienced a steady drop from 3.7 in 1985 to 3.5 in 1990.... Between 1985

Kong hold full-time jobs, depending on helpers to care for their families" (*SCMP* 1988; Wing 1993). Working-class families that had depended on family members (e.g., daughters, mothers-in-law, or mothers) to help with child rearing, cooking, and other housework no longer found this option as available or desirable.

The shortage of space in Hong Kong exacerbated the problem. Smaller living quarters discouraged the formation of large extended households. Employers I spoke to suggested that extended family members were less available to help, and some who had elderly household members still preferred to hire help. Some employers said their mothers and mothers-in-law were "too old" to do such work or that it was unfair to ask relatives to do the work if they could afford to hire someone from outside.

With the growing number of double-income families, the preferred option was to hire help, but in the 1970s it was difficult to locate Chinese domestic workers. Many local women favored factory work, especially when wages were high. As Sankar explains, "in a period of economic prosperity such as in 1973–74, wages rise and industry attracts many women. During these times servant shortages develop. But when industry is slack, as in 1975, many women—especially the middle-aged—are let go or receive so little money it is not worth working. During these periods women return to domestic service in which the wage is relatively steady" (1978a:57–58).

Unlike Malaysian women who in the 1970s mostly preferred paid household work to factory work (Armstrong 1990), Hong Kong women at that time preferred factory work because it provided regular hours, a more independent lifestyle, and a higher social status (Salaff 1981:156–74).[4] Many young Hong Kong women avoided work in private households because it evoked images of bonded servitude. Several young Chinese women I spoke to in the early and mid-1990s said that even the worst cleaning jobs in hotels and department stores were preferable to being a live-in domestic worker. Live-in domestic workers might earn more money (especially if

---

and 1990, the proportion of households with 8 or more members dropped from 3.4% to 1.6% of all households . . . [and the] proportion of households consisting of one unextended nuclear family [i.e., parents and unmarried children] increased from 54.4% to 59.2% . . . households consisting of 1 vertically extended nuclear family [e.g., grandparents, parents, and children] had its percentage share decreased from 13.6% to 11.9%" (HK-CS 1991:6; 1993).

4. Lilly, a Chinese woman in the novel *Sour Sweet*, prefers factory work. "The factory wages were fair. . . . Lilly earned more than she would have done as a servant in either a foreign or a Chinese household where the hours worked amounted to a curfew anyway. The factory work was light in comparison with the unremitting demands a Chinese family would have put on a maid" (Mo 1988:6).

their living expenses were covered by their employers), but better pay did not compensate for the stigma and the "lack of independence" associated with live-in domestic work.[5]

DISENCHANTMENT WITH CHINESE WORKERS

In addition to the growing shortage of local domestic workers and the problem of their rising cost, there was a strong sense among potential employers during the 1970s and 1980s that the "Chinese servants," or *amahs* (paid domestic workers), were "not as good as they used to be."[6] According to an editorial from the early 1970s (which would be echoed by critiques of Filipina domestic workers two decades later), the few remaining amahs were "money-grabbing, unscrupulous and downright difficult," and they had become increasingly particular about the sort of work they were willing to do. "No servant will wash windows, polish the floor or help in moving furniture. A large majority refuse to do any marketing. . . . Offer less than $600 for a full-time general cook amah and she'll laugh in your face."[7] Anticipating problems to come, one employment agency owner predicted that, "in 10 years' time there will be no amahs left. Those working now will have retired. . . . The middle-aged ones will have long gone into the factories" (da Costa 1972).

Several employers I interviewed recalled similar concerns, and many complained about how domineering and demanding Chinese domestic workers had become by the 1970s. Mr. Ho, a man in his late forties who worked in the upper levels of the Hong Kong civil service, explained that he had grown up with Chinese servants. In the mid-1970s when he and his wife were married, they hired a Chinese household worker.

> Because of my income and my wife's income, we were quite well off. And once we were married we organized our own family; we lived elsewhere, not with my own parents, so we needed the service of an amah. In the beginning we tried to employ a reasonable Chinese amah. We tried several times but it couldn't work.

---

5. During the mid-1970s Sankar asked Hong Kong women why they continued to do domestic work. She was told that some women are uncomfortable in the factory setting; one woman felt she was too old to work in a factory; another young woman's mother was afraid of the "kind of people" her daughter might meet in a factory (1978a:58). See also Salaff 1981.

6. See Armstrong 1990 for a similar pattern in employers' complaints in Malaysia. See also Rollins 1985.

7. All dollar amounts refer to Hong Kong dollars unless otherwise noted.

We started employing local Chinese first, but I found it difficult to communicate. Of course there was not a language barrier—I spoke Chinese and they spoke Chinese. But the thing is, a Chinese amah's average age in the 1970s would be in the region of fifty at least, and I was then in my early or late twenties, so to her I was like her son. Whenever I asked her or told her to do anything, "No!" She always corrected me. And if you went on further she would say, "I already had my baby when you yourself were a baby." This sort of thing. So I found it difficult. And if you started some serious, heavy talk with her, she would say, "OK. If you don't like me, I'll quit!" Because there were so many job opportunities for amahs, if they didn't like you they could quit and find another employer. So that was the general trend towards the end of that generation's amah. Instead of listening to what their bosses wanted them to do, they started arguing.

Many of the conflicts that Mr. Ho recalled involved different approaches to child rearing. When he or his wife asked the amah to feed the baby on demand, for example, she refused because she thought the feedings should follow a strict routine. She would say, "No, this is not the correct way." Mr. Ho continued, "How can I be told how to bring up my own child, [or] listen to her tell me what to do?"

The shortage of local labor and the changing needs of Hong Kong households paved the way for the "logical" entry of foreign domestic workers into the colony. Many individuals whom I interviewed thought that the Hong Kong government approved the 1973 policy allowing foreign nationals to come to work as "helpers" in order to encourage locals—specifically middle-class, literate, and educated women—to enter the labor force. At first English-speaking Filipinas were hired by European and Western expatriate families. English speakers better suited the needs of foreigners than Chinese speakers, and they were also much cheaper. Later, the practice of hiring Filipinas became popular among Chinese who spoke some English. Thus, in the 1970s, when this policy was approved, Mr. Ho and his wife were among the first Chinese to hire a Filipina domestic worker. He described his experience with his first Filipina worker: "We got [along] together quite nicely. I spoke English, and she spoke English very well. There was no language barrier. And in the Philippines they are more westernized—so as far as that was concerned we were okay. After I had my first Filipina maid, I said, that was the solution. I would never go back to a Chinese amah." Later on, it is worth noting, Mr. Ho became disenchanted with foreign domestic workers, and he was one of the founders of the Hong Kong Employers of Overseas Domestic Helpers Association, but in the 1970s at least, like many others he was quite pleased with his solution. Filipinas were cheaper, and by "modern standards" they were considered better.

In his study of household workers in Ghana, Roger Sanjek suggests that, "as one traces the links in the world economic chain further and further downward, through international inequalities, through class inequalities, through urban/rural inequalities, through waged/unwaged inequalities, and through male/female inequalities, one comes at root . . . to inequalities among women" (1990:58). If one traces the historical patterns of inequality in Hong Kong, at the root, we find inequality between different classes of local and foreign women. As local women went to work in service and factories, foreign women were hired to do the less desirable household work for lower wages. Ironically, the wages of these foreign workers were sometimes used to hire young Filipina helpers to look after the Hong Kong worker's children back in the Philippines.

IN THE PHILIPPINES

"Compared with Manila, Hong Kong is such a rich and beautiful city," one Filipina told me in the early 1990s. Hong Kong's phenomenal capitalist growth, high standard of living, and relatively low rate of unemployment is often contrasted to the economic instability, growing international debt, high rate of unemployment, and poverty in the Philippines. Although a detailed analysis of the economy of the Philippines is beyond the scope of this study, a brief historical sketch is helpful.

In the middle of the sixteenth century, in order to control a share of the spice trade, Spaniards conquered the Philippine islands in the Malay archipelago of Southeast Asia.[8] In 1898 as the British were claiming the New Territories, Filipinos were struggling to overthrow Spanish rule. The United States declared war on Spain, helped Filipinos defeat the Spaniards, and then declared colonial sovereignty over the islands in 1898. The American colonial period lasted until 1946, when, following Japanese occupation, the war-torn Philippines was granted independence. A new

8. The Philippines comprises over seven thousand islands, about eight hundred of which are populated. Over a hundred different languages and dialects are spoken, and the population includes fifty-five different "cultural groups" (French 1986a). Tagalog (Pilipino) is spoken by 50 percent of the population, and over 50 percent of the population also speaks English. Ninety percent of the people are Christian, mostly Catholic, and slightly less than 10 percent are Muslim.

period of neocolonial dependence began, and the United States established large military and naval bases there.

Following a period of industrial growth between 1952 and 1969, little industrial development took place in the Philippines. Repeated rebellions and internal conflicts threatened national security. Staunchly supportive of anticommunist leadership, the United States contributed military and economic assistance to the country. In 1972 U.S.-backed president Ferdinand Marcos declared martial law and enacted a new constitution through which he was able to reelect himself as president. During the period of martial law, the United States continued to support the Marcos regime, and poured tens of millions in military aid into the country (Kaibigan 1984 [in French 1986a]). Marcos opposed labor organizations and created incentives for foreign investment in the country, but the outflow of capital was extremely high. Statistics suggest that by the late 1970s transnational corporations repatriated as much as 90 percent of their profits (Leahy 1990:25 [citing Briones 1985]).

According to the *Philippine Statistical Yearbook* (1978), the proportion of the labor force employed in industry—in manufacturing, mining, and construction—decreased since the 1950s. Although the percentage of those engaged in agriculture dropped slightly to approximately half of the labor force in 1976, the numbers of those dependent on the land actually "doubled from 4.5 million in 1956 to 8.1 million in 1976" (French 1986a:48; *Philippine Statistical Yearbook* 1978). The price of land skyrocketed, and in some provinces the proportion of landless laborers was as high as one-third (Aguilar 1983 [in French 1986a:48–54]; Custodio 1978). As Carolyn French explained, the economic situation continued to deteriorate during the 1970s and 1980s, creating a serious shortage of foreign exchange, "accompanied by a marked increase in the cost of living, . . . closure of industries and an increase in unemployment . . . [h]igh interest rates, growing trade protectionism among importing countries, and low export prices" (1986a:50–51). By the early 1980s, inflation had reached an average of 32 percent, and the value of the peso rapidly devalued against the U.S. dollar. The real value of industrial workers' wages decreased by about 40 percent and that of agricultural workers dropped over 50 percent between 1976 and 1979 (French 1986a:51). In 1974 the International Labor Organization estimated the unemployment rate to be over 25 percent (Andres 1984). In 1975 over 40 percent of families in the Philippines could not afford "basic nutritional requirements" (Trager 1984:1273). By the 1980s about two-thirds of the Philippine population lived below the poverty line

(CIIR 1987:1).[9] Statistics such as these bolster the popular notions of Hong Kong residents about the "extreme poverty" and "lack of economic opportunities" in the Philippines and the related notion that Filipinos have little choice but to work abroad, and that they—and other Asian workers—are extremely fortunate to have the opportunity to come to Hong Kong.

FILIPINO MIGRANT LABOR

By 1992 at least one and a half million Filipino migrant workers worked legally overseas (not including permanent emigrants), and another estimated half million did not go through legal channels (AMC 1992c:19; APMMF 1991; Tellez 1991). By 2003, according to the International Organization for Migration, over seven million Filipinos (approximately 9 percent of the population) were living outside of the country, over half of whom were temporary contract workers (IOM 2005: 239).

Despite the massive increase in recent decades, Filipino migrant labor is not a new phenomenon. Historically, it is often divided into periods. During the first, 1906 to 1934, farmers with little or no education went to work on plantations in Hawaii and in agriculture on the U.S. mainland. By 1934, when employment opportunities in Hawaii had diminished and Filipinos were declared aliens by new U.S. immigration laws, more than 120,000 Filipino workers had been contracted (CIIR 1987:15–16; Rojas 1990:9). In 1946, seven thousand Filipinos were recruited to work on pineapple plantations in Hawaii, but during the same year the "national origin quota" legislation was passed and only a hundred Filipinos were allowed to immigrate to the United States each year.

During the second period of migration, from 1946 to the late 1960s, immigrants were most often members of the U.S. armed forces or relatives of earlier immigrants (CIIR 1987:16–17). With the abolition of the national origin quota in the U.S. Immigration Act of 1965, large numbers of skilled professionals—doctors, dentists, nurses, engineers—also emigrated to the United States (CIIR 1987:17; Constable 2003a:177–88), constituting a "brain drain" from the Philippines (Carino 1987:316). Around the same time, Filipinos also settled in Europe, and increasingly they went to work as sailors on international vessels (CIIR 1987:16; Rojas 1990:9).

---

9. In 2001 an estimated 40 percent of the Philippine population was said to live below the poverty line. The unemployment rate was 8 percent in 1996, 10 percent in 1998, 12 percent in 2005, and under 9 percent in 2006, with underemployment an even bigger problem (see www.cia.gov/cia/publications/factbook/geos/id.html).

The beginning of the third phase of migration followed Marcos's imposition of martial law in the early 1970s and involved the Philippine government's active promotion of a "labor export policy." Patricia Leahy outlines three global events that affected the migration policy of this period. The first was the increase in oil prices on the world market in 1973–74 and in 1979–80, which was detrimental to the Philippine economy and allowed many Middle Eastern countries to amass huge profits. These enabled them to promote large infrastructural projects built by inexpensive foreign contract laborers (Leahy 1990:27; Rojas 1990:9; see also CIIR 1987:79). The second was the increase in international interest rates in 1979–80, which "automatically increased the Philippines' loan interest payments by US$159 million." The third was the global recession of 1980–82, which resulted in a drastic reduction in the volume of Philippine exports and a drastic reduction in foreign exchange (Leahy 1990:27; see also Briones 1985).

The most recent period of migration began in the 1970s with the labor export policy of the Marcos government, which has been continued by his successors. Initially introduced as a "temporary measure" to ease unemployment and underemployment and to bring in foreign currency, the policy has now become "permanently temporary" (AMC 1992c:20; Rojas 1990:10).[10] Migrant labor "has grown . . . from being a stop-gap measure . . . to being a vital lifeline for the nation," and thus migrant workers are hailed as the "new economic heroes" of the Philippines (AMC 1992c:20).

Foreign workers provide valuable foreign exchange, but there is some question about the extent to which this policy reduces unemployment. Studies of overseas domestic workers in Hong Kong suggest that most were employed before they migrated. Only 25 percent of the Filipinos French surveyed in 1984 had been unemployed in the Philippines (1986b:14), and Leahy's 1988 survey found only 7 percent (1990:6).[11] According to Leahy, emigration creates the problem of replacing emigrants with equally qualified workers. Critics also ask whether the social problems associated with migration and the long-term economic problems created by the dependency on migrant labor are worth it. The "success" of the labor export policy is

10. In a 1992 speech, Philippine Senator Bobby Tanada said, "The Marcos government encouraged the labor export industry as a temporary (stop-gap) measure to reduce the country's unemployment problem and balance of payments deficits. . . . Today the temporary labor export industry has become permanently temporary" (AMC 1992c:20).

11. Carolyn French's research (1986a) included a survey of twelve hundred Filipina domestic workers. The AMC survey (1991) was conducted between June 1989 and June 1990 and included over seventeen hundred Filipina domestic workers.

"achieved at the cost of national dignity and unquantifiable human costs—broken families, uncared for children at home, rootless lifestyles" (AMC 1992c:20; see also Asis et al. 2004, Parreñas 2005).

By the early 1990s Filipino migrant workers were the Philippines' largest source of foreign exchange, contributing about US$4.8 billion annually (AMC 1992c:19). By 2003 remittances reached US$7.6 billion dollars a year, approximately 10 percent of the gross domestic product (GDP) (IOM 2005:232). According to the Asian Migrant Centre, the average migrant worker supports five people at home, and one out of every five Filipinos directly depends on migrant workers' earnings (AMC 1992c:19).

In the 1980s and early 1990s, Filipinas were by far the most numerous among women migrant workers in Asia (French 1986a, 1986b; Fawcett et al. 1984; Leahy 1990), and in 1992 the number of women migrant workers from the Philippines exceeded the number of men (Asis 2003). The majority of Filipino men who are overseas contract workers are employed in the Middle East (especially in Saudi Arabia), although that market has been shrinking since the mid-1980s because of the decline in the region's construction projects (see Margold 1995). Meanwhile, throughout most of the 1990s, the demand for women migrant workers in East and Southeast Asia, especially for domestic workers in Hong Kong, Taiwan, Singapore, and Malaysia, grew. The demand was met mainly by women from the Philippines and Indonesia. Throughout the 1990s, especially since the Asian financial crisis of the late 1990s, the number of Indonesian overseas contract workers steadily increased.[12]

HONG KONG 1997

On July 1, 1997, after ninety-nine years under British control, Hong Kong became a Special Administrative Region (SAR) of the People's Republic of China. "Reunification" was viewed by some Hong Kong locals as a cause for celebration. Others, including some foreign workers, viewed the "handover" with apprehension and more mixed emotions (Constable 1999). Although Hong Kong's unemployment rate had risen somewhat in the years leading

---

12. Whereas the Philippines is said to have had 3.5 million overseas contract workers in 2003 (IOM 2005), Indonesia is estimated to have had 2.2 million in 2000 (Hugo 2002). Until the beginning of the 1990s, most of the legal migrant labor migration from Indonesia was to Saudi Arabia; from 1994 to 1999, more than half was to the Asia Pacific region, and like that of the Philippines it has been dominated by women (Hugo 2002). By the year 2000, Indonesians had overtaken Filipinos as the largest percentage of foreign domestic workers in Taiwan (Lan 2005:216).

up to 1997, and reunification created some uncertainty, overall the political transition had a much less direct negative impact on the economy and the situation of foreign workers than the Asian financial crisis of 1997–98, the global economic downturn of 2001–2002, and especially the outbreak of SARS in 2003.

As described above, in the 1970s through the early 1990s Hong Kong experienced remarkable economic growth. The service sector grew and construction boomed, making up for the shift of manufacturing across the border to China. But since the early 1990s, Hong Kong's economy experienced several marked downturns. The unemployment rate rose to an eleven-year high of 3.5 percent in 1995 (Gilbert 1995) but was back down to 2.2 percent at the end of 1997. It then rose to 4.7 in 1998, to over 6 percent in 1999 during the Asian financial crisis, then down around 5 percent in 2000 and 2001. In 2002 it rose to over 7 percent, then to an all-time high of 8.7 during the peak of the SARS outbreak. It dropped back to 6 percent in 2004 and to 5.2 in early 2006 (Hong Kong Trade Development Council 2004).

The economic downturns were especially difficult for Hong Kong's working class. In certain areas—especially construction and the service sector—the number of jobs declined and wages dropped. Tourism and business travel was severely affected, especially during and in the wake of the outbreak of SARS. Local Chinese women, whose household incomes had declined, often because men were laid off or their wages were reduced, sought to enter or reenter the job market. In some cases this necessitated hiring someone else to do the household work, to care for children and the elderly. According to a newspaper article, middle-aged women—in their mid-thirties and forties—many of whom were illiterate, were finding it increasingly difficult to find work even in 1991. As manufacturing jobs became scarce, many of these women turned to part-time work or no longer worked at all (Forestier 1991). Women who had worked in manufacturing, who had had flexible hours or did piecework at home, were still unable or unwilling to become full-time live-in domestic workers.

When Hong Kong's unemployment reached an eleven-year high in 1995, resentment toward foreign workers and criticism of labor and immigration policies grew. The Labour Department had long required that employers demonstrate an inability to fill jobs with local workers before they could recruit foreign workers, but public complaint mounted, claiming that local skilled, semiskilled, and unskilled workers were being overlooked and that foreign workers were taking jobs that might otherwise be filled by locals.

With the economic downturn, the Labour Department came to view domestic work as a potential source of income for local unskilled and unemployed middle-aged women. Local women—some of whom were recent mainland immigrants and others who had once worked in manufacturing jobs—availed themselves of the government-sponsored "retraining programs" for "local domestic helpers" (LDHs). By 2005, over 94,000 local women had attended these programs, with an estimated 30–40,000 working as domestic workers, charging a fee of HK$50 per hour in 2006. Most local domestic workers are middle aged, have their own household responsibilities, and work only intermittently and part time (Asato 2004; Chun 2004; HK-CS 2001).[13]

In response to growing complaints that foreign workers were taking jobs away from locals ("stealing our rice bowl"), the government began to more strictly enforce rules pertaining to foreign workers. To protect the market for local domestic workers, the government mandated that foreign domestic workers must live with their employers (with some special exceptions for employers who had reasons to petition for an exception), widely publicized the illegality of working part-time for more than one employer, and mounted a media campaign against illegal work (see Chapter 6). To protect the jobs of local chauffeurs, policies dictated that foreign domestic workers could no longer serve as drivers without official government approval that would be granted on a case-by-case basis, and only if their duties were strictly related to "domestic work."

The minimum allowable wage of foreign domestic workers was reduced, with the rationale that foreign workers must "share" the economic burden faced by locals. In 1999 their wage was reduced 5 percent (from HK$3,860 per month to $3,670), and in 2003 it was reduced another 11 percent (HK$400 per month to HK$3,270). Fueling anger among domestic workers was the Labour Department's announcement in 2003 imposing a HK$400 per month levy on employers of foreign domestic workers. The levy was to be used for retraining local workers, thus "penalizing foreign workers to subsidize the local unemployed" (Wee and Sim 2005:185).[14]

---

13. As early as 1995, a newspaper article stated that part-time domestic worker jobs were "becoming popular with [local Chinese] women workers because of the difficulties they face in finding jobs in manufacturing." Elizabeth Tang, general secretary for the Confederation of Trade Unions, is quoted in the article as saying that foreign and local women do not compete because "foreign domestic helpers are all on a full time basis, but local women are very reluctant to work full time" (Palpal-Iatoc 1995).

14. As of 2007, the levy was still being collected from employers, but its legality was being challenged in court.

In 2005 the minimum allowable wage for new contracts was increased for the first time in six years by HK$50, and again by HK$80 in May 2006 and in June 2007, raising it to HK$3,480. Despite many signs of Hong Kong's economic recovery, foreign domestic workers' wages remain significantly lower than a decade earlier.

Despite the increase in the number of local women domestic workers after the mid-1990s, the market for full-time, live-in foreign domestic workers remained strong. Although a temporary dip occurred in the number of foreign domestic workers during and immediately following the SARS crisis, and some observers speculated that local employers could no longer afford foreign domestic workers, the number quickly rebounded.

GROWING CRITICISM AND OTHER ALTERNATIVES

Despite the high demand for and important contributions of foreign domestic workers, and despite the fact that most Hong Kong employers have continued to prefer them to other foreign workers, Filipinas have long been a target of criticism. As the number of foreign domestic workers in Hong Kong grew in the 1980s and early 1990s, there were already some vocal critics. As Hong Kong's unemployment rate increased in the late 1990s, the critics became more vociferous.

Scattered throughout the local Chinese- and English-language newspapers, beginning in the mid-1980s, alongside powerful letters in their defense, were antagonistic letters and editorials that depicted Filipinas as spoiled, overpaid, and more of a hindrance than a help to Hong Kong residents. They were also criticized for not appearing grateful for the privilege of working in Hong Kong.

In addition to the complaints about their use of Statue Square described in Chapter 1, there were complaints of a more general nature. Raymond Wong declared that Filipina domestic workers are extremely spoiled in Hong Kong. He recommended that the government not increase the minimum allowable wage for household work, but instead levy a surcharge on domestic workers to subsidize local hospitals, clinics, and parks (1985). M. S. Chong expressed "heartful support" of Wong for "clearly and loudly" saying what "all of us—the hardworking local middle-class people—know too well, but never mention openly." According to Chong, Chinese employers can "barely bear the unreasonable, unreliable bunch that constitutes the great majority of Filipina maids." Employers hire them "out of despair, as we really have no other choice, as in most cases, the couple who employs them are working from morning till evening. . . . [I]f the Filipina maids are not satisfied with their jobs in Hongkong, they can always return to their paradise to see the conditions of employees over there" (Chong 1985).

A further indication of the growing discontent was the establishment, in early 1986, of the Hong Kong Employers of Overseas Domestic Helpers Association (HKEODHA). This group of a few hundred Chinese employers lobbies the government on domestic worker policies, regulations, and salary issues. The association calls on employers to unite to protect their rights and to defend themselves against the ever-increasing demands and growing problems associated with their "foreign helpers." Despite the social, economic, and cultural advantages of Hong Kong employers over foreign workers, the members of the HKEODHA declare that it is employers who are being exploited. Thus they seek to change government policies that they believe favor the rights of the domestic worker over those of the employer (Sinclair 1995).

Once viewed as a cheap, docile, and ideal solution to the labor shortage, by the late 1980s, Filipinas were considered far too savvy, assertive, and contentious. The high profile of Filipina protests and demonstrations against the New Conditions of Stay that were instituted in 1987 and the Philippine government's temporary ban on approval of new contracts for Filipino domestic workers in 1988 (see Chapters 7 and 9) displeased some Hong Kong employers immensely. In their view, Filipinas no longer behaved as grateful, humble, and accommodating guests but as disgruntled or demanding workers. One editorial clearly expresses the double standard for locals and "guest" workers: "If the local Chinese take the liberty to shout [in public places], it is because Hong Kong is their home; guests and strangers should be more considerate" (Lee 1993b). "Filipinos are in a foreign country," J. Ong commented, "and should be on their best behaviour" (1992). M. S. Chow blamed "vociferous demands and noisy demonstrations" for wearing out Filipinas' welcome. These have "hardened public opinion," and "with a few notable exceptions," Hong Kong Chinese "are unhappy" and "increasingly wary and resentful of these Filipina maids, whose general attitude to work and carefree lifestyle is incompatible with the hardworking ethics and serious attitude of the Chinese" (Chow 1987).

Criticism of foreign domestic workers continued in the 1990s, and sentiments similar to those of Chong and Wong were expressed in the local papers (e.g., Lai 1993; Sinclair 1995; Yuen 1993). Some editorials took on aggressive—bordering on racist—tones. One anonymous letter writer comments on the "very foul smelling Sri Lankan/Indian maids" and the "filthy stench in the air late on Sunday evenings" left by Filipina and South Asian maids (*HKS* 1992a).

Responding to local employers' growing dissatisfaction, agencies provide "tips" on how to maintain docile and obedient domestic workers (see Chapter 4). They provide guarantees, lists of rules, and recommend hiring only workers who are new to Hong Kong. Philippine President Corazon Aquino's short-lived moratorium on contract approval in 1988 created an impetus for agencies to propose alternatives to Filipina domestic workers. Some experimented with women of other nationalities. Nevertheless, during the 1980s many agencies rejected the introduction of larger numbers of domestic workers from Sri Lanka and Bangladesh because of their "cultural differences." According to the director of the Perfect Domestic Help agency, most Chinese do not want South Asian domestic workers: "They don't like them with the skin too dark, [f]or it might scare the children" (Williams and Power 1988).

In the 1980s some considered Thai women the most promising alternative, because their culture is "similar to that of the Chinese." According to employers and agency staff, Thais are not considered as "westernized" or "Americanized" as Filipinos and are supposedly "more passive and submissive" because of their Buddhist background. As an added bonus, one Chinese agency staff member explained, Thai food—as opposed to Filipino food—had become extremely popular in Hong Kong.

Although the number of Thai domestic workers in Hong Kong increased to seven thousand by 1993, there was little evidence to suggest that Thai women would replace Filipinas. Indeed, by March 1994, the recorded number of domestic workers from Indonesia exceeded the number from Thailand for the first time.[15] By the end of 2005, the downward trend continued and the number of Thai domestic workers had dwindled to just over 4,500 (see Table 1.1). When I spoke to employment agency staff in 1994, some said they "no longer deal in Thais" because they are not in great demand. One major barrier was language. Although neither Thais nor Filipinos speak Chinese, many Hong Kong employers communicate with Filipinos in English. Thai women usually speak little or no English. Another problem, according to Chinese employers and agency staff, is that employers fear that Thai women—even more so than Filipinas—come to

---

15. As of the end of March 1994, there were 124,600 foreign domestic workers; 108,400 of them were Filipino; 6,900 were Thai; 7,200 were Indonesian; and 1,100 were Indian (HK-ID personal communication, June 1994).

Hong Kong with domestic worker contracts only as pretext to enter the colony. Employers feared that they might lose their "investment" to the illicit and lucrative local sex trade or the underworld of triads (underground secret societies). Exaggerated though this fear may be, it was enough to deter many employers from hiring Thai workers.[16]

Throughout the 1990s and early 2000s Indonesians gained popularity among Hong Kong employers, and the number of Indonesian domestic workers grew from a mere 6,000 in 1993 to close to 100,000 by 2006 (see Table 1.1). One reason, I was told in 1995 and again in 2006, was because Indonesian workers do not "cause trouble" as Filipinas do. They are less politically organized, and their consulate is reputed to strongly discourage workers from filing complaints against their employers. Employment agency staff also noted that Chinese employers prefer the cooking of Indonesians and Thais to that of Filipinos. Indonesians, many of whom have learned to speak some Cantonese while in training camps in Indonesia, were also considered better suited to provide care for elderly household members who are likely to speak only Cantonese, whereas Filipinas were still preferred by those with small children for their ability to speak and teach the children English. Pei-Chia Lan describes a very similar pattern of "essentialising and naturalising" of the "ethnic differences" between Filipinas and Indonesians by labor brokers in Taiwan (2005). She describes how Filipinas are depicted as *the Westernized other,*" as "outgoing, individualistic, opinionated, and difficult to manage," whereas Indonesians are depicted as *the traditional other,*" as "docile women" who are "obedient, slow and living the simple life" (2005:217).[17]

From the 1980s until at least the time of my research in 2006, mainland Chinese domestic workers were not considered a viable option, despite pressure from some Hong Kong employers. As explained to me by government officials, NGO staff, and local employers, the main reason why mainland women were not sought to work in Hong Kong as domestic workers was the widespread fear that it would be too difficult to "control" or "identify" them and prevent them from settling there permanently. A major concern was that after reunification with China in 1997 Hong Kong would need to defend itself from prospective mainland immigrants. One fear was

---

16. See also comments in the article "Filipinas Are the Favourite Workers," *HKS* 1988.

17. On the racial and ethnic profiling of foreign domestic workers, see also Bakan and Stasiulis 1995; Loveband 2004; Tyner 1999.

that Hong Kong locals might "recruit members of their own families from China as a way of enabling them to stay on in Hong Kong" (Wee and Sim 2005:178). In 1986 Hong Kong's secretary for security, director of immigration, and commissioner of labour expressed opposition to any plan to bring mainland Chinese domestic workers to Hong Kong (Hui 1986). The same view was reiterated in 1993 when Hong Kong Secretary for Education and Manpower John Chan, was quoted as saying that "it would be too easy for mainland workers, many with relatives or family in Hongkong, to integrate into the community and become permanent residents" (*HKS* 1993). The same view was still expressed by government officials in 2006 despite widespread rumors that training centers in mainland China were preparing women to work abroad as maids.[18]

In the course of the 1990s, as they became increasingly critical of Filipinas, members of the employers association began to support "flexibility," "choice," and the option of bringing in mainland workers. Some employers I spoke to were afraid that mainland women would be "even more backwards than Filipinas." One Chinese woman had read in a Chinese newspaper about a Chinese domestic worker from rural Anhui who had accidentally killed her employers' baby by putting him in the electric clothes dryer. By the mid-1990s, spokespersons for the employers association seemed more open to mainland workers. They complained of the cost, aggressiveness, and "cultural differences" of Filipina workers, and said that mainland women would work for less money, cook Chinese food, and speak the local language. Although Philippine President Fidel Ramos received repeated verbal assurance from Chinese government officials that "nothing will change" and that Filipinos would be allowed to remain in Hong Kong after reunification, many Filipinas I encountered were not convinced. They were making alternative plans.

NATURALIZING DOMESTIC WORK

In the 1997 edition of this book, I ended this chapter by suggesting that Filipinas and other foreign domestic workers might eventually be replaced by cheaper and more docile workers from mainland China.

---

18. I was also told by one Labour Department official in the early 1990s that Chinese officials opposed allowing mainland women to work as "lowly maids" in Hong Kong because of the "impression" it would create. In other words, mainland officials—so, at least, this man believed—did not want China to look like a "third world" country in need.

By the mid-1990s the employers association had been pushing in that direction. Chinese nationalist sentiment ("we are all Chinese, after all") and class differences could make the ideological transition from poor Filipinas to poor mainland Chinese relatively easy. During the 1990s until the time of my updated research in 2006, however, despite the growing dissatisfaction with foreign workers, there still existed a strong sense of the logic and appropriateness of bringing Filipinas, Indonesians, and others from "poor" and "less fortunate" regions of South and Southeast Asia to Hong Kong. Besides the economic logic of bringing these women in to fill a lowly economic niche, it was viewed as "natural" for foreign women to do household work.

Unlike the Chinese domestic workers of the past, who by and large shared the same ethnic, national, and racial identity as their employers and whose occupation was largely determined by class factors, Filipinas were increasingly seen as a group whose differences are not simply class based, or even ethnic or cultural, but racially, biologically, and "naturally" consti-tuted. Domestic work, which at one time had few if any racial connotations in Hong Kong, had by the 1980s become so associated with Filipinas that the term *banmui* ("Philippine girl") was used interchangeably with "maid" or "servant." A Filipina journalist commented on the common equation: "A couple of years ago when the editors of [the] Oxford dictionary were preparing a new edition, 'Filipina' was an entry with the meaning 'a female citizen of the Philippines; a servant, or an amah.' Pres. C. Aquino then lodged a formal complaint through the British Embassy and after much controversy the derogatory connotation to the word was deleted. This is the official story as told by the Philippine press" (Layosa 1990a:19).

Indeed, Filipinas in Hong Kong, like some minorities in certain U.S. contexts, may be assumed to be servants by virtue of their racial or national identity (Escoda 1989). For a short period of time in 1986, until outraged protests from the Filipino community and Philippine consulate officials in Hong Kong put a stop to it, a doll called "Filipino maid," with black hair, wearing a domestic worker's uniform, holding a miniature Philippine pass-port and a "lifetime" employment contract, was widely sold in Hong Kong (Constable 2000; Southam 1986a, 1986b; *SCMP* 1986a). In some cases Chinese children referred to domestic workers employed in their homes as "my Filipino." One Filipina domestic worker reported that as she was about to leave on holiday, her male employer explained to his young son that while she is away "Daddy will be the Filipino" (Layosa 1990a).

By the early 1990s, the term "Filipino" had for some people become synonymous with "domestic worker." Since then, as the nationalities of domestic workers have diversified, ideas about their "traits" and the differences between Filipinas, Indonesians, and other nationalities have been further naturalized and essentialized. That household work is viewed as the "logical" or "natural" work for Filipinas or other foreign women (with Filipinas often considered better suited to childcare and Indonesians better suited to care for the elderly), however, does not mean that employers believe that they necessarily do the job well. As we shall see in the following chapter, doing the job well is defined by specific ideas about what constitutes an "ideal" servant.

3 | SUPERIOR SERVANTS

The notion of the "superior" Cantonese domestic servant—inaccurate as it often is, and fueled by a powerful sense of nostalgia—was never far below the surface of the Hong Kong Chinese discourse on foreign domestic workers during my research in the mid-1990s. Complaints and criticisms about foreign workers were common within the privacy of employers' households, but were also broadcast on television, aired on the radio, and expressed in the form of editorials in the local papers. Many statements regarding foreign workers echoed the sentiment that the new "maids" were just not as good as the old Chinese "servants." In the words of a Singapore Chinese man:

> There have been other devoted and excellent servants in the past. Some who come to mind are the black "mammies" of North America's southern states and the nannies of Victorian England. The first exemplified warmth and the second, professionalism. The Cantonese amahs combined both.
>
> There are parallels in the 1980s, notably the ubiquitous Filipinas who work as servants all over the world. The amahs were markedly different from this group as their character, expertise, and loyalty to the families they served made them incomparably superior. (Gaw 1991:xv)

Some conflicts between foreign workers and their employers are connected to recent changes in the Chinese household itself and to larger patterns of social and economic change. Some are common to household workers in many other regions of the world. Others are linked to specific cultural circumstances. Ideal though Chinese domestic workers might appear in retrospect, many of the problems that employers associate with foreign workers also applied to the Chinese workers of old. A comparison of the identity and social status of Chinese versus foreign domestic workers sheds some light on the attitudes toward, and experiences of, foreign domestic workers in Hong Kong. The "ideal" Chinese servant of old, as we shall see, has become a coercive symbol used to control workers who are referred to locally as foreign domestic "helpers" or "FDHs."[1]

AMAHS AND FDHS

Chinese household workers are often spoken of as though they constituted a homogeneous group. In fact, they did not. Chinese "servants" came from a variety of social groups and had different ideas about domestic service and different "master-servant" relationships. Some of the characteristics commonly ascribed to all Chinese household workers apply only to certain types: to *muijai* "bondservants," who were to a large extent considered the property of the master or mistress to do with as he or she pleased; to the *sohei* or *mahjeh* types of sworn-spinster amahs, who were often more independent because they had an external network of support; or to the post-1945 refugee women who were sometimes more dependent on their employers than the sworn spinsters. Popular generalizations about Chinese servants of the past often overlook the distinction between men and women workers and between the free and unfree. To deconstruct the stereotypical, binary opposition one often finds in the discourse on foreign and Chinese domestic workers, it is important to describe some different types.

Andrea Sankar divides Hong Kong servants into menservants, muijai, spinster amahs, traditional amahs, modern amahs, and new immigrant amahs. These heuristic categories are useful, but it is important to note that each contained significant variation, and that several different types may have worked at the same time within the same household (1978a). As Rubie Watson cautions, Chinese households were often highly fluid, and

---

1. Local and foreign domestic workers are both commonly referred to by employers, Hong Kong officials, and many others as "helpers" (i.e., FDH and LDH). When referring to such local usage, I use the term "helper" (or FDH, or LDH). In other instances I prefer to use "worker," in keeping with the preference of local and foreign domestic workers and labor activists who consider the term "helper" demeaning.

servants did not make up a static group. "Clear distinctions among people living together in the same household were not always easy to make; servants . . . were often spoken of as kin, and kin were sometimes treated as servants." Within the households of the wealthy, men were the only ones who "maintained a clearly demarcated and unambiguous position" (R. Watson 1991:232).

MENSERVANTS, SLAVES, AND WORKERS

As Karen Hansen notes, menservants were often fixtures of colonial societies, but little has been written about them (1990:121). The paucity of material may reflect the feminization of housework that has occurred in many societies or the current bias toward perceiving housework as women's work (cf. Hansen 1989, 1990). In Hong Kong today, when people nostalgically recall the servants of the past, they speak of the women. Yet, despite the shortage of studies of menservants, slaves, and household work in late imperial China and in Hong Kong, enough material exists to show that housework in Hong Kong has not always been a female domain.[2]

During the mid-nineteenth century wealthy Chinese families on the mainland commonly relied on free and unfree men and women workers. Until 1949 "China had one of the largest and most comprehensive markets for the exchange of human beings in the world" (J. Watson 1980b:223). When Hong Kong became a colony, domestic workers entered households through varieties of slavery, pawning, or indenture (R. Watson 1991:251; also J. Watson 1980a, 1980b). Most common among the unfree population were *muijai*, often referred to in English as slaves, but more accurately indentured or bonded servants. There were also *hsi min*, male slaves whose positions were inherited along the male line (J. Watson 1980b:245).

As noted in the previous chapter, menservants were most popular in Hong Kong's early colonial history (Sankar 1978a:51–52). European men tended to hire free men as their servants. But since men had ceased to work as household servants in western Europe from the late 1700s until the 1920s, the Hong Kong pattern calls for an explanation (Hansen 1990:123; see also McBride 1976; Hecht 1956). Following Hansen's argument about household work in colonial Northern Rhodesia, European men in Hong Kong might have considered men more suitable because of the tropical

2. Exceptions include Ebrey 1986; Jaschok 1988; McDermott 1981; Meskill 1979; Pruitt 1979; Smith 1982; J. Watson 1976, 1980a, b; R. Watson 1985, 1986, 1991.

heat, disease, unsanitary conditions, and the heavy and strenuous work required of them. European men might have found the idea of "hiring" workers more familiar than "buying" them. European men had opportunities to purchase women servants, but they did not commonly do so.

Men and boys were sold as servants far less often than women and girls.[3] Chinese sons were expected to care for their parents in old age, and were more likely to go out and earn money than daughters. Daughters, often viewed as a drain on the family, were expected to leave eventually. Yet, even the poorest, most desperate Chinese parents might be reluctant to let daughters work for foreign "barbarian" men. Chinese custom required that respectable women be sheltered and controlled; those who worked generally did so for the immediate family or for wealthier members of their extended kin. Bonded servitude was a less desirable option. Reflecting the different standard for men and women, selling a boy was a far more desperate act, and far less common by the twentieth century than selling a girl (see R. Watson 1991:249; see also Meskill 1979:230, Sinn 1994).

Menservants in Hong Kong often did laundry and ironing, general house cleaning, errands, cooking, gardening, and they pulled rickshaws. In Hong Kong, as in colonial Northern Rhodesia, "men servants accompanied travelers . . . cooked and cleaned for [them] . . . , and often served as intermediaries between them and the local populations" (Hansen 1990:121).

During the early twentieth century new opportunities arose for Chinese men to work as builders, porters, and manual laborers, and household work became increasingly feminized. If men worked as "servants," they were errand boys, gardeners, bearers, and rickshaw pullers, more active in the public, male sphere of Hong Kong life. Irene Cheng describes the situation in the early 1920s, when some wealthy families still had a large number of menservants. "A Chinese upper or middle class family included one or more amahs. . . . The wealthier families might also have men-servants performing duties such as those of an English valet, butler, footman, house-boy, or gardener as well as sedan-chair bearers or rickshaw pullers" (1976:47). Note from this description that men's work no longer included cooking, washing, and house cleaning, work that was delegated to specialized women workers.

Chinese men still work as chauffeurs and gardeners in Hong Kong, but at least until the mid-1990s such duties were often performed by foreign

3. *Hsi min* inherited their positions and may therefore have been less accessible to foreigners.

domestic workers. Most men who come to Hong Kong on FDH contracts work as drivers (chauffeurs) and gardeners or do heavier cleaning and household maintenance work.[4] Their numbers are low compared to women. Men are often hired when there is more than one domestic worker and in wealthier households. Although foreign men are hired as domestic helpers, there is a general sense among them and their employers that what they are doing is not really "domestic" at all. Men are rarely asked to wash clothes, watch children, or cook meals, but women are often asked to wash cars and do gardening.

Many Filipina domestic workers have a clear idea about the gender of work and about work they feel they should not do because it is men's work. Some women complained to their employers when asked to wash cars, water gardens, mow lawns, or clean fish ponds. More often, they performed these "male" duties but complained bitterly about it to their friends. Chinese employers told me they could not understand why workers grumbled about doing such tasks or refused to do them even when offered bonuses.

The Labour Department's telephone advice hotline, from which I requested advice in 1994, generally—but ambiguously—sided with the employer's idea about what constitutes "domestic work." One operator, who took me for an employer, said that washing a car, "if it is for family use is okay." Another said that washing cars is not "domestic" work and that a helper should be paid an additional amount of money to wash it. Asked how much, he answered cheerfully, "Oh, it's up to you!" On the topic of gardening, the Labour Department spokesperson said that "if it is not a very large garden," it is certainly reasonable work to require of any domestic worker. "How big is large?" I asked. He said that has not been defined. Other operators reasoned that it depended on the distance from the garden to the house; others answered frankly that there was no clear policy on the matter. When I wrote to a Labour Department official for clarification of what is considered domestic work, his response was, "Domestic work is domestic work." The duties of foreign domestic workers are not clearly stated in FDH contracts. In some cases employers and workers end up in

---

4. In some cases husband and wife are hired by the same employer. In such cases men usually do the gardening, driving, and outside errands, and women do the cooking, cleaning, and childcare. Officially men cannot be hired to *work* only as gardeners or chauffeurs, since these jobs can be filled by local workers. As noted in Chapter 2, as of the late 1990s employers were required to apply for special permission for foreign domestic workers to drive a vehicle, and driving should only be related to household duties (HK-ID 2005).

court over such matters (see Chapter 6). The gendered division of household labor between Chinese men and women workers, which formerly held sway, no longer applies to foreign women workers.[5]

MUIJAI

The report of the Commission on Mui Tsai in Hong Kong and Malaya, defines a muijai as a young girl, around eight or ten years old, who was transferred from her natal family, either directly or through a go-between, "to another family with the intention that she . . . be used as a domestic servant, not in receipt of regular wages and [not] at liberty to leave the employer's family of her own free will or at the will of her parent" (*Report* 1937:22; see also Jaschok 1988; Stockard 1989:28–29; R. Watson 1991:235). In essence, the girl was purchased from her parents, with or without her consent, and then she could be sold again any number of times (Jaschok 1988:8, 45, 70, 72). According to Shellee Colen and Roger Sanjek, even the small element of choice involved on the part of parents helps to distinguish muijai and similar forms of household workers from slaves, who were involuntarily recruited through such means as warfare, raids, or kidnapping (1990a:3).

A muijai's term of service was not specified, but it was generally expected that her master or mistress would arrange her marriage when she reached her late teens, and that thereafter she would be a free person. In many cases she was married as a concubine rather than a wife (Stockard 1989; Topley 1975). The ending of a muijai's obligations to her master at marriage theoretically differentiated the practice from other more extreme forms of slavery, but "for all practical purposes the *mui jai* was treated as if she 'belonged' to her master" (R. Watson 1991:240), and in practice there may have been "very little difference between pawning, indenture, or slavery" (252). The verbal and physical forms of discipline used on a muijai—including beatings, verbal abuse, and threats of sale into prostitution—were, as in the case of slaves, often of the sort that presumed ownership or total control of her body (cf. Foucault 1979:137).

Slavery was officially abolished in Hong Kong in 1844 when Queen Victoria decreed that English law against slavery must be upheld in the colony, but the practice of muijai remained largely unaffected until the 1940s (Jaschok 1988:133). During the late nineteenth- and early twentieth centuries, the majority of nonfamilial laborers in local households were

---

5. From here on, my use of the term *domestic worker* applies mainly to women workers. Some of what I write, however, applies to both men and women workers.

muijai (Sankar 1978a:53). The Anti-Mui-Jai Society was formed in 1921 (Jaschok 1988:84, 149; Smith 1982), and in 1923 it succeeded in pressuring the British government to prohibit the sale and purchase of muijai. In 1929 all muijai owners were "called upon to register their mooi-jai, pay regular wages and release them from their bonds at the age of 18 years" (Jaschok 1988:75, 136–39; R. Watson 1991:236). Both Rubie Watson (1991) and Maria Jaschok (1988) provide ample evidence that the practice of muijai continued at least until World War II. Among wealthy Chinese, the practice continued under the guise of "adopted daughters" many years after it was officially abolished (Jaschok 1988:101; R. Watson 1991:241). One Chinese employer described how she "hired a muijai" in the early 1960s. Her amah, then in her fifties, insisted that she get a muijai to help with the housework. As this employer explained, "We had to hire a muijai . . . to help her. It wasn't technically a muijai. They were forbidden. But we got one."

According to Sankar, muijai were the "lowest status servant in a Chinese household" (1978a:51). Jaschok's detailed case studies suggest that muijai were bought by people from different social strata and those in wealthy households often had far better situations. Some were treated as veritable slaves, but others did the lighter housework while the paid servants were left with the heavy and menial work (1988:96).

The sale and resale of muijai was not uncommon. Jaschok cites examples of girls who were trained for a few years and then resold at a profit as muijai or, more often, as prostitutes or concubines or secondary wives. Yip Min-yuk, an amah who was a ritual specialist hired for wedding rituals and celebrations, bought muijai as investments (Jaschok 1988:10–16). In the Canton Delta region of Guangdong Province, sworn spinsters also bought muijai to work for them and as investments that could later be sold as secondary wives (Stockard 1989:28–29).

The choice of a marriage partner for a muijai was "almost exclusively motivated by money considerations" (Jaschok 1988:107). Often they were married to older men—tailors, shopkeepers, hawkers—who could afford a reasonable bride price. If the bride price was not considered sufficient, muijai were often sold into prostitution (107–8). In cases where a muijai stayed with the family for life, it was often to become a concubine of the master. Her former position as a muijai meant that she posed little threat to the position of the first wife and the other concubines (1988:107).

Both Maria Jaschok and Rubie Watson note that among the wealthy, benevolent motives are cited as part of the justification for purchasing muijai (Jaschok 1988:98; R. Watson 1991:245). Charitable motives were less likely to be expressed by poorer masters, who were more likely to view these girls as a cheap source of labor or an investment to cash in on in times of hardship. When muijai were "bought" *(maaih)* they were thoroughly examined. As one female informant reported, the buyer "would examine and discuss her as one discussed the merits of a work-horse; her teeth were inspected, and she underwent medical examination to assess her potential work performance in the household" (Jaschok 1988:98–99).[6]

There are certain similarities between muijai and foreign domestic workers. Both resemble "commodities" in the way they are inspected, bought, traded, owned, generally objectified, and treated as economic investments. The work requirements and the extremely low status of foreign domestic workers resemble those of muijai more than those of Chinese amahs. Another striking parallel is in the extremely harsh forms of discipline that both types of domestic workers have experienced.

In Hong Kong today, Chinese and non-Chinese express amazement about the abuses that foreign domestic workers experience at the hands of their employers. I met women at the mission who had been underpaid, forced to do illegal work, beaten, starved, locked inside rooms for days on end, and verbally and physically assaulted. The image that remains most vividly etched in my mind is of a woman who came in one Sunday afternoon with a mark covering her upper arm and part of her face in the unmistakable shape of an iron, where her angry employer had branded her. Horror stories about the cruelties experienced by foreign domestic workers are also common in the daily papers (e.g., Batha and Finlay 1994; O'Neill 1993).

Such atrocities are inexcusable and, in a sense, unexplainable under any circumstances. Yet they do seem somewhat less inexplicable when we realize that such abuses are not new or directed solely toward *foreign* domestic workers. Although there is often an underlying—and sometimes overt—racial hostility toward foreign workers in Hong Kong, it is clear from the history of the muijai that these abuses did not originate as "racial incidents," as some have suggested. They may have evolved into expressions of racial and ethnic tension, but this is an acquired meaning, not the simple cause of the abuse.

Favorite punishments meted out to muijai included "beatings with the handle of a feather duster or a split cane, burning with heated tongs or

---

6. Selection of a concubine also entailed a thorough inspection of the "merchandise," but one that focused more on her sexual appeal than her ability to work (Jaschok 1988:15–16).

lit matches, tying up the mooi-jai for long hours, and not giving her food" (Jaschok 1988:102–3). Regardless of whether it was early in the morning or late at night, the girl's services were expected at a moment's notice. Filipinas, like muijai, are often not paid their wages, fed leftovers, forced to work long hours until they become sick with exhaustion. When they fall ill, they are punished with beatings and kicking.

The uses to which muijai were put also resemble the illegal work often required by the employers of foreign domestic workers. Contracts stipulate that the FDH must work only for the employer who signed the contract, but employers of foreign workers, like those of muijai, "loan them out to friends," put them to work in markets or factories, and keep their earnings (Jaschok 1988:103). Despite these similarities, however, the foreign domestic worker in Hong Kong is most often compared to the Chinese amah.

AMAHS

The meaning and origin of the term *amah* is debated (see Chan and Kwok 1990:204–5; Gaw 1991:87–89). It may be derived from the Portuguese word *ama* (nurse), or it may be an Anglicized form of the Chinese *ah mah—Ah* being a common name prefix, and *mah* a term of endearment meaning "little mother," which was sometimes used to refer to a worker who looked after children. Others say *amah* originated in the Chinese term for wet nurse, *nai mah*, literally, "milk mother". As Mimi Chan and Helen Kwok explain, the word has "become more general in meaning and is used to refer to any female domestic, and not only those who take care of children" (1990:205).

Amah is not often used when speaking Chinese but has long been used by Chinese who speak English and by English speakers in Hong Kong, Singapore, and Malaysia. In Chinese, Chinese household workers are generally referred to as *gungyahn*, literally, "workers" or, more figuratively, "servants." Chinese household workers of the past might also have been referred to as *mahjeh*, literally, "mother" and "older sister." This term was sometimes applied to Chinese women who wore a distinctive suit of black trousers and a white top, but more accurately it referred specifically to the *sohei* from the Shunde region of the Pearl River Delta area of Guangdong Province, who had participated in a hairdressing ceremony that marked their special status as sworn spinsters and who had been dependent on the silk industry for their livelihood (Stockard 1989:70; Constable 1996). Chinese in Singapore described mahjeh as prettier, classier, and better dressed than other amahs. They normally wore their hair "in a single loose plait or occasionally unplaited" and were considered "more relaxed, less severe, and more 'stylish'" (Gaw 1991:91). Spinster amahs also had a reputation for having a "professional" commitment to their work.

In the past, most households had several amahs and they were often referred to by their duties. The woman responsible for the cooking was a *jyufaahn* (cook amah); the one who looked after young children (similar to an English nanny or an Indian ayah) was called a *chaujai* (baby amah); the one responsible for washing and ironing was *saitong* (wash amah). The amah who did washing and general cleaning and tidying was called a *dajap* (cleanup amah). The "all around servant" who might be the only servant in a less wealthy household, might do cooking, washing, cleaning, and also childcare, and would be referred to as a *yat geuk tek*, literally, "one leg kick," or "general amah." Most well-off households would have had at least a cook, a baby amah for each child, a wash amah, and a general amah. They might also have drivers and gardeners and personal attendants, either muijai or paid servants (see Gaw 1991:91, 111–12). In the 1950s Mr. Ho's family, which was, according to him, "rich but not very rich," had a baby amah, a *yat geuk tek*, and a gardener.

M. Jocelyn Armstrong notes that in Kuala Lumpur, the term *amah* is commonly used to refer to domestic workers, regardless of whether they are Chinese, Malay, or Indian, but the workers themselves prefer to be called housekeeper or houseworker, or to be described as "working for a family" (1990:150). Editorials in Hong Kong's English-language newspapers sometimes use the term *amah* to refer to Chinese and foreign domestic workers, but it is also applied more specifically to Chinese women who received wages for their household labor as opposed to muijai. *Amah* may loosely refer to any woman domestic worker, but most foreign women in Hong Kong do not like to be called amahs and claim it refers only to Chinese women.

Strictly speaking, amahs were a special type of Chinese household worker that included sohei and other types of sworn spinsters and post-1945 women refugees from Guangdong. Traditional amahs, like foreign domestic workers today, were usually *jyu ga gung* (live-in workers). In this they differed from the Chinese domestic workers today, who may occasionally be called amahs, but who usually work part-time and return to their own homes every day.

During the 1920s and 1930s, as pressures against having muijai mounted and they became more difficult to recruit, spinsters and unmarried or widowed women arrived from the Canton Delta to seek other forms of paid employment.[7] With the depressions that hit the silk industry during the early part of the twentieth century and its eventual collapse in the 1930s, land once used to grow mulberry bushes for raising silkworms was shifted to cash crops such as sugarcane and tobacco (Gaw 1991:25, 28; Sankar 1978a:55–56; Stockard 1989:5–6, 164–65, 169). By the 1930s "with the world depression, the growing significance of the synthetic fiber industry, the Japanese occupation, and civil war, sericulture—the economic basis of sworn spinsterhood—collapsed," and spinsters turned "to domestic service in Hong Kong, Singapore, and Macau to support themselves and their families" (Stockard 1989:169). According to a 1934 report, "After 1929, more than 100,000 women formerly engaged in some phase of the silk industry were without work" (Stockard 1989:169). Women from the delta region thus emigrated to urban centers to look for jobs.

The group that Sankar calls "traditional amahs" includes pre-1945 immigrants, such as sohei or sworn spinsters from Shunde, and post-1945 refugees. Women who were not sworn spinsters were usually widowed, unmarried, or otherwise separated from their families. Sankar defines the "traditional amah" by "her adherence to the classical standards of the master-servant relationship" (1978a:54). She "unquestioningly dedicates her life to the master's family in return for which she expects, but does not always receive, respect and care in sickness and old age" (54).

One main difference between muijai and traditional amahs had to do with the wage and the relative freedom of the latter. As Sankar notes, there were important social distinctions between the spinster amahs and the amahs who migrated to Hong Kong during the same period of time but who did not belong to sworn sisterhoods. Members of sisterhoods had some clear advantages over other women servants. They were not as vulnerable to their employers' demands because the sisterhood formed a sort of "primitive labor union" (Sankar 1978a:56; 1984). They were also less dependent on their employers for care and support in illness and old age. Sisterhood networks "helped women migrate from the silk area into the cities . . . trained the women in various skills . . . and assisted them in finding jobs and in relocating if their work situation was unsatisfactory. . . . Members

7. Amahs came mainly from the following counties of Guangdong: Shunde (Sundak), San-shui (Saamseui), Dongguan (Dunggun), Nanhai (Naahmhoi), Panyu (Punyu), Xinhui (San-wui), and Zhongshan (Jungsaan) (Gaw 1991:25; Sankar 1978a:55; Stockard 1989:195–99). These are not all silk-producing regions, but areas in which "delayed transfer marriage" or forms of marriage resistance were practiced (Stockard 1989).

[also] established job definitions and minimum wages for each job" (Sankar 1978a:56). According to Sankar, "traditional free servants" often had little choice but to remain with employers who maltreated them since finding a new employer could be difficult. But if women who belonged to sisterhoods were maltreated, sisters lent them economic and emotional support and helped them find new jobs, and other sisters refused to work for the offend-ing employer. Sisterhoods organized loan associations, and sisters often pooled money to buy property and retire together (1978a:56).

Domestic workers who belonged to sisterhoods often had more control over their work conditions than those who did not, but sisterhoods could be more or less formal organizations. More formal ones involved a ritual and swearing-in ceremony; less formal ones entailed simply introducing a prospective member to the other members for approval (Gaw 1991:127; see also Ho 1958).[8] Although sisterhoods ideally served the functions Sankar describes, women who were not sworn spinsters might have similar advan-tages. They could, and often did, draw on family and village networks to bring new servants to their employer's household, and although they did not necessarily retire in a home with their "sisters," they could also, like sworn spinsters, invest in real estate on their own, with friends, or through a son, daughter, nephew, or other relative back home, thus paving the way for their later retirement and care.

Dr. Linn, a Chinese woman in her forties, described a "very clever" sohei who once worked for her family; Ah Lee had wisely invested in real estate and now lived in a flat with several sisters. Mrs. Chin, a professional woman in her early fifties who grew up with Chinese domestic servants, described the two amahs who worked for her after she was married. These two women illustrate the blurred line between sohei and other types of amahs.

Ah Ching came to Hong Kong from Shunde in the 1930s to work for Mrs. Chin's father-in-law. She was not a sohei but a young widow with a son. After several years, Ah Ching became a baby amah for the boy who later became Mrs. Chin's husband. After his marriage, Ah Ching went to work for the newlyweds, and when the Chins had their own children, Ah Ching became their baby amah. After working in Mrs. Chin's household for about

8. In Singapore, the term *jimui* (sister), once referred strictly to sworn spinsters and their sisterhoods, but "in later years, all formalities were dispensed with; good friends simply referred to each other as *chi mui [jimui]* or 'sisters'" (Gaw 1991:127). Janice Stockard and her informants also use the term *jimui* loosely to refer to fictive "sisters" who belonged to the same "girls' house" in the native village but did not necessarily take part in a formal ritual to become sworn spinsters (1989:31–41). See also Ooi 1992:84.

twenty years, in the 1970s, Ah Ching injured herself and then went to live with her son and daughter-in-law.

> The daughter-in-law was perhaps not ideal. They lived in a very small flat in Kowloon somewhere. Altogether there were five grandchildren, so you can imagine how crowded it was. And . . . after a while, we suddenly heard that she had gone to the Sha Wan Drive old people's home. . . . Most Chinese people don't like to be in old folks homes. They think that it's a great disgrace if their son is not filial, and they think of it as a rejection. But we kept consoling her and she kept consoling herself. She's a very brave woman. And it's very hard to get into this home. It's extremely clean. Extremely nice and friendly. . . . and she always says how lucky she is.

Ah Leen came to work for Mrs. Chin and her husband a few years after Ah Ching did, and stayed with the family for over twenty years. Ah Leen was not, strictly speaking, a sohei, for she had been married. Her marriage, however, was never consummated, and following a pattern of "compensation marriage," she left her husband and provided him with a replacement (Stockard 1989:48–69).[9] As Mrs. Chin remembered, Ah Leen said when she was very young she was forced to marry a man she "disliked intensely from the first moment" she saw him, and so she fled and earned some money to buy a concubine to replace herself. The concubine and her son were "very good" to Ah Leen.[10] Ah Leen invested her wages in building a house in Dongguan. When she eventually retired, she went to live in Dongguan where her "son" had become an important Communist Party official. Mrs. Chin reported that Ah Leen's son drives her around, and she

> is very happy. . . . The son now recognizes her as a mother. . . . He's very good, and when she dies he will take care of her tablet. . . . Dongguan is one of the most prosperous industrial regions in southern China, so her house has appreciated a great deal in value. She rents out one floor to a shopkeeper and

9. Compensation marriage normally refers to a situation in which a "wife" refuses to consummate the marriage or serve as a wife but instead provides her husband with another wife to serve as her replacement. Her income is what allows her to arrange for this "compensation." Dongguan is mainly outside the area where Stockard commonly found delayed transfer marriage and compensation marriage. It is interesting to note that if Ah Leen's age was estimated accurately by Mrs. Chin, she was born at least two decades after the "heyday" of compensation marriage. See Stockard 1989:127–29.

10. Ah Leen's abdication of childbearing did not mean that she forfeited parenthood. As Stockard explains, "secondary wives provided children to compensating bridedaughters as well as to their husband. The sons of secondary wives were responsible for attending to the tablets of deceased first mothers" (1989:69).

makes something like a thousand yuan off that. She's quite comfortable, well off, and she comes out to visit Hong Kong quite often.

Although she was not a sohei, Ah Leen resembles one. At first Mrs. Chin felt pressured by her demands. Ah Leen was a "big, loud and domineering" woman. She "demanded all her rice and quite a salary for the time. She was quite able bodied, and already [Chinese amahs] were becoming a rarity." Ah Leen often spoke to her "sisters" on the phone, and Mrs. Chin heard her give them all kinds of advice concerning work and their employers. Echoing Sankar, Mrs. Chin explained that the sisterhoods, including Ah Leen's very informal network of friends, seemed to her "very much like labor unions." She felt she had to concede to their demands, "whereas in the old days—or in the bad old days—in my father-in-law's time, they cost only a few dollars. Food was so scarce back then that you could get a thousand muijai if you had just a bit of money."

Amahs were on the whole better off than muijai. They earned a wage and were, at least in theory, free to leave their employers and negotiate their conditions of work (cf. Jaschok 1988:101). This does not mean that their work conditions were ideal. In the 1950s Mr. Ho's baby amah, Ah Sam, received a wage of HK$60 per month. As he explained, this was not considered a good wage, but amahs "could survive," and they were satisfied.

> They have always been given housing and food. Not necessarily servant's quarters, but at least a bed to lie down. And definitely food. If you asked me what the treatment was like, I would say it varied a lot—from being abused like a muijai, raped or locked in the house—to very nicely treated. My amah—I think she was treated the way she should have been. No more. No less.

Despite Mr. Ho's protestations, however, not all amahs were satisfied. When Elsa came to Hong Kong, she worked for several years with a Chinese cook amah who took her aside and complained that she was being cheated by their employer. According to this amah, foreign workers had it much better. "You are lucky you have a contract," she told Elsa; "you have more benefits. Me, I have been in this family for quite a long time. I was the one who raised the children, and look at me now."

Although, according to the ideal, the employer's family was responsible for the amah in illness and old age, in practice, as Sankar points out, employers could not meet the demands of supporting their own parents, let alone their servants (1978a:54–55). The benefits an amah received depended on the emotional pressure she could exert on her employer and the extent to which she could convince them that she really was "like one of the family." Mr. Ho did not keep in touch with his family's amahs. Some amahs, he explained, "have a very close link with the family they work for, even for quite a long period of time after they retire, even when they are very old and until they die. Some do. But that depends on individuals." If a retired amah comes to visit at New Year, employers may give her *leihsih*, a red envelope containing "lucky money," and now and then she might be invited out for a meal, but few employers feel responsible for looking after their old family amahs once they have retired. For a fortunate few, like Ah Leen and Ah Lee, old age has meant returning to the mainland to live with relatives or moving into flats in Hong Kong with "sisters." But more often, as in Ah Ching's case, retirement has meant entering an old age home.

Although some employers say they would prefer to hire Chinese amahs if they were still available, not all feel that way. Mrs. Chin has employed a Filipina domestic worker for three years and is far happier with this arrangement than she was with any of her Chinese amahs. Ah Ching, Mrs. Chin's husband's baby amah, behaved in many ways like a mother-in-law to Mrs. Chin. She insisted on eating at the dinner table with the rest of the family; she called Mr. Chin by his given name; and she passed herself off as the children's "grandmother." Mrs. Chin's sisters asked her how she could tolerate this "mother-in-law figure" in her house. Mrs. Chin said she felt like the outsider. "After all, I'd only known my husband for eight years, and Ah Ching had known him all his life!" Once the children grew older, the Chins did not need a baby amah, but they did not have the heart to let Ah Ching go. Ah Ching worked the family attachments in her best interest; no one dared get rid of her because she was "like family."

One of the biggest differences between Filipina domestic workers and amahs, according to Mrs. Chin, is that foreign women eventually "marry and go home, so they don't form these definite commitments and attachments." With foreign workers, there is "a professional attachment which makes the relationship easier" than with amahs. It is worth noting that "professionalism" has different connotations when it is ascribed to sohei and other traditional Chinese amahs and when it refers to foreign domestic workers. As Kenneth Gaw and others apply the term to Chinese amahs, it suggests that domestic work is a career or a profession, more than just a means to earn money. It implies that amahs took pride in their work. Their relationships with employers, however, are characterized not as professional but as pseudofamilial. Filipina domestic workers are not considered professionals pursuing a career, but their relationships with employers may be viewed as more professional, based on a contract, not on an emotional or personal bond. The relationship between foreign workers and Chinese employers, unlike the traditional one between Chinese servants and their employers, entails no expectation of a lasting obligation or commitment.

Besides muijai and traditional Chinese amahs, Sankar identifies "modern amahs" as "wage laborer[s] who [are] not willing to exchange salary or benefits for favors" (Sankar 1978a:56). These Chinese workers fall into two groups, those who work full-time and live in their employer's homes and those who work part-time several hours a week for one or more families. The first type had become very rare by the 1990s.

Full-time Chinese domestic workers could demand higher wages than foreign workers. One Chinese cook, for example, earned HK$6,000 per month in 1989, while the Filipina domestic worker who was in charge of childcare and housecleaning earned just under HK$3,000. Compared with full-time local Chinese domestic workers, foreign workers are relatively inexpensive. Their starting salary in fall 1993 was HK$3,500 (approximately US$450) per month, plus room and board. According to employment agency staff, the wage of a full-time, live-in Chinese worker could be up to twice that amount.[11]

At the time of my early 1990s fieldwork, most Chinese domestic workers worked part-time and collected an hourly wage. In 1993 I was told that Chinese women could earn up to HK$70 per hour, and foreign workers HK$30–60. In 2006 the hourly wage for local women who did part-time domestic work was normally HK$50 per hour. During the period just before Chinese New Year, when women sometimes cleaned intensively in teams of two or three, the normal wage went up to HK$75 per hour. Officially foreign domestic workers are not permitted do part-time work, but in the cases I knew of they earned HK$30–40 per hour. Chinese women often work when employers are out and do not typically develop a sentimental relationship with them. "Whereas the traditional amah welcomed sentimental attachment to the employer's family, the modern amah is wary of such entanglements," since they can result in "invasions of her privacy

11. The Filipina domestic worker Mr. Ho hired in the mid-1970s earned around HK$550 per month. Although he speculated that Filipinas would have been "happy" to work for far less, he believed that the minimum wage was pegged at a higher level to protect local workers. Setting Filipinas' wages too low could put Chinese domestic workers out of work.

and ultimately lead to increased demands on her time" (Sankar 1978a:57; cf., Romero 1992:126–29).[12]

Foreign workers risk fines, imprisonment, and deportation if they are caught doing illegal work. In the early 1990s officials usually turned a blind eye to part-time work, but by 1995, with the reported rise in the local unemployment rate, there were more crackdowns than before. The mission estimated that in the early 1990s approximately a third of all foreign domestic workers have done part-time work. Indeed, most of the Filipinas I met had worked on their "day off" for one or two employers, sometimes with the approval and "permission" of the main employer. According to one agency owner, this is "one of Hong Kong's worst-kept secrets." As noted above, this rate had likely dropped considerably after the mid-1990s.

AMAHS AS "SUPERIOR SERVANTS"

The few remaining full-time elderly and experienced Chinese domestic workers in Hong Kong in the early 1990s did not fit the traditional image of the dedicated, obedient, and subservient amah. Their small numbers and anachronistic style turned them into important status symbols; they could demand more money and perks. Often only the wealthiest could afford to hire them (cf. Romero 1992:112–19; Rollins 1985:104–6). Some employers met their demands because Chinese amahs were a rare commodity and they symbolized not only economic success and class identity but also Chinese ethnic, cultural, or racial superiority.

By the early 1990s these few remaining older full-time Chinese domestic workers were on the whole far less subservient and more domineering and demanding than their predecessors. For that reason, Mr. Ho explained, many Chinese preferred to hire foreign workers. One employer flatly stated that Chinese amahs know what they are worth and constantly remind you that they can get another job elsewhere if their demands are not met. She recently "made the shift to FDHs" when her last Chinese worker retired. As she explained, "amahs have become so rare that they can virtually name their price. The fear now, though, is that if you can find one, you never know when one of your so-called friends, will offer her more money, and

12. The greater freedom and flexibility of part-time Chinese domestic workers resembles that of Chicana domestic workers described in Romero 1992. Although Chinese local domestic workers normally work alone, I was told that at Chinese New Year they sometimes form collectives, working in groups of two or three, and charge HK$75 per hour for each worker.

she will leave to go and work for them." The loyalty that Gaw and others commonly attribute to *all* Cantonese domestic workers is thus rare among the remaining few. Loyalty has, in many cases, been replaced by a desire for economic gain—a common enough theme in Hong Kong but one that goes against the popular notion of the traditional Cantonese amah, whose devotion to her employer's family was supposedly not motivated by economic necessity or greed.

As we have seen, there have been many different types of household workers in Hong Kong's history. Amahs, to which foreign workers are most often compared, did not form a homogeneous group. Nevertheless, employers commonly ascribed to them two main virtues that they claim foreign workers lack: Chinese amahs of the past "knew their place" and were, above all, "loyal servants." Despite many examples to the contrary, this nostalgic view still holds. Mr. Ho, for instance, spoke of the amahs he remembered who

> would rather stay with one family than to go and look for different families. Job hopping was nonexistent in those days. . . . Some amahs even stayed with a family for more than two decades or generations. They started when they are young, or maybe in their mid-thirties, and then end up retiring in the same family. So they used to be able to see their young employer growing up, and their kids, and then another generation. The link was very strong.

This nostalgic bias is typical of many Chinese in Hong Kong, whether they hired Chinese domestic workers in the past, grew up with them in their homes, or were raised in less wealthy households without servants but believe they know what they were like.

Certainly Chinese domestic workers were, on the whole, extremely hardworking. But were they really more hardworking than foreign domestic workers or any other domestic workers the world over? Were they really warmer, more expert, and more loyal? The answer to these questions is, in my view, a qualified "no." Although it is not my intent to criticize Chinese domestic workers of the past (who deserve the belated but well-earned appreciation), it is important to place the nostalgic and romanticized image of them in perspective. Cynical though it may sound, "tributes" to the amahs of the past do little to erase the hardships and exploitation they endured. A critique of the imagined superior servant is crucial because only by understanding the discourse that surrounds amahs are we able to deconstruct the opposite and more insidious stereotype of the lazy, selfish, and greedy foreign workers.

Chinese amahs of the past are viewed as the antithesis of the foreign worker, a symbol that opposes the past to the present and recalls a time when Hong Kong seemed wholly comfortable in its status as a colony, a time when servants "knew their place." As a colony that never fought for independence, Hong Kong of the 1990s was in an awkward situation. As one Chinese woman explained, reunification with the mainland is "like leaving your adopted parent—the only parent you ever knew—and being given back to your birth mother." Being "given back" to China, as opposed to gaining or receiving independence, raises issues of identity. Reunification with the mainland—which has itself undergone phenomenal sociocultural, political, and economic transformations over the past decades—inevitably stirred up concerns and questions about the degree of Hong Kong's Chineseness. In this context, the imagined Chinese amah glorified a time and place—well away from Communist China—where there was no guilt about wealth, power, or class difference.

"FDHs" in contrast, symbolize a rapidly changing global terrain in which local cultures take on postmodern qualities (Appadurai 1991). Building on the metaphor of war and illness, foreign women are said to be "taking over," or "invading" the city and threatening to "infect" the new generation of more "traditional" and "naïve" Indonesian domestic workers with their activism and assertiveness. Unlike the good servants of the past who are remembered as quietly performing their duties and remaining outside the public eye, Filipina workers are seen as loud, aggressive, boisterous, and brash. They make demands and they stand their ground.

Contemporary Chinese local domestic workers (LDHs)—whose numbers increased in the late 1990s and early 2000s—have neither the economic benefits nor the prestige associated with the last remaining Chinese amahs. Most of them work part-time for low hourly wages for employers who do not need or cannot afford the help of a full-time live-in foreign domestic worker. As local domestic workers become organized and assert their rights, they too may evoke negative comparisons with the imagined superior servants of the past.

For Hong Kong's upper- and middle classes, the Chinese amah has become the symbol of an idealized past in which power, status, and class differences were unquestioned. The image of the loyal, humble servant who passively acquiesced in her master's every wish can also be viewed as a tool with which Hong Kong people (not only employers) try to control and subdue contemporary domestic workers. Cantonese amahs are thus a metaphor for control and domination and a tool with which to put present-day workers "in their proper place."

4 | THE TRADE IN WORKERS

Filipina domestic workers are a valuable source of income for hundreds of recruitment and placement agencies in the Philippines and in Hong Kong, an important source of labor for Hong Kong employers, and a crucial source of foreign capital for the Philippine government. It is therefore in the shared economic interest of agencies, employers, and governments on both sides of the China Sea that Filipinas continue to be docile workers. This chapter describes recruitment and the role of agencies in Hong Kong and the Philippines in preparing Filipina domestic workers for the Hong Kong market.

Although agencies, employers, and governments all attempt to mold women into docile and obedient domestic workers, the women themselves are also involved in the disciplining process, both as willing accomplices and as unknowing victims. The extent of self-discipline and attempts to— or ability to—resist the control to which they are subjected are important questions underlying this chapter and those that follow.

SATISFACTION GUARANTEED

As of the mid-1990s about two-thirds of all Filipina domestic workers in Hong Kong were hired through one of several hundred Hong Kong employment agencies.[1] Over two-thirds of the seventeen hundred Filipinas in the Asian Migrant Centre study conducted in 1989–90 were hired through one of 115 Philippine employment agencies and 79 Hong Kong counterpart agencies (AMC 1991:28).[2] Carolyn French's survey of twelve hundred Filipina domestic workers found that almost three-quarters of them had located employers through government or private recruitment agencies in the Philippines and their Hong Kong counterparts (French 1986a:137). Until mid-1994, domestic workers and employers could also locate one another through personal contacts, as in the case of Elsa and Belle's first employers, but that year the Philippine Overseas Employment Administration (POEA) issued a memorandum popularly known as "MC 41," which effectively banned "name hiring" and required that all domestic workers be hired through licensed agencies (MFMW 1995). According to the Labour Department, as of June 1994, there were 481 registered employment agencies in Hong Kong that dealt with foreign domestic workers. Twelve years later, by July 2006, the number had more than doubled and there were 972 such agencies.

In the late 1980s, over 100,000 Hong Kong households employed domestic workers. According to 1988 figures, the "typical" employer's household had four or five members, including at least one child under twelve years old or an elderly person over sixty-five. Virtually all employers were middle income or above (in 1993 they were legally required to have a yearly household income of no less than HK$150,000). Most employers surveyed by the Hong Kong Census and Statistics Department preferred to hire live-in workers because they could require the worker's services anytime, day or night (HK-CS 1990:57–66). Some employers hired a domestic worker to perform one principal duty such as cooking, cleaning and ironing, or childcare, but about two-thirds hired domestic workers to perform a combination of duties (HK-CS 1990:65; see also AMC 1991:37).

As of the year 2000, according to a government survey, over 200,000 Hong Kong households (over 10 percent of the total of 2.1 million households) employed domestic workers; 88 percent of these employed foreign

---

1. By mid-1987 there were approximately 900 agencies in the Philippines, most of them in the Manila area (*SCMP* 1987a). By 2003, out of over 2,820 licensed recruiters in the Philippines that dealt with land- or sea-based recruitment, over 1,040 recruited domestic workers for overseas markets (Wee and Sim 2004:7).

2. The percentage of Thai domestic workers hired through agencies was much higher, closer to 85 percent, but few of the Indian and Sri Lankan domestic workers used agencies. They depended much more on personal contacts (AMC 1991:28).

domestic workers (HK-CS 2001). Households that employed foreign domestic workers in 2006 were required to have a monthly income of HK$15,000 per month (HK$180,000 or US$23,000 per year), just below the median monthly household income of HK$16,500.

Prospective Hong Kong employers usually hire domestic workers through an agency chosen on a friend's recommendation, from an advertisement, or because of its convenience or proximity to home or work. The prospective employer then visits the agency—many located in glitzy office buildings in Central District or Tsim Sha Tsui or on the ground floor of upscale housing estates in the midlevels of Hong Kong island—and describes to the staff his or her specific requirements. The employer is then referred to individual applicant files. In the 1990s, employers could see candidates on video monitors; by 2006 video clips were available online, and most agencies arranged for interviews with candidates via live computer video conferencing. If a worker is selected, the agency coordinates the necessary paperwork with a counterpart agency in the Philippines, Indonesia, or elsewhere. For the employer, the entire procedure usually takes three or four months. Most employers do not meet workers ahead of time but hire them on the basis of their application materials.

One role of the Hong Kong agency is to convince potential employers that their domestic workers—their "products"—are superior to those of their competitors; that they are better qualified, better trained, and more obedient. Much of the rhetoric I heard from agency staff in Hong Kong was geared toward attracting new customers and guaranteeing the satisfaction of old ones. One owner boasted that his agency dealt almost exclusively with "direct hires," workers who had not been in Hong Kong before. For many employers, this is a major selling point. He would not accept applications from "finish contracts," women already in Hong Kong whose contracts were expiring.[3] The workers listed at this agency were all "hand-picked" by the Chinese owner or the director in order to "guarantee" the most obedient, honest, and hardworking candidate possible. This agency, in operation since before 1980, has a reputation for being very selective and for providing a guarantee: if dissatisfied within the first three months,

---

3. The term *direct hire* sometimes refers to a person who is hired without the use of an agency. More often it is used to refer to a domestic worker who is hired directly from the Philippines, and who has never worked in Hong Kong. In other words, a direct hire is generally not a "finish contract." These terms are used as nouns; e.g., "she is a direct hire, not a finish contract."

the employer receives a "free replacement." An employer who terminates a worker's contract must provide her with an air ticket home and is then given four and a half months in which to choose a free replacement.

The director of another Hong Kong agency whom I spoke to in 1994 also recommended that employers negotiate overseas direct hires, rather than local finish contract workers, although his agency dealt in both types. Overseas hires, the agency representative explained, were "on sale" because the agency was celebrating its thirteenth anniversary. As he put it, "We are having a promotional bargain of 15 percent off." The special price to the employer was HK$4,080, which included the cost of a one-way air ticket from Manila. For a local finish contract worker, the cost to the employer was HK$3,600, which included the Philippine Consulate notarization fee and a forty-day guarantee for the employer. The guarantee at this agency was similar to those of other agencies. It ensured the employer a half refund within forty days or unlimited replacements within the first forty days. The overseas hire was also guaranteed for one year. If the worker performs poorly, or if either employer or worker terminates the contract within the first year for any reason, the employer need only repay the Philippine Consulate handling fee (HK$425 at the time). The one-way air ticket would still be covered, and the employer need not repay it. The agency representative boasted in 1994 that his was the only agency that videotaped the "entire" interview (which lasted about five minutes). The other agencies, he claimed, "only record the girl introducing herself." His agency staff travel far from metro Manila, "to many of the smaller islands and small towns out in the provinces" to select the best possible women.

The rapid turnover in domestic workers—contracts are often terminated before two years are up—does not present a problem for recruitment agencies. Domestic workers are valuable commodities. The greater the number of domestic workers and the more rapid their turnover, the more profitable is the agency's business. Although many agencies offer "free replacements" for unsatisfied employers, it is the employer, not the agency, who is generally required to pay the domestic worker's return ticket home. Chances are good, moreover, that when a worker is terminated, she will return to the same agency, willing to sign away months of yet-to-be-earned income to try her luck again.

The similarities between domestic workers and other types of commodities should be evident. The domestic worker is marketed as though she were an inanimate household appliance: She comes in various models, goes on sale, includes a warranty, and can easily be replaced if the customer is not satisfied. Like a washing machine or a refrigerator, a domestic worker has little say about the household she is delivered to or the job she is expected to perform. Nor is the salesperson, except in rare instances, particularly concerned about the product once it has left the shop. Increasingly, through computer searches, prospective employers can enter the specific characteristics they are looking for in a worker, including age, marital status, children, education, languages spoken, and so on.

Although Hong Kong agencies say they act in the best interest of employers and workers, it is clear that their own interests come first. In refusing to accept applications from finish contract workers, for example, some agencies might seem to be bypassing valuable workers. Those who have already worked in Hong Kong know their way around, have a better sense of what they are getting into, and may have a network of friends who give them support and therefore may not be subject to the loneliness or culture shock of many new arrivals. But agency personnel and many of the employers I spoke to saw these very qualities as disadvantageous. According to one agency owner, "Most people don't want an FDH who has already worked locally. The ones who are new to Hong Kong are more subservient, and less wise and cunning than those who have been here a while. Those who have been here know the ropes, and may be very difficult." A Filipino staff member at an agency in Central made a similar statement: "The advantage of a direct hire is that she is new and you can break her in the way you want. A finish contract knows her way around, but she may not be as easy to break in." An employee at another agency explained:

> The smart ones and the ones who have been in Hong Kong for some time negotiate the terms of their contract and try to bargain with the employer for their terms—such as their own room, a certain day off, and so on, while the ones who are direct hires from the Philippines are offered their terms by the employer. The local girls offer the employer terms—like they will stay out at night and won't clean cars, or they want a room with an air conditioner.

Thus, finish contract workers are not in the best economic interest of agencies, but they can be advantageous for employers and workers. One advantage is that employer and worker can meet in person before signing a contract. They can conduct their own interview, and the employer need not make a decision based solely on a file of papers, a videotaped interview, or a live interview over the Internet. The advantage to the domestic worker is clear: An interview allows her a chance to assess the employer. When workers are in the Philippines, they know little about their prospective employers. Employers are not required to provide as much personal information as workers, and what they do provide to the agency—regarding income, occupation, and special needs—is not usually told to the worker. In many cases, workers I spoke to had no idea of their employer's occupations or household composition ahead of time. Agency staff decided what limited information would be relayed to the worker. The domestic worker's file, in contrast, was an open book, available to anyone who walked in off the street.

The tips and advice agencies offer to employers help to promote a high turnover in workers. At one large agency a staff member said that no matter how attached to a domestic worker an employer and her family has become, they are strongly advised to keep the worker for only one contract or two at the most. One reason is that after five years with the same employer, the worker is legally entitled to a salary bonus called long-service pay. Another reason stated by agency staff is that, through time, even the best domestic worker will "begin to slack off in her duties and take advantage of her employer." What this staff person neglected to mention is that if all employers kept the same workers for several contracts, the agency's business would be greatly diminished. If the worker's contract is not renewed, the employer will return to the agency to find a new one. In dealings with prospective employers, Hong Kong agencies profess to have the best interests of the employer in mind, but, in fact, they persuade employers to act in the best interest of the agency.

Hong Kong agencies claim they do everything possible to satisfy the employer-customer, but they make few claims regarding the satisfaction of the worker. The underlying assumption shared by most agency staff and many employers is that foreign workers are lucky to work in Hong Kong regardless of the circumstances. Advising employers to hire new domestic workers and not to renew contracts is clearly not—nor do agencies claim that it is—in the best interest of workers. Changing workers every two or every four years, regardless of how satisfied employers are with their work, is also not in the best interest of the employer. Such a change requires additional training, personal readjustments, and expense on the part of both the worker and the employer.

PACKAGING THE PRODUCT

Agencies in the Philippines, Indonesia, and elsewhere serve as "partners" or "counterparts" to Hong Kong agencies. The primary stated role of the Philippine or Indonesian agency is to provide a steady pool of candidates. Agencies must thus convince women whom they recruit or who come to them that the agency can provide them with good jobs.[4] Just as Hong Kong agencies present themselves as champions of the employers' interests, recruitment agencies in the Philippines or Indonesia present themselves as advocates for prospective domestic workers. Despite the kindness of certain agency personnel and the stated patriotic or humanitarian motives of specific agencies, recruitment agencies are money-making operations. Their success depends on their ability to generate and "package" products that will satisfy would-be employers. Since many Hong Kong employers prefer women who have not previously worked in the colony, agencies must maintain a continual fresh stock of potential workers.

Agencies in the Philippines and elsewhere are involved in the initial stages of furnishing workers for the Hong Kong market. These agencies help to transform women into domestic workers. Whether a manager of a marketing firm, a schoolteacher, a university degree holder, or a rural housewife who has not completed high school, whether married or unmarried, in her teens or in her forties, a woman undergoes virtually the same homogenizing process intended to produce a single product: a hardworking, submissive, and obedient domestic helper.

Approaching an agency in the Philippines or meeting a recruiter in her town or village is likely to be a Filipina's first step toward securing employment as an overseas worker. The "typical" Filipina domestic worker is in her late twenties or early thirties and unmarried. She supports several family members in the Philippines, and her primary stated reason for going to Hong Kong is economic, although a desire for pleasure, adventure, and independence may also be factors. She is most likely Roman Catholic, has at least a high school education, and speaks English, as well as her national and regional dialect. She may have been an office worker or a professional in the Philippines, or she may have been unemployed. About one in three Filipina domestic workers is married, and they typically leave two or three children behind to be cared for by relatives in the Philippines (AMC 1991:9–20, 26; see also French 1986a).

4. Although I did not conduct research in the Philippines, domestic workers I spoke to suggest that agencies in the Philippines do not distinguish themselves by the particular sorts of employers they can locate, beyond specializing in certain regions of the world such as Hong Kong or the Middle East.

MARLENE

Marlene's narrative helps to illustrate the employment process from the worker's point of view (AMC 1991:15). Like almost a third of Filipina domestic workers in Hong Kong, Marlene has a university degree. Hers is in commerce from a local university in Iloilo, a central Philippine province on the island of Panay. Like many college graduates, Marlene was unable to find a job after graduation; so she decided to work overseas to help her family. Her first job was in Singapore. She told an interviewer in 1990 about her first approach to an agency in Manila in 1984:

> The agent, by the name of Mila, told me to submit my autobiography and to pay a deposit, and they would work out my papers for a job as a domestic helper in Singapore. . . . From 1985 to 1988 I worked as a maid in Singapore. I started with the salary of S$250 (US$125) monthly. During my last year with them my employer made me work for two houses, and my salary increased to S$400 (US$200). I later learned that the other family I was working for paid my employer S$300. I told myself, I could find this kind of money in the Philippines, why should I make a buffalo of myself for ungrateful masters? I returned to Manila in 1988 and with my savings I started a small eatery for factory workers. On the side I sold Avon cosmetics and tupperware. (AMC 1991:85)

During the late 1980s, the price of food in the Philippines soared, and Marlene was unable to pay her bills and her debts. She then learned that domestic workers in Hong Kong could make more than in Singapore.

> I went to see Mila in Ascend [the name of the agency] and she recommended Annie to me. Annie is a Filipino Chinese married to a Hong Kong Chinese. For a small fee she agreed to get me an employer in Hong Kong and work out my papers much faster. I agreed and she took my papers.
> The next day I went to her office where 37 other girls were also waiting. All of us submitted our autobiography. Then we were brought to the video room for an interview. All of us sat down in a line in front of the video camera and were interviewed. Some of the questions were:
>
> Q: Tell me about yourself, where you were born, grew up, family background, etc.
> Q: What were your duties and responsibilities as a maid? . . .
> Q: What would you do if you didn't know how to cook a dish?
> A: I will ask my employer for instructions and make sure I learn it the first time.
> Q: What are your likes and dislikes? What kind of employer do you like, don't you like? What are your hobbies?

Q: If something terrible happens to your family while [you are] in Hong Kong, what would you do?

A: I would consult my employer for advice. If it is not so serious I will request my employer to allow me to make a call. If my presence is needed, it will depend whether my employer will allow me to go home for some time. If they refuse, I will obey them.

After the video taping I paid Annie Peso 1,500 (US$65). . . . The program was shown to prospective employers in Hong Kong and each employer picked out from the 37 girls in the show. I was among those chosen by these employers. The contract was prepared and once it was signed, I paid Annie another Peso 6,500 (US$283). In addition I spent for the processing of papers at the Labour Department (POEA), for visa fees, medical certificate and predeparture orientation. This amount was a little lower than the standard processing fee since I already had a passport.

Processing took two and a half months and I arrived in Hong Kong on the 2nd of March 1991. Before leaving Manila, I signed a promissory note saying I would pay Annie HK$6,000 and Mila HK$1,300. These amounts would be deducted from my monthly salary. All in all I would have spent Peso 36,000 (US$1,335) for getting the job in Hong Kong. Peso 10,000 (US$370) would go to Mila and the Peso 19,000 (US$705) to Annie.

Since I arrived I have been paying Annie HK$2000 (US$256) every month, until I finished the last payment of HK$1,500 in June. I also learned that my employer also paid Annie for getting a maid for them. (AMC 1991:85–87)

GIVING THE RIGHT ANSWERS

Some of the questions and procedures that Marlene described are typical of many types of job applications. She had to answer questions about her previous work experience and her education and to share her views on various work-related topics. Like a teacher who is asked pedagogical questions, a domestic worker is asked how she feels about children and whether she likes to cook. She is also asked, however, either during the interview or on the application form, to answer more personal questions concerning her age, marital status, religion, financial situation, and salary at her previous job. She must provide information about herself, her children if she has any, her husband's and her father's occupations and salaries.

Application forms are fairly standard at most agencies. Besides this basic information, an applicant is usually required to comment on her previous work experience. One applicant, asked about her childcare experience, wrote: "Can give baby bath, sterilize bottle, feed baby, change diapers, give medicines, supervise play." For a question about cooking abilities, most applicants listed *adobo*—a popular Philippine dish—and other things such as "beef stick, maggi soup, spaghetti." Application files often include copies of high school diplomas and marriage certificates. Most agencies require a short essay, and some encourage individual expression. At one agency, applicants included informal snapshots of themselves. One woman enclosed a large photograph of herself and the little girl she took care of in Singapore. The handwritten caption at the bottom of the photograph read: "I love the little children very much." At one agency, applicants were instructed to "tell something personal" and explain why they want to work in Hong Kong. Almost all of the essays at that agency took the form of a letter to prospective employers. A typical essay read:

> Dear Sir and Ma'am in Hong Kong,
>
> My father is a farmer and my mother is a housewife. We live in Isabela. I want to be a domestic worker because I want to work very hard to help my family earn money so we can send my younger brothers and sisters to school. I promise to work very hard and faithfully and to be honest and obedient if I can work for you in Hong Kong. When I work for you I promise that I will stay in Hong Kong and finish a two year contract.

Among other questions on the application forms are: Do you drink or smoke? Are you willing to eat only Chinese food? The "correct answers" to many of these questions, I was told amidst peals of laughter at the mission, are common knowledge. "If a woman wants a job badly enough, she doesn't drink or smoke, and she would be happy to eat anything that the employer gives her!" In response to a variety of possible interview questions, the best answer is that "the employer is always right," or "I would be sure to discuss it with my employer and ask his or her advice/permission!" Although economic hardships can be mentioned, the applicant should not sound as though she would be working solely for the money. Many women told me they were coached by experienced friends or relatives who had already "passed the test."

Beginning with their interactions with agency staff, Filipinas, like domestic workers elsewhere, learn to exhibit deferential behaviors toward their employers (see Rollins 1985:155–206). Some Filipinas said that they do not "really" consider themselves inferior to their employers but that they "play along" (cf. Rollins 1985:107). But to view such reservations about deferential behavior as resistance may assume more than is warranted (Scott 1990:23–24). Some domestic workers internalize a sense of inferiority, which can begin with the application process. In learning how to answer such questions "correctly," no matter how much a woman feels she is just "playing along," she begins to learn how to fit herself into the employer's desired mold, in some cases even by adjusting her age and personal history.

Many agencies accept only applicants with two years' prior experience as a domestic worker, although Hong Kong government regulations are flexible in this regard. Some applicants alter their pasts and transform the housework they did in their own homes into "paid domestic work" for a relative. Letters of reference are, perhaps needless to say, easy to come by. Although it goes against the common assumption among domestic workers, the owner of a Hong Kong agency told me that most employers prefer to hire married women because they think they are more "stable," often in more financial need, and "less trouble than single girls." I met some women who had claimed they were not married and that they had no children because they believed that most employers preferred to hire women without too many responsibilities back home, and indeed, some employers I spoke to shared this view.

Age is another factor that domestic workers "adjust" to fit themselves into the necessary mold. Although the Hong Kong government has no minimum age restriction, in 1994 the Philippine government imposed a minimum age of twenty-five for first-time domestic workers. Two underage Filipinas I spoke to said they were not concerned, because they could "easily fake" their age. Acosta and two other Filipinas who were over forty had had their birth certificates altered to become "younger" candidates. As Acosta explained, she wore her hair long and her skirts short in order to play the part of a woman in her thirties rather than her forties. Even before the minimum age was introduced, two women in their teens said they were a few years older than they were because they believed employers would consider them too young. Information I collected from recruitment agencies suggests that most employers prefer workers between twenty-five and thirty-five.

Other forms of self-imposed "packaging" include claiming that one's children are older than they really are or exaggerating the degree of confidence one feels about the childcare situation at home in the Philippines. Many women leave their families in the care of relatives, and although they worry about how their children are being raised, they believe they must give the impression of stable, long-term security, that they will not need to leave suddenly to take care of some emergency back home.

DOCILE BODIES

A number of anthropological studies look at the way in which women's bodies are disciplined through work and medical practices (e.g., Ginsburg and Rapp 1995; Martin 1987, 1994; A. Ong 1987; Ong and Peletz, 1995). Recruitment of Filipina workers also involves certain forms of body discipline. Like biographical and personal data, physical features may be altered to conform to an accepted mold. Applicants are fitted into uniforms, examined, photographed, x-rayed, measured, and evaluated. They are often advised to make themselves "look the part." Agency staff members advise women to come back after they have lost twenty pounds, trimmed their fingernails, cut their hair, removed makeup and jewelry, and changed their shoes. An applicant is usually photographed at the agency or asked to submit photographs of herself. These generally include a close-up of her face and a "full body" shot of her standing, usually wearing a standard pastel pink or blue striped "maid's uniform" with a white collar and white apron. Uniforms may be rented or borrowed from the agency for the photograph or video session. A woman is advised to wear comfortable shoes, little or no makeup, and to cut her hair short or tie it back. As I was told by agency staff in Hong Kong and by domestic workers, a prospective worker must look neat and tidy but not so attractive as to put off women employers.

In some cases, videotapes and files are sent to Hong Kong to be reviewed by agencies there. In other cases, Hong Kong staff visit counterpart agencies in the Philippines and "handpick" applicants.[5] One Hong Kong recruiter used a special form to comment on each applicant he met. He also gave an overall evaluation and "grade" to each applicant on appearance, personality, and spoken English and comprehension, scoring them excellent, very good, good, fair, or poor. In most of the two hundred files I looked through at that agency in 1994, women received mainly scores of "good." Well over half of the applicants had one score of "very good," most often in the category of "personality." No applicants received "excellent" in any category, and only a few received "fair" or lower. For every five hundred applicants on file at

---

5. Agencies in the Philippines can be owned only by Philippine citizens, but often they are owned by Filipinos of Chinese descent or Filipinos married to Chinese.

the counterpart Philippine agency, this Hong Kong agency picked roughly a hundred. The files of those who "pass the interview" are then brought to Hong Kong to show to prospective employers. Most applicants are placed within three months. If an applicant is not hired within six months, her file is rejected. She is then offered the chance to repay certain fees and to "redo" her file and resubmit her application.

Under "appearance," none of the applicants whose files I saw received more than a "good" rating—even some who might have been considered beautiful. When I made this observation to a Chinese worker at the agency, she laughed and shook her head incredulously as if this idea was preposterous. Another staff member explained that the rating of an applicant's appearance might be influenced in part by the fact that "people—women employers in particular—don't want to hire domestic workers who are beautiful, for obvious reasons." Those whose appearance was rated as "fair" usually included the interviewer's written explanation that they had acne, visible scars, or birthmarks or, most often, were "rather dark."[6] The file of a nineteen-year-old Filipina, for example, read, "She's rather dark, but well built and looks like a hard-working and obedient helper." Asked why it was necessary to remark on an applicant's complexion, the staff member confirmed what I had already heard from various other sources: that many Chinese employers do not like to hire women with darker skin because "they scare the children." As she explained, "If the children see them it will make them cry." Stories often circulate among domestic workers of women whose contracts were abruptly terminated at the airport, the moment the employer laid eyes on them. The explanation, I was told, is that the employer "saw how dark her skin was" or "how beautiful she was" and didn't want her around.[7] Filipina applicants try to look neat and tidy, but not beautiful or well dressed (cf. Rollins 1985:147, 167, 200).[8]

At an early stage in the application process, a woman must submit to physical examinations and medical tests. These are required by the Hong Kong government and by the Philippine government. The employment contract states that "the Helper should submit his/her medical certificate to the Employer

---

6. In this context, *fair* meant "mediocre" rather than "attractive."

7. I was also told that Filipina and Thai domestic workers who "look more Chinese" (sometimes of Chinese descent) are preferred by employers who intend to have them work outside the house, illegally, in an office, restaurant, or factory.

8. As Judith Rollins explains, among the outward signs of deference or subservience employers are likely to appreciate is the appearance of not being "too educated or too intelligent, too materially well off, or too attractive" (1985:147).

for inspection" and advises employers "to scrutinise the medical certificate before sponsoring the Helper's application for an employment visa for Hong Kong" (HK-ID 1993d:2). Many employers require another medical examination and pregnancy test once a domestic worker arrives in Hong Kong.[9]

During medical examination, a woman's body is invaded. Specimens are taken to test for various forms of hepatitis, syphilis, herpes, HIV, and other diseases. She receives a pregnancy test. She is x-rayed, weighed, and measured. Her "ideal weight" is recorded alongside her actual weight. Medical information then becomes part of her application file. The employer can then evaluate her on the basis of her state of health as well as her physical appearance and her physical build.

Written comments by agency staff often make reference to a woman's weight and build. The "ideal weight" for a thirty-nine-year-old woman who is five foot three and weighs 156 pounds was marked at 129 pounds. The interviewer wrote, "She can be expected to handle heavy household work, but she is overweight and I hope she reduces her weight a bit." A thirty-three-year-old applicant was described as "quite plump. I think she can cope with household work well if she reduces her weight." This applicant's height was five foot one, her weight 141 pounds, and her ideal weight was marked as 121 pounds. A thirty-seven-year-old, five-foot-tall, 146–pound woman was also deemed overweight. According to her file, her ideal weight should have been 116 pounds, but the agency director wrote, "She is plump and jolly, but quite agile despite her size. She should cope with hard work quite easily." A forty-seven-year-old woman with four children was said to be "strong and well-built. She can handle all the heavy household work and heavy household duties too." Once a woman is hired, her employer may also pressure her to subscribe to a particular bodily ideal, for example, by having her go on a diet. The striking similarities between the physical scrutiny and examination undergone by foreign domestic workers, concubines, and muijai should be obvious.

ECONOMIC CONTROL

From the moment a woman steps into an employment agency in the Philippines she is subject to—and, in many cases, willingly participates in—forms of discipline that she is unlikely to have experienced before. The way she is treated is designed to elicit from the start of the process a sense

9. One extreme case I encountered at the mission was of a domestic worker taken for a physical exam and pregnancy test who was, without her knowledge, given an abortion. She was filing criminal charges against her employer.

of dedication, loyalty, and sacrifice, a sense of how to present herself as a domestic worker. One important means through which this transformation is accomplished is economic: through the economic commitment required of an applicant, the economic obligations she incurs, and the economic rewards she envisions.

Most Filipinas go into debt to find jobs in Hong Kong. Almost three-quarters of the women in French's survey borrowed money to go abroad; two-thirds of these borrowed from relatives, and the rest from friends or friends and relatives or other sources (1986a:137–39). In 1984 the average amount paid to come to Hong Kong was 6,283 pesos (approximately US$387) (1986a:139).[10] The 1989–1990 AMC survey found the average amount paid to recruitment agencies by Filipina domestic workers was 18,542 pesos (US$850) (1991).[11] Some women paid as little as 1,500 pesos and others as much as 35,000 pesos, but most paid the equivalent of about two months' wages. Some of the respondents to the AMC study were unwilling to divulge the source of their loans to pay recruitment fees, but close to half received the money from their relatives. As noted by several of my informants, some Filipinos took loans "through the 5–6 system, a popular but exorbitant money lending process, where for every 5 pesos loaned, one pays 6 pesos back, after a month" (AMC 1991:34).[12] The AMC also found that roughly half of the Filipinas surveyed took out loans of some kind after they arrived in Hong Kong. Almost half were bank loans, and a third involved "passport mortgage," giving one's passport as collateral for a loan (1991:58–59).[13]

Interviews with agency staff and domestic workers who arrived in Hong Kong in 1993 suggest that agencies in the Philippines charged between thirty thousand and forty thousand pesos on average (close to three months' salary) at that time. Occasionally, the mission's volunteers encoun-

10. In 1984 when French's study was conducted, US$1 = 17.52 pesos (CIIR 1987:2); in 1993 US$1 = 25–30 pesos.

11. According to the CIIR report on Filipino migrant workers of all sorts, the average amount paid in 1981 was between 6,582 and 7,768 pesos (1987:9–10).

12. Citing material collected in the late 1970s and early 1980s, another study of Filipino migrant workers states that "few pawned their land or borrowed from private money-lenders or banks" to get the money necessary to go overseas because their rates were so exorbitant. As the study explains, "debt, once incurred, is extremely difficult to clear in the Philippines, because the standard level of interest set by private moneylenders is 20% per month" (CIIR 1987:10–11).

13. This type of loan is particularly risky not only because it is illegal but also because the domestic worker often finds herself in even greater debt trying to retrieve her passport if her contract or her visa is about to expire. It is in such situations that a domestic worker may become especially prone to take up illegal work, including, in some cases, prostitution.

tered women who had paid over fifty thousand pesos. The maximum legal fee that the Philippine government officially allows Philippine agencies to charge for placement and documentation was pegged at five thousand pesos in 1983 (CIIR 1987:26). When agency employees were queried about overcharging, they said that five thousand pesos did not come close to covering the necessary costs and that all agencies overcharge. Philippine government personnel, I was told, were aware of this practice but chose to ignore it because otherwise the agencies could not function and the government would lose a valuable source of income. Newspapers indicate that Hong Kong agencies also charge clients more than the legally stipulated maximum of 10 percent of a month's wages. A point to stress here is that debts and economic obligations make workers reliant on their earnings and, by extension, more dependent on maintaining good relations with employers, who hold the power to terminate their contracts and return them, in debt, to the Philippines.

Employers and domestic workers sometimes end up paying duplicate fees. A worker may be required to pay for her air ticket, visa, processing, and medical examination fees. By Hong Kong law, employers are supposed to reimburse foreign domestic workers for these expenses.[14] But if employers pay the agency, the domestic worker may never be reimbursed. The Hong Kong agency, in turn, can claim to have paid the agency in the Philippines, thus shifting the blame. When Mrs. Chin decided to hire Rina, she discussed the necessary fees with a woman at the agency, who said to her:

> "*You* don't have to worry. You are the all time favorite type of employer for these Filipina maids. [Rina] will pay *any* amount to come work for you." She said, "You are the all time favorite. . . . You are not ancient. You have no old person at the house—no *ah poh* to watch her. You are out all day." She said, "You are fashion." Her English wasn't so good. She said, "You are fashion"—fashionable—so [Rina] knows she will get hand-me-down clothes.

Mrs. Chin, apparently unaware that she was legally obligated to pay Rina's airfare, magnanimously offered to "pay half." The agent insisted that it was not necessary and that Rina would "be happy to pay any amount" for the opportunity to work for her "all time favorite" employer. Aside from showing

14. A domestic worker is required to provide her employer with receipts to prove that she has paid the fees herself. In many cases women either lost or never received receipts; so their expenses were not reimbursed. This is also the case for women who try to claim reimbursement from their employers for food. If they cannot provide receipts, the Labour Tribunal officer will not award recompense.

how the agency gained Mrs. Chin's goodwill by flattering her and allowing Rina to foot the bill, this example illustrates how a worker is expected to make economic sacrifices to get a job.

Through her willingness to make financial commitments to get to Hong Kong in the first place—by borrowing money from parents, relatives, and loan agencies to pay recruitment fees—a woman begins to fit herself into a mold of economic dependence, inferiority, and subservience, qualities that are desired and expected in a domestic worker. Financial and emotional indebtedness both help ensure that a worker remains "in her place." Expressions of economic inferiority are a form of deferential behavior that employers often require of workers (see Rollins 1985:147, 196–97, 157–73).

These qualities are expressed in a woman's willingness to pay the agency whatever fees are asked. Costs may continue to mount as the application progresses. As one domestic worker described her experience, it was as if she were being asked to jump one hurdle after another, and after she jumped each one successfully, she was told how much closer she was to landing the job. Then she was asked for more money in order to continue the process. Acosta described her sister's experience. In 1992 she was required to put down fifteen thousand pesos to begin the recruitment process and prepare her file. Then she was required to pay another fifteen thousand to have her file shown to prospective employers. Finally she was pressured for another fifteen thousand to "complete the process."

Comments written in applicants' files also allude to their financial circumstances and suggest that poorer applicants are more attractive to employers. In the case of a thirty-two-year-old woman with two children, the interviewer wrote, "She is determined to work in Hong Kong *for the welfare of her children.*" A twenty-four-year-old whose father was a farmer was described as a "pleasant looking very simple person *from a poor family. She can be expected to work hard.*" A twenty-four-year-old with one child, whose husband was a police aide, was "a sensible person. *She really needs to work in Hong Kong to earn money because her husband's income would not suffice.*" Of a forty-one-year-old with three children, whose husband was a farmer, the interviewer wrote "(She's rather dark)—A provincial lady, *comes from a poor family and determined to do a good job. She knows hard work and she will do everything possible to work and work.*" A thirty-four-year-old widow with three children was "quite tall and well built. *Being a widow all she needs is financial support from her employment.*" Of a thirty-seven-year-old with three children ranging in age from twelve to fifteen years, and whose husband occasionally worked as a driver, the interviewer wrote, "She is strong and well built and can carry heavy loads. She is a person who *has a strong desire to work because of her family's needs.*" Another thirty-seven-year-old, with five children, was described as "rather dark" but "quick to respond for her age of 37. *She is badly in need of work in Hong Kong because [her] husband is jobless*" (emphasis added).

Agency interviewers' comments suggest that widows, married women with unemployed husbands, or women who are poor or urgently in need of money to support their families may be more likely or more willing to work hard. Many employers feel more comfortable with domestic workers whose economic status is unambiguously inferior to their own. Women from poorer families are more attractive to employers who are anxious to maintain a clear class boundary between themselves and a domestic worker and to those who want the worker to feel especially grateful to have a job. A woman with financial difficulties in the Philippines is likely to be more dependent on her employer and is more likely endure an employer's abuse.

Without a doubt, economic motivations are fundamental in a woman's decision to work in Hong Kong. But domestic workers are not from the poorest sector of the Philippine population. Very poor women are unable to afford the costs of emigrating. According to French, two-thirds of the women she surveyed cited "lack of money" as their main reason for emigrating; others cited adventure or family problems as the main reasons (1986a:131). Seventy-five percent of the Filipina respondents to the AMC survey said they came to Hong Kong for economic reasons, but over 8 percent said they came out of a desire to "travel" or out of "curiosity," and another 15 percent came because they considered the job a "stepping stone" (1991:26). French's data suggests that roughly a third of Filipinas surveyed did not need to borrow money to go to Hong Kong, and almost a fifth of those in the AMC study cited themselves as the sole source of funds from which to pay the agency.

A domestic worker is in an awkward and ambivalent class position. In the Philippines she may have been poor or unemployed, or she may have been a highly educated professional. She may have paid her own way to Hong Kong, or she may arrive there deep in debt. Her earnings may be used to hire a domestic worker back home, and thus she may simultaneously be both a domestic worker and an employer of a domestic worker. On arrival in Hong Kong, regardless of her previous position, she is usually expected to be "just a maid" or a *banmui* (Philippine girl) and to accept the "baggage" that accompanies this label, including a presumption of her economic inferiority. *Ban* is the final syllable of the Cantonese term for "Philippines," and *mui*, as in *muijai*, means "younger sister" or "girl." Innocuous as the literal translation of the term may first appear, the condescending implication of the diminutive is that Filipinas are merely cheap and available "girls," in contrast to *gungyahn* (worker), the term that is usually reserved for Chinese workers (see also Jaschok 1993:1).[15] When used as a form of address for mature women, the term *banmui* carries the same sort of connotations as "girl": perpetual immaturity, inferiority, and submission (see Hansen 1989, 1990; Rollins 1985:158; Romero 1992).

Middle-class employers more often equate Filipina domestic workers with muijai than with the "professional" Chinese amahs of the past. A domestic worker's contract may be reminiscent of the transaction papers that marked the sale of a muijai. The agreement between employers and Chinese amahs, in contrast, was verbal and personal. Families of foreign domestic workers—like the parents of muijai—are often viewed as desperate for money. As Su-lin once asked me, why else would a Filipina be allowed to go so far away to do such demeaning work?

From a domestic worker's point of view, her class identity does not, or should not, change upon arrival in Hong Kong. When she visits the Philippines each year, well dressed and loaded down with gifts, she is received not as a "poor maid" but as a wealthy woman returning from abroad. But unless her remittances are invested in land or other assets, her economic transformation is only temporary, lasting only as long as she works abroad and continues to remit money or until she returns home as a "one day millionaire."

EDUCATION

Since the 1970s, the Philippine economy has been such that despite training as a teacher or a degree in agriculture or commerce, many Filipinos cannot find work. If they do, the salary is often so low that it is impossible to support a family. Filipinas who become domestic workers are often highly educated, sometimes more so than their employers.[16] French's study suggests that almost 50 percent of all domestic workers had a high school education, and an additional 38 percent had attended college or university or received some sort of postsecondary education. Five years after French's

15. Although *gungyahn* was once unabashedly translated as "servant," today it has taken on the somewhat more honorable meaning of "worker," most likely influenced by the use of the term in mainland China.

16. Like West Indian domestic workers in New York (Colen 1990) and Latina domestic workers in the San Francisco Bay area (Salzinger 1991), domestic workers may come from "middle-class" backgrounds and are sometimes far better educated than their employers.

study, the AMC found that the educational level of domestic workers had increased. Of the Filipinas surveyed, nearly all had completed secondary school. Almost two-thirds of those surveyed had attended college or university or had received some sort of tertiary education, and almost half of these had earned a college certificate or university degree (1991:15). Despite this trend, agency staff members claim that employers prefer to hire less-educated domestic workers.

The earliest employers of Filipina domestic workers in Hong Kong, as noted, were mainly foreigners living in the colony. These employers considered Filipinas' English-language skills and education an advantage. Higher levels of education did not conflict with European ideas about the proper status of domestic workers. Most westerners were familiar with the idea of au pairs from the same socioeconomic class as the employer, or nannies who are to some extent considered professionals in their own right (Gathorne-Hardy 1972).

For Chinese employers, with a cultural tradition of segregated and hierarchical servant-master relations, the expectation is significantly different. Many middle-class Chinese employers consider the English-language abilities of Filipina domestic workers beneficial, and many expect "helpers" to tutor their children. But agency staff and members of the employers association both insist that many Chinese employers favor less-educated domestic workers because they "know their place." As the owner of one of Hong Kong's biggest employment agencies explained, today the "high education of FDHs has come to be seen as an objectionable quality" because an educated domestic worker is more likely to "put on airs" and to present herself as "too good" to do what is expected of her. One staff member explained that her agency prefers women "from the provinces" who have little education. In her words, "The applicants with higher education . . . argue more with their employers. . . . Some even have the gall to ask their employers how many degrees *they* have."

From the standpoint of employers and employment agency staff, the ideal worker is not a "professional" or the social equal of her employer. She takes her employer's superiority for granted. Education, like wealth or financial independence, is antithetical to Chinese ideas about domestic servitude and can seem threatening to employers. Education is a traditional Chinese means of attaining political power and prestige. To a woman employer with little education or one who views her education as validating her recent upward mobility, the "downward" mobility of an educated worker can seem to undercut her self-image and put primary cultural values into question.

The comments written in applicants' files support the idea that education and "intelligence" are not valued by employers. In the scores given to prospective domestic workers, personality was the category in which women received highest ratings. Most of those who received "very good" in this category were described in the written comments as "gentle" and also "quick" and "cheerful." A few were described as "bright." More often those with a score of "good" or "very good" for personality were described as "not very bright." The staff member I asked explained that "gentleness" did not refer to her way of handling children or fragile objects, as I had assumed. It meant that she was "soft, kind, and obedient." "Gentle," in this sense, is closer in meaning to "docile, meek, and pliable"—qualities that I was told are all especially desirable in a domestic worker. "Not very bright," she said, often refers to girls "from the provinces" who are "not too smart or educated or sly." Being "not too bright," she explained, can be a good thing, and these women may be especially well suited to work in small households or for first-time employers. They will "just *follow* the instructions they receive," she explained, and will not ask questions or take advantage of their employers as the bright or educated ones might. A much larger household may need a "brighter" domestic worker because she will have to be better organized and work more quickly.[17]

Additional Conditions

Besides exhibiting a willingness to adjust her demeanor, body, personality, experiences, and to accept certain financial commitments, a prospective worker may also be expected to be willing to accept less than ideal work conditions. At the agency a prospective worker may be asked if she is willing to work for an employer who cannot provide her with a private room, who expects very long working hours, or who lives in a more remote part of the New Territories. Most applicants know that the "correct" answer to these questions is "I will be happy to take any job you can find for me, ma'am." Other conditions that applicants may feel pressured to accept include agreeing to do illegal work such as cleaning more than one flat, working for an employer other than the one who signed the contract, or working outside the house in an office or factory. Many are unaware that such work may be illegal and that the official government contract supersedes any agreements made with the agency or the employer.

17. As Rollins has also observed in the United States, employers prefer less-educated and less well-informed domestic workers because they are "more easily controlled" (1985:196).

A woman may be asked to sign various documents, including unofficial contracts and "oaths" at agencies. At one agency applicants were required to sign the following, fairly typical, list of rules.

1. On your day off, you must be back home by 10:00 P.M. and you can never stay out overnight.
2. You can never ask for a salary advance or borrow money from your employer.
3. You can never receive collect international calls from your friends and relatives.
4. You can never use the telephone for international calls.
5. You can never use the phone without permission from your employer.
6. You can never bring your friends and relatives to the house of your employer.
7. You can never beat the children of your employer.
8. You must be willing to adopt the ways your employer wants you to do the housework.
9. You must be willing to take care of children the ways your employer wants you to.
10. You must never go out without permission unless there is an emergency.
11. You must take care of your personal hygiene very well.
12. You must take your shower once a day before you take your rest at night.
13. You must brush your teeth at least once a day.
14. You must keep your fingernails short and clean.
15. You must keep your hair clean. Wash your hair at least twice a week.
16. You must perform all your duties as tidy as possible.
17. You must be hardworking. You must never use your work hours to do personal things.
18. You must be kind and patient to children.
19. You must be polite and respect all people in the family of your employer.
20. You must be honest and perform your duties faithfully.
21. You must not argue with your employer.
22. You must not show your temper to your employer or his/her children.
23. You must not use any personal belongings of your employer.

24. You must not take away any possessions of your employer or his/her family.
25. You must pay utmost attention to any instructions given by your employer.
26. You must follow every lawful instruction given by your employer.
27. You must not let strangers in unless you are under supervision of your employer.
28. You must inform your employer of any mistakes you commit.
29. You must not attend any religious rituals other than simple prayer before rest at night in the house of your employer.
30. You must contact [your agency in Hong Kong] whenever you have any problems in Hong Kong.

Applicants who did not agree to this "Code of Discipline" were not processed.

Another agency's rules were less stringent but included "I shall not mind sharing a room with my employer's children if required; I shall observe absolute cleanliness; I shall refrain from smoking; I agree to another medical check-up if my employer requires one." Another list paid closer attention to work-related issues. Workers agreed to "adhere to the working schedule prepared by employer; to serve all visitors tea or coffee; and to keep the house clean and tidy at all times." In addition, workers must "maintain a pleasant and cheerful personality at all times; avoid make-up and fingernail polish; only wear shorts and nightgowns in the servant's quarters." The agreement states that "Personal hygiene is strictly emphasized; that smoking or drinking alcohol are not allowed; and that the clothes of the maid should be washed separately from those of the employer and children."

Agencies may require women to take courses in home economics, or enroll in weeklong training courses where, as one agency director explained, they are taught "basic courtesy and skills." They may be taught childcare techniques, how to use appliances, and cooking. Until 1993, women were required only to take a daylong or half-day government-sponsored, predeparture orientation course. Several domestic workers described it as a waste of time. They were taught how to plug in a vacuum cleaner and how to run a washing machine but nothing about their legal rights or about Hong Kong organizations that might provide help and guidance. Beginning in 1994, a new two-week training program was introduced by the POEA. One domestic worker cynically commented, "it may be better, but it's probably just a way to get more money out of us."

INDONESIAN WORKERS

By the mid-1990s, the Indonesian government was following in the footsteps of the Philippine government. Women who could go to work as domestic workers overseas were recognized as a profitable resource, and mechanisms were developed to deploy them. Through the licensing fees charged to recruitment agencies, and the remittances and fees that women pay for passports, documentation, and training, the Indonesian government gained much needed currency, especially as the Asian financial crisis hit Indonesia hard in the late 1990s. Recent studies show, however, that those who stand to gain the most from overseas workers are the recruitment agencies, the government, and the employers. One recruiter interviewed by the AMC (2005), explained that until the early 1990s, Hong Kong employers still paid most of the recruitment fees. In subsequent years, however, as the number of recruitment agencies multiplied, the competition between them grew, and recruitment agencies shifted many of the costs away from the employers and to the workers.

Recent surveys, research, and anecdotal evidence all demonstrate that by the early 2000s the situation for Filipina domestic workers in Hong Kong had greatly improved, and that Indonesian domestic workers were far more vulnerable to a variety of abuses—especially underpayment and overcharging—than their Filipino counterparts (AMC 2001, 2005; ATKI 2001, 2005; Petersen and Lee 2006; Wee and Sim 2004). Carole Petersen and Peggy Lee argue that many Indonesian domestic workers in Hong Kong fit the international legal definition of "debt bondage" (2006). According to several recent surveys (AMC 2005; ATKI 2001, 2005), over 40 percent of Indonesian domestic workers in Hong Kong are paid below the legal wage, and over 90 percent are overcharged recruitment fees.[18]

The problems of underpayment and overcharging are related to the recruitment process in Indonesia. Whereas Filipinas are free to remain at home while they await employment abroad, Indonesian women must stay at "training camps" that are run by recruiters—for which they are sometimes charged exorbitant rates. Since 1996, the Indonesian government has officially required "training." Training, of course, can potentially be very

---

18. The 2005 survey of 1,017 Indonesian domestic workers by the Asian Migrant Centre found that 42 percent were underpaid and 97 percent were overcharged (AMC 2005). The 2005 study of 2,777 Indonesian domestic workers by the Association of Indonesian Domestic Workers (ATKI) found that 53 percent were underpaid, and 93 percent overcharged (AMC 2005).

beneficial, providing women with language classes (Cantonese if they are headed to Hong Kong, Mandarin if they are going to Taiwan, and English or Mandarin if they are going to Singapore, for example), cooking lessons, and experience using household equipment. Training also increases the competitive edge of Indonesian workers relative to other nationalities, but it often does little or nothing to teach workers about employment regulations, their rights, or what to do if they face difficulties abroad. Moreover, as Vivienne Wee and Amy Sim argue, such training camps often resemble illegal forcible detention (2004:10–12).

I did not visit Indonesian training camps (also known as "recruitment centers"), but women speak readily about their experiences and researchers have reported on the situation (AMC 2005; see also Lan 2006). Women typically remain in the camps for three to six months, but some have had to stay there for up to a year or more as they await overseas employment. Most women work as part of their "training"—some clean the homes of the recruiter and their acquaintances, others work at restaurants. According to the AMC study, women were paid either paltry wages of US$3 to $16 a month for this work, or not paid at all. Although some women reported that the conditions at the camps are reasonable, others reported crowded conditions, insufficient food, and various forms of physical abuse (Wee and Sim 2004:11–12). One woman described how dozens of women were crowded into one room, slept shoulder to shoulder on dirty straw mats, and had to share one shower and toilet. They were locked in and not permitted to leave the camp, not even to visit family members. If they became ill, they were required to pay for their medical expenses. Some women reported receiving no training whatsoever while at the camp, whereas others described long hours of endless language classes (AMC 2005).

Women must typically remain at the camp until they have secured a job. When a job is offered to her, she is expected to take it with no questions asked. She is given a number of forms to sign; sometimes this includes receipts stating that she has received her full salary for 24 months. Women report that forms may be in a language they cannot read, or that they are not given time to read them or a copy of their own to keep. In some cases women are told what salary they will receive abroad, but they are unaware that the wage is below the legal minimum wage. In other cases they know it is below the minimum wage, but are told that if they want a job they must agree to the lower wage. If she is perceived as a "trouble maker" she will not get a job or she risks remaining for more months at the recruitment center. Women are usually required to sign promissory notes in Indonesia or shortly after arrival in Hong Kong that indebt them to a finance company. They are thus forced to take out a "loan" to repay the recruitment debts, although they never actually see the money they have borrowed. Women are often unaware of the full implications of their indebtedness and are unaware that such payments to recruiters is illegal in Hong Kong (Wee and Sim 2004; Petersen and Lee 2006; AMC 2005).

Many women do not know ahead of time that they will be charged as much as the equivalent of seven months' salary for their training, medical examinations, and travel documents. The Hong Kong government stipulates that employment agencies can charge workers only the equivalent of 10 percent of one month's wages (HK$340 in 2006). Although Hong Kong counterpart agencies claim they are not involved in this process and do not profit from it, they often facilitate the signing of the loan agreements and help arrange the repayment. In some cases, employment agents take workers directly to the loan agency to begin the payment process. In other cases, they have arranged with employers to automatically deduct the amount and pay it to the loan agent (even though it is illegal for employers to make such deductions). In some cases (knowingly or unknowingly) the worker has signed a form that allows for automatic deduction from her account. As is the case with Filipinas, indebtedness renders workers more vulnerable to exploitation. Rather than lose a job, be sent back home, and go even further into debt because of the late fees and climbing interest rates, workers are more likely to put up with abuses and try to keep working until they can begin to save some money.

By 2006 nongovernmental organization (NGO) staff, domestic workers, and domestic worker activists had begun to actively publicize the problem of overcharging of Indonesian workers and to demand that the Hong Kong and Indonesian governments do something to alleviate the problem. Hong Kong agencies, however, have learned to cover their tracks, and on the surface it may appear that they have done nothing illegal. Agency staff members claim that they are kindly assisting workers in arranging the repayment of their loans. Activists argue that recruiters have disguised illegal agency fees as loans. A representative of the Hong Kong Labour Department explained to me that because the problem has its roots abroad—that most women make or sign such agreements in Indonesia—there is little that the Hong Kong government can do about it. Hong Kong activists, however, argue that the Hong Kong government should more actively and conscientiously investigate the ways in which Hong Kong agencies are implicated in the process of overcharging, and that the Indonesian government should stop facilitating an exploitative mechanism through which the government and the recruiters profit at the expense of workers.

As I have argued in this chapter, foreign domestic workers are a critical source of revenue for their home governments and for employment agencies in Hong Kong, the Philippines, Indonesia, and elsewhere. Workers are often regarded as resources by their home governments or as commodities that are marketed and traded by employment agencies. Indonesian training camps, as described above, are one context in which employment agencies aim to train and discipline workers even before they go abroad. In January and February 2007, as this book was going to press, Philippine President Macapagal-Arroyo faced severe criticism from Filipina domestic workers and migrant worker activists. She had referred to overseas domestic workers (or Household Service Workers), as "supermaids" and introduced new legislation that would require all domestic workers to take part in (and pay for) an intensive "cultural and language training" before going to work abroad. Domestic workers and activists did not consider the training requirement a welcome form of protection that would serve the needs of workers but rather as a "burden for workers" and a way for the government and employment agencies to "extort" more money from them. In Hong Kong and Manila thousands turned to the streets in protest of new POEA requirements (APMM 2007; UNIFIL 2007).

The following chapter turns to forms of discipline that take place within the intimate space of the employer's home.

5 | HOUSEHOLD RULES AND RELATIONS

Instructions and guidelines that women learn from agencies and training programs in the Philippines and Indonesia take effect within the context of employers' homes in Hong Kong. Employers also introduce new forms of discipline to control domestic workers' bodies. Such discipline is meant to establish "uninterrupted, constant coercion, supervising the processes of the activity rather than its result" (Foucault 1979:137). In other words, controls are not simply directed at the product of a domestic worker's labor but extend into her most private domains. Her body, her personality, her voice, and her emotions may be subject to her employer's controls. The following sketch illustrates a number of bodily and other forms of discipline that take place within the household.

CATHY

Cathy is from the Philippines. When I first met her in 1994, she was nineteen years old. Her innocent, cheerful, and youthful appearance belied the difficulties she had recently experienced. In the shade next to Saint John's Cathedral she began to tell me her story. She is the youngest of six children, and her mother is a widow. She completed secondary school at seventeen. A promising student, she hoped to study management in college and eventually start a small business, but her mother could not afford the educational costs. So Cathy decided to go to work as a "helper" in Hong Kong. She first had to overcome her mother's resistance. "I explained to her that I want to go to college. . . . If I can earn some money, I will finish one [two-year] contract and then go back home and continue my studies."

To avoid employment agency expenses, Cathy asked her sister, who had already worked in Hong Kong for six years, to help her find an employer. A friend of her sister's recommended Ms. Leung, a woman in her late thirties who ran a small textile business. Cathy was assured that Ms. Leung would be a good employer, for she was supposedly single and living alone in a small middle-class flat. Thus all indications were that Cathy's workload would be reasonable.

Cathy's sister met her at Kai Tak airport the October evening of her arrival in 1992 and took her to her employer's house. Cathy was surprised to find that the "single" woman lived with her husband and daughter, but she was reassured by Ms. Leung who said kindly that she would be treated as a "younger sister."

Despite such reassurances, Cathy's situation was not good. She was required to work sixteen hours a day and to do "illegal work" outside of her employer's home. She was not paid the legal wage stipulated in her contract. As Cathy explained:

> It's written in the contract 3–2 [HK$3,200]. But when I got to Hong Kong . . . [Ms. Leung] said to me, "Your salary is 2–3 [HK$2,300], but don't worry, I will just add [to it] if your performance is good until it reaches minimum [wage]." She promised me, so I expected her to respect that promise. But for six months, no. She didn't add to my salary. So she only gave me 2–3. But in fact I only received 2–1 [HK$2,100], because she opened a bank for me but she did not give HK$200 every month. The account was in her name and my name—a joint account. [Now] my bank book is with her so I cannot get my money. My bank book—my documents—she took them all. So I still cannot get my money from the bank.

Cathy's work followed a rigid daily schedule beginning before seven o'clock in the morning and ending close to midnight. Her duties included washing, marketing, cooking, cleaning Ms. Leung's flat, and looking after two dogs. In addition to such "official" duties, she was also required to clean Ms. Leung's mother's flat, Ms. Leung's friend's flat and office, and Ms. Leung's office, and to serve as a messenger. Even on her "rest day"— which was rotated each week, thus curtailing her ability to meet her sister and her friends—she was required to make breakfast, take the dogs out, and do many other household chores.

Ms. Leung gave Cathy a detailed list of rules to follow. She was forbidden to wear makeup, fingernail polish, or perfume; she could not wear dresses or skirts, only pants; and her nine o'clock curfew was strictly enforced on her day off. She was not permitted to use the phone, and was threatened with a deduction of HK$10 from her pay, even for free local calls. Ms. Leung specified the days when Cathy could wash her hair and monitored the length of her showers. When Cathy ate with the family, she was served last. Other times, she complained, she was given leftovers and rarely received enough to eat. The rest of the family slept in air-conditioned quarters, but the room where Cathy slept, which also served as a storeroom, was sweltering hot in the summer and leaked when it rained.

HOUSEHOLD WORK AND OTHER WORK

Among the differences between the controls experienced by foreign domestic workers in Hong Kong and those experienced by other types of workers is the isolation of being a foreigner and an outsider who lives and works in a private home. Domestic workers are usually far outnumbered by the members of the employer's household. Such factors increase vulnerability to abuse or exploitation. Most factory workers are expected to abide by rules of conduct and dress, follow timetables, and perhaps fulfill work quotas dictated by their employers, but they work together for the same employer for a set number of hours a day, usually under similar conditions. Domestic workers, by contrast, with few exceptions, have different employers and work conditions, and live in the place where they work, so that work time is often difficult to distinguish from time off.[1]

The relationship between a household worker and her employer is potentially far more intense than the relationship between other workers and their employers. A domestic worker works in the employer's personal and private domain and thus observes behaviors to which only the closest family members are otherwise privy. The Hong Kong Institute of Household Management in Manila instructs women who plan to work in Hong Kong to "maintain a SAFE DISTANCE" from their employers. "If you become too familiar with your employer, you may answer back or abuse [*sic*] without knowing or intentionally doing it" (HKIHM n.d.:3). The domestic worker, unlike her employer, is expected to behave "professionally" at all times. In

---

1. The fact that domestic workers all have different employers also impedes labor activism and creates unique challenges for labor unions.

other words, the emotional outbursts of the employer and the employer's family should be ignored or taken in stride, but a worker's anger, frustration, and other emotions are to be concealed and repressed.

One Philippine agency advises workers to "be patient and tolerant to your employer when you are being scolded for your mistakes. Be willing to adjust to your employer's way of cooking, working, and way of living. . . . Be polite and always SMILE. Greet your employer 'GOOD MORNING' 'GOOD NIGHT.' Say 'PLEASE' 'THANK YOU' 'I AM SORRY.' . . . Avoid crying. It is bad luck to your employer."[2] Crying, displaying "long faces," touching employers with any part of a broom, sweeping the house on the first day of the Lunar New Year, wearing all white or all black—colors associated with death—are all behaviors that domestic workers are warned against for the bad fortune some employers believe they will bring (cf. Maglipon 1990:8; see also Jaschok 1988:100).

Echoing employers' demands, the Hong Kong Institute instructs domestic workers to begin the day by "saying 'good morning' to everybody. Even if they don't answer you, continue doing this." Filipinas are taught that, "even a difficult employer can be won over by a hardworking and pleasant maid." In addition, "a maid should never shout [at] an employer. Always speak in a normal, pleasant voice. Also, when called . . . respond immediately" (HKIHM n.d.:2). The burden of patience and flexibility is placed entirely on the domestic worker. She is expected to adjust to her employer, not vice versa.

One important difference between household and factory workers—especially factory workers who commute and do not live in a factory dormitory—is that factory workers can usually draw a sharper line between their place of employment and their home, between places where work rules do and do not apply. In some ways, live-in domestic workers are like military recruits who share the same place of work and residence and to whom the same rules apply twenty-four hours a day. Military officers are bound by many of the same regulations as their recruits, however, and some emphasis is placed on the notion of leading by example. Employers of household workers are not bound by their own rules. As in a factory, the employer creates rules specifically for the worker. Rules thus highlight the status differences between the two groups. In the case of domestic workers, rules do not usually apply to anyone else, except occasionally to immature

2. I thank George Edwards of the Hong Kong University Foreign Domestic Helper Project for this example.

members of the household. Rules for children change, however, as a child becomes older, whereas rules for the domestic worker remain the same whether she is eighteen or fifty-five.

HOUSEHOLD RULES

A domestic worker is viewed—and is expected to view herself—as a "maid" at all times, but especially in her employer's home. She must obey her employer's rules, even at night and in her own room. She may be told when and where to bathe, what time to go to bed, and what she can and cannot wear. Only on her day off is she at all free to express herself outside of the role of domestic worker. But even on her day off she is under the watchful eye of the public.

Jane, a Filipina in her mid-forties who has several children, had been a domestic worker in Hong Kong for fifteen years in 1993. When I met her, she had just received a month's notice because her employers were moving to Canada. Since her employers were willing to document their situation with the Labour and Immigration Departments, Jane was allowed to process a new contract in Hong Kong rather than return to the Philippines. Thanks to her good "release papers," she had interviews with several prospective employers. After one interview she rushed excitedly to the mission office, not because the interview had gone well but because she had another list to add to my collection. "Where's Nicole?" she shouted, "I have a good one for her!" A volunteer read the list aloud, interrupted by jeers and a chorus of dissent. The list included many "rules" that contradicted the official contract, such as requiring chores on the "rest day" and imposing curfews. Other rules included:

- You are not allowed to rest and lean on sofa of parlour and your employer's bed.
- A maid must always be polite and greet the employer, his family members, relatives, visitors as soon as meeting them by saying: GOOD MORNING, GOOD DAY, GOOD AFTERNOON, GOOD EVENING, or GOOD NIGHT (before going to bed), SIR, MADAM etc. Don't forget to say THANK YOU at appropriate times.
- DO NOT use any nail polish on fingers and toes. DO NOT put on makeup, even when you are going out to do the family shopping. Your hair must be short and tidy. DO NOT wear tight jeans and pants and low-cut T-shirts while you are working. DO NOT go to the parlour in pyjamas.

- Must take bath daily before going to bed. Hand wash your own clothes separately from those of your employers and the children (especially the under-wear), unless your employer allows you to wash your own clothes by the washing-machine together with theirs.
- You will be required to sleep and attend the baby and elderly, even during night time.
- Use separate towels for different purposes, such as (a) sweeping floor, (b) cleaning furniture, (c) cleaning dining table, (d) washing oily dishes, (e) washing cups, (f) washing basin, (g) washing toilet.
- Washing of car and caring for pets (e.g., dogs & cats) are part of your duties with NO EXTRA ALLOWANCE.
- You give very bad impression to your employer if they see you chatting or laughing with your Filipino friends outside their house or down the street. Therefore, NEVER gather with other Filipino maids near your living place, especially when you are bringing their kids down to the street to catch the school bus or going to the market.
- DO NOT write any letters during your working days, do it on your holidays.

Jane accepted a job offer from another employer whom she expected to be far less controlling.

Cathy received an interesting but not unusual assortment of regulations from Ms. Leung. Some rules pertained to her physical appearance (e.g., no nail polish), or to the specifics of household work (e.g., when to wear rubber gloves, to dry dishes before putting them away). Several reflected her employer's economic concerns—restrictions on use of the phone, requiring her to pay replacement costs for broken dishes, limiting her use of hot water. Such rules help establish the worker's inferior position. Unlike the other members of the household, the domestic worker must ask permission to use the phone, the television, the air conditioner, or to attend to "personal matters" when she has completed her work. Like immature members of the household, she is told when to go to bed and what time to come home. The final rule on Cathy's list takes the form of a threat:

> The employee must not be misconduct himself [*sic*]. The term misconduct includes insolence, persistent laziness, immorality, dishonesty and drunkenness. Misconduct will justify summary dismissal if it directly interferes with the interest and business of the employer or the employee's ability to perform his services. And all the expenses, including the air ticket, doctor fees, application fee, every thing paid for you in advance for coming to H.K. the

employer shall have the right to claim back all the charges and deduct in your salary while you break the contract or found dishonesty at anytime [*sic*].

According to Hong Kong law, an employer does not have the right to reclaim expenses. Another employer's list ended with a similar warning: "If you are not satisfied with working in this house, you have to give a one month's notice before you can quit. If we are not happy with your work, we can send you back to the Philippines right away according to the contract" (CIIR 1987:104). Again this "rule" inaccurately represents government policy.

CONTROLLING TIME

Rules not only govern a domestic worker's behavior and attitude, they also control her use of time and the pace of her work. The Hong Kong Institute teaches, "There is not [*sic*] place for LAZINESS in the job you have accepted. There is a difference between a lazy and a slow person. We tend to do things here [in the Philippines] at a slower pace due to the hot weather but in Hong Kong where the weather is cold, people move fast and this is what they expect to see in other people" (HKIHM n.d.:2). Women are told to "Learn to CLOCK WATCH. Schedule [your] time and work. . . . During your FREE-TIME, rest if you must, but be ready to answer the door or telephone. Sew clothes or other special chores like repotting some plants and cleaning kitchen cupboards" (HKIHM n.d.:3). The idea that domestic workers need to be taught the "value of time" and how to "budget time" bears a strong resemblance to the capitalist discipline imposed on workers, as described by E. P. Thompson (1967).

Just as the confluence of home and workplace makes it more difficult for household workers than factory workers to separate work spatially, it is also more difficult temporally to distinguish time on and off. Many domestic workers I met were told by their employers that after completing assigned tasks, they should "find" more work to do. One worker I spoke to prided herself on her efficiency and speed. Her employer agreed that she did good work but told her that when she "finished," she should either find more work or redo what she had done: "I didn't hire you to sit around and do nothing."

Ms. Leung's list of rules illustrates the minute controls an employer can have over a worker's time. She claimed the right to change Cathy's day off without notice and to dictate that Cathy be home by nine in the evening. Cathy was told that all her work had to be finished before bed. After work, she "must turn off the light and sleep within one hour at ten o'clock."

Domestic workers are usually expected to follow timetables and work schedules. The timetable, as Michel Foucault writes, is "based on the principle of non-idleness" and was designed "to eliminate the danger of wasting [time]—a moral offense and economic dishonesty" (1979:154). The timetable allows the employer to control and budget the domestic worker's time. It also prevents the worker from using her time more efficiently to create "free time." Regardless of whether the floor or windows appear clean, they must be cleaned at the scheduled time. In most cases workers are not allowed to judge for themselves whether a job needs to be done, they are merely required to follow the schedule. Many domestic workers are not permitted to write letters or take care of their own business on workdays or during work hours regardless of whether they have "finished" work. It is as though the employer has "bought" the domestic worker's labor power and time, not simply hired her to carry out specific tasks.

Most employers impose restrictive curfews, demanding that a domestic worker return home by eight, nine, or ten in the evening on her day off, even though the official contract states that employers must "notify the Helper before the beginning of each month" as to the dates of the weekly rest days, and that "a rest day is a continuous period of not less than 24 hours." Employers often rationalize curfews as being for the domestic worker's own good or claim that they impose them out of a concern for her safety. Domestic workers—often mature and responsible women—more accurately view such restrictions as unfair, overly restrictive, and patronizing or "maternalistic" (Rollins 1985:173–203).

Recalling the wealthy owners of muijai who saw themselves as benevolent, many employers claim that they are different from other types of employers since they serve as the domestic worker's "guarantor." As one explained to me,

> A guarantor . . . has to pay all her lodging, food and [guarantee her] safety. Safety is the most important. Now that is one misunderstanding with the girls. . . . Some girls want to stay outside. . . . They want to come home late. The employer will ask them, "Oh, next time please come home earlier." She will be very unhappy. "This is my holiday. Why will you not allow me to?" But one thing they do not understand [is that it is] because they live in the same house. If she did not come home, the employers would have to wait for her. They could not go to bed. Another thing is that they worry about her because the guarantor is responsible in case she had an accident outside. The employer would be responsible for her, so she looks after her like her own son and daughter. But the maids don't understand.

For domestic workers whose duties include care of infants, small children, or sick or elderly family members, work hours may extend through the night. Jane's prospective employer specified that she would be required to attend to the babies and the elderly, even at night. As was often the case with the traditional baby amah, foreign domestic workers often share rooms with children and provide bottles, diaper changes, and comfort when a child wakes up in the night. Domestic workers are commonly expected— like the muijai or amahs of the past—to serve refreshments at mahjong parties, which may take place several nights a week. Although the employer who has been up until the early hours of the morning is free to sleep in late, the domestic worker is still expected to prepare breakfast for the children, walk the dog, or resume her normal duties at six or seven in the morning. A domestic worker may theoretically be "allowed" to go to bed whenever she pleases, but if her "bedroom" is in the living room where the family watches television until late, or on the floor of the kitchen, she cannot go to sleep until the rest of the family does because of the noise, interruptions, or lack of privacy.

Domestic workers sometimes find their use of time monitored by a household member who remains at home. This is often an older member of the household such as the employer's mother or mother-in-law or the woman employer if she does not go out to work. Occasionally a Chinese amah supervises the foreign worker. Some employers phone or "check in" on the domestic worker periodically. Workers who have a choice much prefer to work in households where no one is home during the day.

Detailed timetables provide the best example of extreme controls placed on workers' time. Some timetables include daily, weekly, biweekly, and monthly duties. Employers make up their own schedules or adapt them from books such as *The Maid's Manual* (Gaff 1983) or from those of friends or agencies. Along with her list of rules, Ms. Leung gave Cathy one of the most detailed lists of duties I have ever seen. Monday's schedule was as follows:

6:30 A.M. Wake up, prepare breakfast for Pucci [Ms. Leung's son].

6:50 A.M. Feed Bobo [the dog] (two cups of dry food and one glass of milk.) After that bring him to the toilet. But make sure [its] in the right place. Don't let him [go to the] toilet in the house and the building.

7:30 A.M. Prepare breakfast for Mr. and Mrs. [Leung].

8:00 A.M. to
12:00 P.M. Wash all the cups and dishes. Wash clothes, use washing machine. Clean the living room (including all the windows,

<table>
<tr><td></td><td>furniture, mirror, television, hi-fi, fans, table, chairs and books. . . .) Clean the floor (especially the corner and the gap).</td></tr>
</table>

At office:	Arrive office at 12:30 P.M. After lunch wash bowls and dishes. Rest one hour (1:00–2:00 P.M.). Clean all the tables, chairs, machine, showroom (all the surfaces). Clean the floor.
5–5:30 P.M.	Go back to home and buy meat for dinner.
Evening:	Wash all the meat and vegetables. Prepare dinner for Bobo, bring him to the toilet and take the rubbish to the street. Prepare dinner. After dinner clean up all the bowls and dishes. Clean the floor. Iron clothes.

This same schedule is repeated each day of the week with additional daily variations between 8:30 A.M. and noon. Saturday's schedule included the usual chores, but at 9:30 A.M. Cathy was required to go to Ms. Leung's mother's house and to cook, clean, iron, and mop there.[3]

Domestic workers, unlike most factory workers, commonly work more than ten hours a day and receive no overtime pay. According to French's study of a hundred Filipina domestic workers, only 15 percent worked ten or fewer hours a day; 40 percent worked eleven to thirteen hours a day; 30 percent worked fourteen to sixteen hours a day; and 10 percent worked over sixteen hours a day (1986a:186). According to a 1991 AMC study, over 75 percent of domestic workers surveyed worked over fourteen hours a day; only about 3 percent of Filipinas worked less than eleven hours a day; over 50 percent worked twelve to fifteen hours a day; almost 30 percent worked sixteen to seventeen hours a day, and 4 percent over eighteen hours a day (1991:38–39).[4] According to the AMC 2005 survey of 1,017 Indonesian domestic workers, 47 percent worked for more than eight hours a day, and according to the ATKI 2005 survey of 2,777 Indonesian domestic workers, 45 percent worked twelve hours a day or more (AMC 2005; ATKI 2005).

Domestic workers and representatives of their organizations often express concern about unlimited working hours. Employers, however, often

3. For another detailed schedule of duties, see CIIR 1987:103–4. Almost every minute of the worker's time is accounted for. At 6:45 "take breakfast alone," at 7:00 prepare breakfast for the family and boil water, at 7:20 dress the son for school, at 7:30 feed him breakfast, at 7:55 take him to the bus stop, at 8:15 dress the daughter and give her breakfast, at 8:30 clean the bathrooms, tidy the bedrooms, sweep and mop all floors, etc.

4. A higher percentage of Filipinas than Indian, Thai, or Sri Lankan domestic workers in the AMC study worked fourteen to fifteen hours a day, but a higher percentage of non-Filipinos worked sixteen or seventeen hours a day (1991:39).

strongly opposed any limit on hours. One reason employers say they hire foreign workers as opposed to local ones is that foreign workers live in and can be called on to work at any time (see also Chun 2004; HK-CS 2001). Mrs. Yang, a working mother of three young children, expressed the view of many employers when she said that she would not hire a worker who was restricted to ten hours a day. "Families—working wives—they really need someone who will sleep in, stay. Why do they have to give them the house to live in? Why do they have to allow them to have the bed? Only because they need to have someone to stay in."

Some employers accuse domestic workers of exaggerating the number of hours they work, claiming that it is impossible to count work hours since domestic workers "work intermittently" and spend part of the day "resting." According to Mrs. Yang,

> You cannot keep account of family work. . . . For family work, as you know, [there are] some things you have to do in the morning and some things you have to do in the evening, like the meals: breakfast, lunch, and dinner. How do you count the time? And actually if you count their rest, when the babies go to sleep, they should rest too. I mean, family work is not work in the factory! I mean, we have many part-time servants in Hong Kong. When they do the part-time they really work! Not like the domestic workers in the house now.

In an editorial in the *South China Morning Post*, A. Lam expresses a similar view:

> It is unfair to say that they [FDHs] have to work an average of 15 hours a day. It all depends on their own efficiency. . . . For those helpers whose employers are working and will not stay at home, have they thought of the free time they have during the day?
>
> If, for example, a domestic helper's employers leave home at 8 am and return home at 8 pm for dinner, the helper has 12 hours on her own. If she can organize her work better, I'm sure that she could have about three or four hours free time within that 12 hours. One of the reasons for their long working hours, and I think most employers would agree with me, is because most of them do not organize their work. (A. Lam 1993)

These statements suggest that "housework" is not considered "real work." Even employers who were once full-time "housewives" feel justified demanding extremely long working hours of paid workers. What Lam and Mrs. Yang do not seem to realize is that many domestic workers are not given the option to budget their time more efficiently. Housework, moreover, is never "finished." The more a domestic worker does, the more she must do.

Domestic workers who seemed most satisfied with their work were those who felt they were allowed more independence and responsibility. They could budget time however they liked as long as the required work was done well, and they could use their "spare time" as they liked. Elsa, Belle, and other volunteers at the mission were workers who completed their tasks quickly, efficiently, and to the satisfaction of their employers. When they finished work, they were allowed to decide how to spend their time.

A Chinese social worker, a counselor to foreign domestic workers and employers, spoke to me about possible differences in the "forms of discipline" used by Chinese and Western employers.

> Some of the girls may prefer to work with Western employers instead of Chinese employers because they think the Chinese employers are more strict. [The Chinese employer] will give all of the instructions to you and they expect you to do it in her way. But most of the Western employers don't. They just let you to do your work, and as long as you can do the work, it's OK. So they do not provide so many instructions to you and they just let you cook whatever you like, and they let you do the work whenever you like as long as you can finish all the work before you sleep. But sometimes it's good for the workers because they think they are free and they can do whatever they like as long as they can finish. And also they have much more freedom and autonomy to do the work and also the way to do the work. But for the Chinese family most of them may expect [the domestic worker] to work in their way, to cook in their way. How to do that, how to do that! "You have to follow *my* instructions how!" So some of the time, most of the helpers, when they come to us they say, "Any Western employers? Do you have any European employers, any American employers?"

Workers I spoke to frequently made similar generalizations about the differences between Western and Chinese employers and expressed their preference for non-Chinese ones including non-Chinese Asian employers (French 1986: 21; see also Wee and Sim 2004:14). But I also encountered workers with strict and harsh Western employers, and others with flexible and lenient Chinese ones. Further research would be necessary to draw any overarching conclusions about the different forms of discipline used by Chinese employers and those of other nationalities and cultural backgrounds. The main point here, however, is that workers often respond negatively to direct supervision and specific controls and more favorably to less overt forms of discipline that they commonly associate with Western or non-Chinese employers.

PHYSICAL APPEARANCE

Some of the workers I knew were required to wear uniforms when their employers expected guests, but relatively few had to wear uniforms all the time. In the 1990s, women could occasionally be seen wearing "maid's uniforms"—another obvious form of body discipline—at the market, on the train, at the post office, or at school bus stops. These are typically knee-length, loose-fitting dresses with short sleeves and a collar. For everyday wear they may be pastel colored or have small stripes. The more formal version is black with a white collar and an apron. Domestic workers often express pity or sympathy for women who must wear uniforms. Many workers dislike uniforms and consider them demeaning or embarrassing, but as Jane's prospective employer's list specified, "If your employer requests you to wear uniforms you must obey and you have no right to refuse."

Maria, whom I met in the mission-run Kowloon shelter, explained that some women oppose their employer's uniform requirement. "We have one woman like that here," she explained. "Her employer requested that she wear a uniform, and she said, 'You want only that we look smart so that when you have a visitor they will see us in uniform, so they will think it's a rich family.' We don't like to wear uniforms. . . . Because they can identify you, you are a maid!"

Studies in the United States and elsewhere suggest that domestic workers are often well aware of their roles as status symbols (Colen 1986:57; Coley 1981:238; Kaplan 1987:98). Workers of different class and racial backgrounds can be especially effective for affirming the employer's status (Rollins 1985:129; Romero 1992:112). Uniforms and other visible markers help distinguish workers from employers and heighten their ability to serve as status markers (Glenn 1986:158; Romero 1992:113; Tucker 1989:269). Hong Kong employers were also concerned that Chinese amahs be identified as such. Mrs. Chin was extremely annoyed that Ah Ching could successfully pass herself off as the children's grandmother.

Even if they are not required to wear uniforms, foreign domestic workers are usually told what to wear. Some employers allow workers to wear whatever they choose, but more often they are told to wear pants that are not too tight and shirts with high necks and at least short sleeves. Skirts and dresses must usually cover the knees. Some employers specify that proper shoes—as opposed to "slippers" or "thongs"—must be worn. One worker was told by her woman employer that it reflects poorly on the employer if she is seen going to the market in slippers. Acosta (introduced in the preface) described an employer who criticized her for dressing like she was going to a disco, rather than as a maid.

Indonesian domestic workers, most of whom are Muslim, sometimes face additional problems related to their dress. Whereas many of them dress in ways that are indistinguishable from Filipinas (i.e., jeans and T-shirts) or in baggy hip hop styles, others prefer to dress in more distinctly Muslim styles. Those who are religiously observant participate in daily prayers that require them to bathe and wear modest dress (*hijab*)—which includes a headscarf and a long loose gown (*jilbab*). The vast majority of Indonesian domestic workers have Chinese employers, some of whom do not allow them to wear modest dress in the house, whereas others prohibit them only from performing prayers. One Chinese employer described his and his wife's discomfort the first time they saw their Indonesian domestic worker wearing an all-white head cover and long white gown for prayer. Since white is the color that is traditionally worn by Chinese for funerals, she appeared "frightening and inauspicious." Some Indonesian workers are forbidden from wearing headscarves or long gowns at all in their employer's home because their employers claim they get in the way of their ability to work. Some Indonesian women who are not permitted to wear them at work take great pride in sporting a variety of long, elegant pastel-colored gowns and white or colored headscarves on their day off.

Employers also attempt to control domestic workers' hygiene and bodily appearance. Almost every part of a worker's body, literally down to her toes, may be subject to the employer's control. As noted, the use of makeup and perfume and the length and style of hair are often subject to an employer's control. The length of fingernails and toenails and even the frequency of nail cutting may be prescribed by an employer. Few of the women I spoke to had been told that they could wear whatever they liked; most had at least some restrictions imposed on them. Christina experienced harsh restrictions.

CHRISTINA

Christina was in her late twenties and had worked as a domestic worker in Malaysia for three years when she came to work in Hong Kong in January 1993. On a steamy afternoon we met in the crowded two-bedroom shelter in Western District where she was staying with fifteen other Filipinas whose contracts had been terminated and who had nowhere else to go. We sat in the crowded corner of one dark room, on top of a tall pile of thin mattresses that would later be spread out from wall to wall for women to sleep on. As we talked, a three-week-old baby cried softly and was passed from one woman to the next. His mother had given birth alone, and since the birth had not been officially recorded, she had difficulty obtaining a passport to allow him to go back with her to the Philippines. As a result both remained in the shelter.

Christina began her story. Her roommates already knew it well and interjected parts of it for her. She had arrived at Kai Tak airport a bit tired but excited at the prospect of her new job. Her employer, Mrs. Wong, a woman in her mid-thirties, was there to meet her. In the car, as they headed away from the airport, Mrs. Wong began to recite a long list of duties and regulations. "On your day off you must be home by 8 P.M. You cannot wear dresses or skirts, only pants. You must keep your shoulders and upper arms covered at all times, and you cannot wear makeup, fingernail polish, jewelry, or perfume." She told Christina that she must have short hair. At the time, Christina's hair was long and she wore it loosely tied back in a ponytail that reached a third of the way down her back. "Yes ma'am. But I can keep it tied back and pull it back tighter to make it smaller." Christina tried politely to reason with her employer. Mrs. Wong firmly pronounced that Christina's hair *must* be short because she would be working with small children.

Before reaching the flat, Mrs. Wong parked the car in front of a "barber shop." As Christina described it, "It was the sort of place where old men go to get their hair cut." Mrs. Wong said something in Chinese to the barber and left. Christina was upset, but felt she had little choice but to obey her employer if she wanted to keep her job. So she tried to communicate with the barber, in English and with gestures, the kind of shoulder-length cut she would like. He understood and gave her a reasonable haircut, but when Mrs. Wong returned she was furious and insisted that he give her a "man's cut." She watched and waited while the barber cropped off Christina's hair. One of Christina's friends commented: "*Bruha* [witch] obviously didn't know you'd look even more beautiful with short hair!"

For the next two days Christina worked hard washing clothes and dishes, cleaning windows, and scrubbing the walls and floors as her employer scrutinized her work. Shortly before midnight, when Christina had been there less than three days, Mrs. Wong began to shout at her loudly, saying that Christina could not have ever worked as a maid before. She then ordered her to leave the house. One of the last things Christina remembered Mrs. Wong shouting was that she was still entitled to three free replacements from the employment agency. Christina had worked for her employer for less than three days. She now did "aerobics" (i.e., illegally worked part-time) when she could and patiently awaited her hearing at the Labour Tribunal.[5]

HYGIENE

A type of bodily control that many Filipinas find extremely annoying relates to bathing. At least fifteen different women told me that their employers dictate that they follow the Chinese custom of bathing in the evening, before bed. Most were required to bathe after ironing, or some other work, in the evening. Some workers were assigned a specific time to bathe.

Bathing in the evening runs counter to Filipino custom. Several women explained that in the Philippines, they would bathe in the morning and sometimes in both the morning and the evening. Bathing in the evening, when one is still hot from work, they believe, makes one more susceptible to colds, bronchitis, pneumonia, or *pasma* (trembling/shivers). They believe it can make the veins in the hands or legs "bulge" and can cause permanent varicose veins. Jane showed me the bulging veins on her hands and explained that this happened only after she came to Hong Kong. Maria said, "I had to iron many, many [clothes], and then I had to hand wash [more clothes] again. So we have, you see [she points to her hands] veins. I didn't have hands like this in the Philippines! Because if we iron in the afternoon we never even take a bath or wash our hands, our parents get angry at us. . . . Because we will get colds, rheumatism, arthritis."

In the Philippines, I was told, parents and elders advise young girls to rest for at least an hour after ironing, or preferably to wait until the next morning to bathe so as not to become ill. Back home, one worker explained, she was not allowed to wash the dishes if she had just ironed. Her employer, however, always made her wash dishes, iron, and then bathe. The worker interpreted the order as dangerous to her health. Another worker said that forcing her to bathe in the evening was just another way in which her employer tried to destroy her health and beauty. Acosta advised friends who had to shower in the evening to threaten their employers with the medical bills that might ensue should they become sick.

5. For another analysis of Christina's situation, see Constable 1997.

Cathy was particularly upset about her bathing situation. Mrs. Leung criticized the length of her showers. Cathy quoted her, "'Why when you take a bath do you take such a long time? It takes you one hour—a half hour or something?' She said, 'Why? Why?' She said to me, 'In the Philippines you do that?' 'Yes,' I said. 'Well you're in Hong Kong already. You can follow what I want!' 'Okay,' I said." Mrs. Leung would not allow Cathy to bathe before going out on her day off. She told Cathy to wash once a day, in the evening, and would not allow her to wash her hair every day. I asked Cathy to describe her usual bathing pattern in the Philippines. "My hair and my body every day! In the morning, I wash it all—hair and body and everything. . . . Every day [in the Philippines] I clean my body at least twice a day, but at my employer's it's only once. One time, and in the evening! So it's terrible! So she said on my day off I cannot take a bath normally. So every week I would bring some clothes and I go to my friend's house just to take a bath."

Acosta's first employer would not let her wash her hair every day as was her custom in the Philippines, and if she came out of the bathroom with wet hair the family members laughed at or scolded her. Cora explained that Filipinos prefer bathing daily, usually in the morning, and that they will wear their clothes only once. Summing up the situation she said, "to the Chinese we are being spoiled and not behaving like maids."

Food

The most common complaints I heard from domestic workers related to food. Many Filipinas commented on their difficulties using chopsticks and their disgust at the customary communal dish, which everyone dips into with his/her own chopsticks. Some women continued to use spoons as they did in the Philippines, despite criticism or teasing. Others found it difficult to get used to Chinese food. Elsa described how her stomach turned the first time she saw "the way the blood is left in the steamed chicken." Employers, conversely, complained about the smell of Filipino food. Indonesians face some different food-related problems. Most of the Indonesian domestic workers are Muslim and therefore do not eat pork, but pork is especially popular among Hong Kong Chinese and a staple of Cantonese cuisine. Although domestic workers are not forced to eat it, they are often required to shop for it, prepare it, and cook it. If the employer's family is eating pork, the domestic worker may be given the choice of eating that or nothing. One Indonesian domestic worker explained that each day of the week, when the family ate pork, she made due with eggs.

The main food-related problem, which I heard repeatedly, concerned quantity. According to Maria Jaschok, the owners of muijai thought they were "always hungry, and ate too much" (1988:109). Employers of foreign workers described them in much the same way, sometimes pointing out that Filipinas are, by Hong Kong standards, overweight. Filipinas, conversely, often think that Chinese are "too thin," and that their employers eat very little.

In most parts of the Philippines, I was told, rice constitutes an important part of every meal. Especially for those who are expected to work hard, three solid meals that include rice are considered essential. In Hong Kong, domestic workers are often expected to eat a slice of bread or toast for breakfast, or perhaps a bowl of "watery rice" cereal (*juk* or congee). Employers, Filipinas note, are often in a great rush to get to work in the morning. To their amazement, employers sometimes skip breakfast, or are satisfied with just a cup of tea or coffee. For lunch, especially if the employer is not at home, a worker may be expected to eat just a bowl of noodles. One woman I met was given only three dry packets of instant noodles a day, one for each meal.

When domestic workers complain to their employers that they need more food, they are sometimes told that they should eat less and lose a bit of weight. By Hong Kong standards, Filipinas may be overweight, but in the Philippines, I was told, it is desirable for a woman to be "chubby." Chubbiness (as opposed to obesity) is considered attractive and a sign of good health. Maria and Elsa both noted that when they came to Hong Kong their complexions suffered and they lost fifteen pounds. Very few women were pleased when they lost weight, and most were happy to put it on. Putting on weight was reassuring to their families back home, evidence that they were getting along well in Hong Kong.

Rina's employer described her as "much slimmer and more attractive when she first started to work for us." Rina, in contrast, was pleased that she was regaining the weight she lost when she lived with her first employer. She had been miserable and anxious and was not allowed to eat what she wanted. Like many others, she associated her weight loss with stress, hard work, lack of food, and an uncaring employer. She felt that her recent weight gain reflected well on Mrs. Chin.

Cathy complained that her employer did not give her enough food and gave her overripe fruit and leftovers that no one else wanted.

We ate together. Using chopsticks and no serving spoons. Sometimes the bone of the chicken was all that was left for me. I ate the same food as them but there wasn't enough. When we went to a restaurant there were only small bowls, so they ate just a little. . . . Not like in the Philippines. There we eat twice the rice, and for breakfast, lunch, and dinner. But here they eat just bread. Only one piece of bread and it's okay [for them]. For me it's okay, but at least at lunch and in the evening I need some vitamins and some nutritious food so that I can work. Sometimes . . . we eat just one kilo of cabbage and HK$5 of pork for a family of four! Fried only, because they like fried food. And sometimes just fried eggs for dinner. Not much. It was very strange for me at first, because in the Philippines I never ate like this. Because I ate well in my family.

The employment contract specifies that domestic workers should be provided with "food free of charge" and "if no food is provided, a food allowance of not less than HK$300 a month." The contract does not stipulate how much food an employer must provide. Some employers apparently think that if they provide any food at all, they need not provide an allowance. Most workers I spoke to in the 1990s did not receive any food allowance, and those who did received no more than the minimum of HK$300 a month (less than US$1.30 per day). For some, the food allowance was meant to cover meat and vegetables, whereas the employer provided rice, sugar, tea, soy sauce, and other common ingredients. For others, HK$300 was meant to cover everything for the entire month, and even in the early 1990s most found that it was not enough. The figure of HK$300, which has remained unchanged in the employment contract from the early 1990s until at least 2007, is a tiny amount given that Hong Kong has one of the world's highest costs of living. As if in recognition of this insufficiency, the Hong Kong Institute advises women that "if FOOD ALLOWANCE is given, use your money to buy your food supplies. Do not complain about [buying] food with salary received. A small part of your salary can buy more than enough food than one wishes to eat" (HKIHM n.d.: 3).

Food and eating arrangements vary greatly. Some women eat with their employers and are pleased to do so; others experience discomfort or embarrassment even at the thought of it. More often domestic workers eat separately in the kitchen. Whereas some workers express a preference to eat with the family, others are relieved to be allowed to eat on their own.[6] Some are permitted to cook their own food in the employer's kitchen, but others, like Acosta, were not allowed to cook Philippine food because members of

---

6. For a fascinating and provocative discussion of domestic workers and commensality in Singapore, see von der Borch 2006.

the employers' family did not like the smell of it. When cooking Chinese food, workers are usually required to follow specific instructions. As Elsa explained, buying the wrong cut of beef, or slicing the meat or the vegetables the wrong size, shape, and direction for a particular dish sent one of her employers into a rage. For a broccoli and beef dish, the broccoli and the beef are cut a particular way; for a tomato and beef dish, the meat is sliced in a different way. Some domestic workers assist in preparing the food—they wash, chop, slice, pare, and peel—but leave the actual cooking to the employer. Employers can determine not only what a domestic worker cooks for the family meal but also what, where, when, and how much a domestic worker eats.

TERRITORY AND HIERARCHY

The delineation of territories and the use of space within the house serve as status markers and means of discipline. Although employers and workers occupy the same household, certain privileged spaces may be off limits to the worker or may be entered only for work. Jane's prospective employer's list indicated that although she would be required to clean the living room and dining room, she would not be permitted to relax or eat there. In extreme cases, workers cannot sit or lean on any furniture but their own bed and chair. One worker was told to clean the vinyl-covered dining room chairs with rubbing alcohol after she sat on them. Others were chastised for walking in front of the blower of the air conditioner, or in front of a fan, because it would blow the domestic worker's "air" onto the employer.

In some cases domestic workers have their own "quarters," often a small, windowless bedroom and a small bathroom, separated from the rest of the flat by the kitchen or a hallway. The "servant's bathroom" typically has less "modern" fixtures than the family bathroom, a squat toilet rather than one with a seat, and a shower or faucet that drains into a hole in the floor, rather than a separate bath or shower stall. If the domestic worker does not have a separate bathroom, employers often designate certain times for her to use theirs. Many workers are not allowed to keep their things—soap, shampoo, towels—in the family bathroom. In one case, an employer insisted on providing the worker with generic brands of soap and shampoo that could easily be distinguished from the more expensive brands used by the rest of the family.

Many domestic workers do not have private rooms. Some, like Cathy, slept in the family storeroom. Often the "servant's quarter" or "amah room" in a Hong Kong flat resembles a large closet. It is often without electrical fixtures, and even if the rest of the flat is air conditioned, often this room is not. In some apartment buildings, there is a separate back door, back stairs, or a back elevator that is most accessible from the kitchen and the "servant's area."

Despite the lack of privacy, some workers consider themselves fortunate to share a bedroom with their employer's children because they are less isolated from the rest of the family and because their rooms are usually nicer. The bedroom may be small, but it is often more comfortable and has better lighting than servant's quarters. Elsa once shared a room with her employer's two young daughters while the Chinese cook amah slept in the servant's quarter near the kitchen. Elsa was pleased with this arrangement because she was not "kept at a distance" from her employer's family. As she explained, "My room was much better [than the Chinese amah's] because I am staying in my employer's vicinity. And you know what? If my employer is watching TV, and it's English TV they sometimes asked me to watch downstairs [with them]! And we talk, and we make up stories about what we are watching. Or if it is a beauty contest we rate the contestants—like that!" Indeed, Elsa's situation was infinitely better than those of workers who sleep in a hallway or on the kitchen or bathroom floor.

Another indication of the difference between employers and workers in relation to household space is that employers are free to come and go as they please, but workers are not. In the most extreme but not uncommon cases, domestic workers may be locked inside the flat or in a room of the house. I met several workers who were locked inside the flat (without a key) whenever their employers went out. One worker told me of her friend who was locked in the flat for several weeks while her employer was on vacation. Her friends had to pass her food through the spaces in the locked metal gate. At the mission, I read files of several workers who were locked in a flat. Although many employers say they lock them in to keep the domestic workers safe, it is obviously not in their best interest. If it were, workers could lock the door themselves or be given a key. Clearly this practice has more to do with control, keeping the worker in the house and curtailing her freedom.

Like a Member of the Family

Although many do, not all domestic workers resent or complain about the controls placed on them by their employers. Linda, a thirty-year-old who was wearing a neatly ironed T-shirt and pair of blue jeans when Acosta and I met her at Chater Garden one Sunday, is one example. She worked for four years in Abu Dhabi (in United Arab Emirates) before coming to Hong Kong in early 1992. She told us she had no complaints about the jobs and employers she had had, and the pay was good in both places. She was happier in Hong Kong because her sister was there. Her Hong Kong employer enforced many strict rules regarding work and dress codes. Some were written, but most were explained to her verbally. One rule was that she must go to bed at 9:30 and wake up at 6:30. Even if her employers were still awake, she had to be in bed or in her room with the light out at 9:30. On her day off she had to be home by 8:30.

I asked her how she felt about all these rules, and she said, "I tell her, 'Thank you, ma'am.'" Acosta was as surprised by Linda's response as I was and asked her if she minded these rules. Linda answered "No. Why would I?" I answered that some workers in similar situations felt they were treated like children. "No, ma'am, I don't mind," she explained, "because my employer is looking out for me like she does her daughter."

Linda eats with her employer's family. As she described it, they all serve themselves from the main dishes at the center of the table, but her food is placed ahead of time in a small side dish next to her bowl. Linda said this "special treatment" is probably because her employers noted her shock and disgust at this practice the first time she ate with them. A more critical observer, however, might wonder if this is another example of an attempt to establish the worker's place as a subordinate member of the household rather than an expression of concern. As James Watson has noted, eating from the same pot serves as a symbol of shared identity among members of the same Chinese lineage (1987). Conversely, being served separately may symbolize exclusion.

Some domestic workers, as described above, prefer to keep their distance from their employers, and many of them are more comfortable eating apart from them. But in Hong Kong, as elsewhere, domestic workers often express a desire to be treated "like one of the family" (see Anderson 2000; Childress 1986; Romero 1992:122–26; von der Borch 2006). As Mary Romero explains, one meaning of this "family analogy" is that the domestic worker is treated "with respect," as a "family member" as opposed to a "non-person" (1992:124–25). In Chinese society, as Rubie Watson has shown, however, there is a high degree of "inequality among brothers" (1985). The family analogy has a coercive side to it, moreover, for it serves to "distort working conditions" and disguise the exploitative side of the relationship (Romero 1992:123).

Many Filipinas expressed their awareness of the coercive side of the familial analogy with a popular joke. This joke, I was told, is often heard in Statue Square, but I learned it as I chatted with a group of domestic workers at the mission. Two women were comparing work situations. One woman complained of overwork, and the other grumbled about her early curfew. A third woman suddenly cut in and said in a serious tone of voice, "So you're a member of the family too, eh?" Then the crowd all burst out laughing. Observing my puzzled expression, Cora explained the humor.

The joke I heard was the punch line of a more elaborate joke. Because the longer version of the joke was so widely understood, the punch line was all that was necessary to evoke laughter. The original joke, as it was told to me, goes like this:

> A Filipina domestic helper arrives in Hong Kong at the home of her new employer. The employer says to her, "We want to treat you as a member of the family." The domestic helper is very happy to hear this. On Sunday, the helper's day off, her employer says to her, "You must work before you leave the house on Sundays because you are a member of the family." And the employer adds, "And you must come home in time to cook dinner for the family." "But sir, ma'am, I would like to eat with my friends today, because it is my day off," says the helper. "But you are a member of the family," says her employer, "and because you are a member of the family, you must eat with us."

Domestic workers who say they would like to be treated "like a member of the family" refer to the way they are treated by their own families in the Philippines, not as the joke implies, when the rhetoric of "family" is coercive.

Mrs. Leung told Cathy she would treat her like a younger sister and said, "You can treat me as your elder sister and my husband is your elder brother, and my daughter—you can treat her as your younger sister." As Cathy reflected, it sounded nice. "But later I think they treat me sometimes lower than an animal. It was May—that was summer and we have a small dog that time. . . . My room is very hot and I have no electric fan. But our dogs have a fan! They bought it for the dog. . . . They all have air conditioning. But in my room, even an electric fan I don't have."

Relationships with certain family members may be close, but some fairly typical conflicts can develop. The employer's mother or mother-in-law, if she lives in the home, often does not get along well with the domestic worker.[7] Mrs. Chin was considered an ideal employer because she was out all day and had no mother or mother-in-law in the house. A "pohpoh" at home all day "is constantly watching to see that her son is getting his money's worth."[8] The tension in this relationship is reminiscent of the tension that once existed between a Chinese mother-in-law and daughter-in-law. The daughter-in-law, however, now goes out to work, and the criticism she once endured—over her household duties, her cooking, and her way of raising the children—is transferred to the domestic worker. The situation is different, however, because a domestic worker, unlike a daughter-in-law, lacks the support of the husband, which can help to counterbalance the conflicts with his mother (see M. Wolf 1968, 1972).

Filipina domestic workers may also bear the brunt of generational conflicts between elderly members of the household and their adult children who—often because they speak English—are the ones who give instructions to the domestic worker. If an employer goes against his or her parents' wishes and instructs the worker to put less oil, salt, or soy sauce in the cooking, to prevent the children from going outside before they finish their homework, and to do the marketing three times a week rather than every day, the pohpoh may direct her dissatisfaction toward the domestic worker. Criticism of the domestic worker, however, does not automatically free the woman employer from her mother-in-law's criticism. She may still be held responsible for not having trained, instructed, or disciplined the domestic worker properly.

According to many domestic workers, children are also a source of conflict between employers and workers. As one Filipina explained, workers are in a double bind. If a worker loves the children, and the children become fond of her, the mother may become jealous and try to undermine the relationship (cf. Rollins 1985:99–100). To put the domestic worker in her place, some mothers, I was told, tell their children that the domestic worker is "just your maid." Some parents will not punish their children for hitting, kicking, or verbally abusing the domestic worker. One reported, "Children are very impolite because they are the same as their parents. Their parents show them how to treat the Filipinas like their *gungyahn* [servant]. So if the parents growl then the children will growl too."

---

7. Filipinas and other foreign domestic workers often refer to these "old women" generically as "pohpoh," "ah-poh," or "grandmother." In Cantonese *pòhpó* refers to one's maternal grandmother. Filipinas apply the term to the mother of either a man or woman employer.

8. An old Chinese family amah can be viewed as a similar source of conflict.

Jealousy on the part of the woman employer, I was told by both domestic workers and some Chinese informants, is a common problem (see Constable 1996, 1997). As a Chinese social worker from the Catholic Centre explained, women employers are often mothers who work outside their homes for the first time. They may be insecure about working and leaving the housework and childcare to someone else. When they realize that their children are getting attached to the domestic worker, they sometimes feel that their position in the family is being undermined. Especially if the domestic worker is young and attractive and if they are also worried about their husbands' being attracted to the worker, women employers may become jealous or hostile.

Mrs. Chin knew "some women who feel jealous or threatened" by their domestic workers. She speculated that, "some uneducated people may feel threatened" because they think Filipinas are "desperate enough to do anything to come to Hong Kong. They fear their maids want to ensnare whatever ugly husband they might have." As Mrs. Chin points out, there is a popular fear in Hong Kong that foreign domestic workers will go to any length to find a man to marry for the economic benefits.

In the past, male members of the household entered into sexual relations with muijai and other Chinese domestic workers (Jaschok 1988), and at least among the wealthy and elite, extramarital liaisons were expected. But such relationships were unlikely to result in divorce, and only in rare circumstances would such a liaison disempower the first or primary wife. Chinese wives in Hong Kong today, influenced in part by Western romantic ideals, are far less likely to view their husband's affairs with nonchalance.

Elsa's Chinese employer did not perceive her as a threat, but she confided in Elsa her fear that her husband would take a "mistress" as his brothers, father, and uncle all had. Like domestic workers described by Romero, Elsa was expected to listen and to express sympathy, to do "emotional labor" for her employer (1992:105–11). As Judith Rollins points out, confiding in a domestic worker is not necessarily a sign of "equality" between the employer and worker. As a member of a different class and social group, a domestic worker may be a "safe confidant." Confiding in her "may, in fact, be evidence of the distance in even the closest of these relationships. Employers can feel free to tell domestics secrets they would not share with their friends or family precisely because the domestic is so far from being socially and psychologically significant to the employer" (1985:166–67). Elsa said she would usually just listen, nod, and try to empathize with her employer:

"It's not because I'm a rich person that I'm happy," she would say. "No Elsa, I'm not actually happy." And after I saw it, I really understood. [My employer] had much money, but she was not happy, because she didn't like some of the Chinese ways. She was a jealous-type woman. Most of the brothers of her husband had another wife, and she told me that she didn't like that. She was afraid that in the near future her husband would imitate his brothers. It's very sad. Some of the Chinese men they are—you know—are very kind natured—they are not shouting at their wives, they are very good husbands. But you cannot say how good they are because they have to get another woman. It is the infidelity of rich people. They can get so many women— they can get three wives—like that! I have observed that. And she told me that she doesn't like that. She told me that all the brothers of her husband have two wives because they are millionaires. From Monday to Friday the husband is with the first wife, from Saturday to Sunday the first wife will bring her husband to the second wife. Strange isn't it?

Although she had gained her confidence, Elsa never really considered her employer a "friend."

When she went to America to arrange her things because the eldest son was going there to study in America, my employer he was not sleeping in the house. And he was playing a trick on us—both maids. Because one time when we came in the house I observed that my employer, the male employer, he put out his shoes, pretending that he came back that night. And so me and my cousin were laughing because he mistakenly put two different kinds of shoes! We were laughing because we didn't care if he is staying out. We will not tell to our employer. It's not our business. But we kept laughing and laughing.

Despite the emotional labor she did for her employer, Elsa managed to maintain some "professional distance" (cf. Romero 1992:126–27). Her first commitment was to keep her job, so she refused to get caught taking sides between her two employers.

Belying the egalitarian implications of being "like a member of the family," domestic workers are often required to address women employers as "ma'am" or "Mrs. Lee." Women employers may refer to themselves or be referred to as "mistress." Men employers are most often referred to as "sir" or "master" or "Mr. Lee." Often domestic workers view them as their silent allies or as henpecked by their domineering wives. Although most domestic workers receive instructions exclusively from women employers and interact mostly with them, men employers are more often the ones who sign their contracts. Most share a sense that men employers are neutral or allow their wives to make decisions regarding domestic work, but many seem to think that the man is more on their side. So as to not incur the wrath or jealousy of the woman employer, many workers are careful to avoid, as much as possible, any interaction with men in the household.

CLASS AS A SOURCE OF CONFLICT

Since the 1980s, employers of foreign domestic workers have come mostly from middle-class Chinese families, and many grew up in households that could not afford to employ domestic workers.[9] Employers today may be upwardly mobile, or aspiring to be, but most are not Hong Kong's most wealthy or elite. Their middle-class status is often recent and may appear quite precarious to them. As discussed in Chapter 4, an employer's class position may seem uncomfortably close to that of many Filipina domestic workers and can thus be a source of conflict. Women employers often work as schoolteachers, bank tellers, shop clerks, or office staff, occupations that some Filipinas held before coming to Hong Kong.[10] The growing appeal of Indonesian domestic workers since the mid-1990s is likely to be linked not only to their ability to speak Cantonese (and thus communicate with the elderly members of the household) but also to their rural or working-class background and their relative lack of education compared with Filipinas and compared with most Chinese employers.

One Filipina domestic worker with a degree in education (who hired a helper back home) felt that her employer, a schoolteacher, acted cool and condescending toward her. In the Philippines, she said, her woman employer could have been her friend or a teacher at the same school, but in Hong Kong "she is my employer and I am just her maid." Other domestic workers, like some of their employers were, until recently, "housewives" who worked in their own homes.

Certain conflicts between employers and workers may be directly related to the assumed economic inferiority of domestic workers. From the employer's point of view, the main problem is that the worker will not accept her

9. The required household income for hiring a foreign domestic worker in 2006 was HK$15,000 per month, below the median monthly household income of HK$16,500 in early 2006.

10. An African American domestic worker explained to Rollins that lower- and middle-income employers are most concerned with maintaining the economic "inferiority" of domestic workers. "The people with real high incomes don't care what you got or what you're doing. But someone just making it, just across that border in Brookline, just barely got there, they don't want to know you've got a home, a car, and don't let them know you've got kids in college!" (1985:197).

inferior status or behave as deferentially as she should. This conflict can exacerbate other problems. In describing their various "more serious" complaints, domestic workers who came to the mission for advice often interjected their hurt feelings about employers who shouted, scolded, shook a finger at them, and called them "only a maid," "just a poor maid," or worse. As one employer bluntly stated, "Of course Filipinas are poor. Why else would they become maids?" Domestic workers often resent being labeled poor and sometimes take offense at such an attitude.

If domestic workers receive the wages, food, and lodging stipulated in their contracts, if they can pay off their recruitment debts, and if they can remit a reasonable portion of their salary home, then their families may be quite well off, particularly by Philippine standards. A domestic worker's salary in Hong Kong—as both domestic workers and employers were quick to note (but for very different reasons)—may be more than that of a doctor, lawyer, or politician in the Philippines.

The following excerpt of a conversation I had with Dally and Rosa, two workers who were staying at the mission-sponsored shelter in Kowloon, illustrates the tension domestic workers feel when their employers label them "poor."

D: The thing I don't like about them [the employer and the employer's family], sister, is that they always tell me that I am stupid. I am the very worst maid in their house. And then I say, "Okay, okay." And then they always said that I am very poor in the Philippines. And then they said also that our country is very poor. But actually I am not very poor in our country, but I accept it. I say, "Yes ma'am, yes ma'am." I say to them.

N: Why do you say, "Yes ma'am," if it isn't true?

D: I don't like that many arguments and shouting. So she will leave me alone. I don't mind. But I *want* to say, "In the Philippines I have much land— but you, even one cup of land you don't have!"

N: Your family has a lot of land in the Philippines?

D: Yes.

N: So if you can save money, will you buy more?

D: Yes. Yes, sister.

R: Investment in the Philippines *is* more land. My employer tells me that Filipinos is devils. I was there one month! . . . I say, "I've only been here one month and you only know me! Why do you generalize? Why you say that *all* Filipinos?" I say, "You know, we are not beggars in the Philippines! We are rich in the Philippines, you know?" I said to her, "Before I come here, do you know what is my job in the Philippines? I am a promotions manager in a business in Manila."

Rina can also be included among the financially better off domestic workers. Her family is in the jewelry business, and before coming to Hong Kong she worked as an office manager in Manila. Her two sisters, two sisters-in-law, and several other relatives also work in Hong Kong as domestic workers. Her aunt had just arrived to work as a domestic helper in Hong Kong, Rina explained, "not because she needs the money" but "because she wants to see Hong Kong." When Rina returned from a holiday in the Philippines, she brought a videotape of her brother's wedding to show to Mrs. Chin's family. Mrs. Chin was surprised at the extravagance of the affair. She described it to me:

> When Rina's brother was married there was a tremendous feast in the Philippines. I think they may be quite well off in the Philippines! They own a farm with lots of ducks and—she showed me photographs and all that. When her brother was married she went home and brought all these gifts, and when she came back she brought one of those home movies of the whole wedding. And she very unselfconsciously, you know, put it in our TV set and showed it to us. I'm very polite. I sat through the whole thing. And then, you know, my husband was struggling to be very polite and making comments. But my children disappeared—to my embarrassment—in the middle of the performance. But she was obviously very proud. She wanted to share this experience and all this. I think she's quite well off. I don't see that there's any cause for resentment. She was an office worker in metro-Manila—accounting—or something, and made about five hundred dollars a month—which was not too bad.

Fortunately for Rina, her relationship with Mrs. Chin was a secure one. Mrs. Chin and her husband both came from an elite and privileged background. Rina's display did not evoke any sense of class insecurity. If anything, they were amused by what they considered a rather conspicuous display, an attempt to impress them that was more befitting of the middle class than of the truly wealthy. Other employers might not have taken it so well.

More often domestic workers are like Dally and Rosa. They want to tell their employers a thing or two—that they own land, that they have a house (not just a tiny flat), and that they have maids of their own in the Philippines—but they refrain from doing so because their employment depends on maintaining the pretense that they are "just poor maids."

Photographs

Filipina domestic workers congregate under the "black statue" in Statue Square on Sundays, summer 2005.

Crowds of Filipina domestic workers gather in under the shade of the Hong Kong Shanghai Bank in Central District on Sundays, June 2005.

Hawkers openly sell food in the square on Sundays in 1993. By 2005 this was a rare sight.

Protestors in Chater Garden call for a wage increase and for abolition of the two-week rule, August 1993.

The window display of a shop in Worldwide Plaza that sells domestic worker uniforms, 1994.

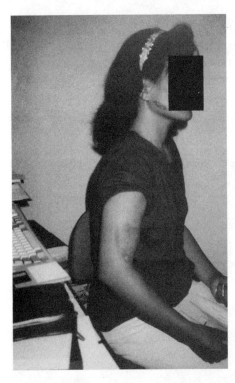

A client at the Mission for Filipino Migrant Workers displays her burn marks, 1994.

Indonesian domestic workers, members of the Indonesian Migrant Workers Union and KOTKOHO, rally outside the Indonesian Consulate on May 15, 2005, to demand an investigation into the death of Suprihatin.

A domestic worker waves a banner bearing the names of migrant worker organizations at the final march against the WTO on December 18, 2005. Note the "No WTO" written onto her "I ♥ HK" T-shirt. Photograph by Peter Constable Alter.

An Indonesian domestic worker waves anti-WTO balloons and a banner at Victoria Park, Causeway Bay, December 11, 2005. Photograph by Peter Constable Alter.

Indonesian domestic workers dress up to protest the commodification of workers at one of the HKPA anti-WTO rallies in Victoria Park, Causeway Bay, December 2005. Photograph by Peter Constable Alter.

Indonesian domestic workers prepare for the final protest march against the WTO in Victoria Park on December 18, 2005.

Filipino and Indonesian members of the Asian Migrant Coordinating Body joined the prodemocracy march on July 1, 2006, the anniversary of Hong Kong's becoming a Special Administrative Region of the People's Republic of China. WISER stands for Wage Increase, Social services, Employment protection, and Rights of workers.

A domestic worker at the July 1, 2006, prodemocracy march holds a sign in protest of the increased visa fee.

6 | DISCIPLINED MIGRANTS, DOCILE WORKERS

Foreign domestic helpers are by definition temporary residents of Hong Kong, and as such, their rights and privileges are different from those of permanent residents. Their ability to deal effectively with work-related problems is limited by their status as outsiders. The contract presumably guarantees certain rights, and it is assumed that because foreign domestic workers have contracts they are better off than workers without them. In practice, however, many of the conditions of the contract are difficult to implement or are interpreted to favor the employer. As a Hong Kong attorney and advocate for foreign workers, Melville Boase, has written, "No matter what fine words one may have written on paper, they only have significance or meaning if they can be enforced" (1991:90).

Domestic workers, furthermore, may be unaware of their rights or of how to report their grievances. Even if they know about their rights and the official recourse open to them, many choose not to act because the personal and financial costs involved in filing an official grievance against their employers often outweigh any benefits they stand to gain. In the majority of cases domestic workers, unlike many of their employers, do not have the financial resources, the time, nor the confidence to pursue their claims through the maze of Labour and Immigration Department officials, hearings, tribunals, courts, and offices.

This chapter describes some of the experiences, particularly the obstacles, faced by foreign domestic workers in their attempts to realize the rights ostensibly guaranteed by their contracts. These experiences illustrate the ways in which many Hong Kong government policies and regulations are interpreted and enforced in a spirit contrary to the international labor conventions on which Hong Kong policy is ostensibly based. Hong Kong laws and policies primarily serve the interests of employers and the larger state apparatus. They deter workers from pursuing their rights, ensure the continued availability of an affordable pool of foreign workers, and aim at maintaining domestic workers as temporary and docile migrants.

FELICIA

Before meeting Felicia, I looked over her file at the mission. Hers appeared to be a simple and straightforward case of termination without notice and without a month's pay in lieu of notice. She was twenty-three years old, single, had no children, and came from the Philippine province of Isabela where her family owned a small amount of land. Felicia had paid an agency fifty thousand pesos out of her parents' savings to come to Hong Kong, where she began to work for the Puns, a young couple living in an exclusive part of Hong Kong, in early February 1993. From the start, Mrs. Pun, who did not work and stayed at home much of the time, seemed very particular and scolded Felicia a lot. Felicia worked long hard hours, but Mrs. Pun complained about her cooking and cleaning. In one incident shortly before her termination, Felicia had been asked to remove a stain from the collar of a shirt; she scrubbed it with a brush because she had been instructed not to use bleach. After she ironed the shirt, the stain was still visible. When she saw it, Mrs. Pun became furious.

After she had worked for only eighteen days, Felicia was presented with an airplane ticket back to the Philippines, and eighteen days' wages, but no pay in lieu of notice as stipulated in the contract. She then had the choice of either returning home to the Philippines within two weeks of her termination or filing a complaint with the Labour Department.[1] Believing that

---

1. Cases involving violations of the "conditions of stay" under which the visa was granted (including terms stated in the contract) are directed to the Immigration Department, which handles cases of illegal work, endorsement, or overstaying (AMC 1992a:38–39; MFMW 1991:21–23). Labor-related cases that involve monetary claims (e.g., under- or nonpayment of wages, no rest days) are referred to the Labour Department (MFMW 1991:15–17).

she had been treated unfairly and that she should have been given notice, Felicia filed a complaint. The Labour Department then scheduled a conciliation meeting for April two months later. Meanwhile Felicia returned several times to the Immigration Department to apply for a visitor's visa to allow her to extend her stay. Each time she paid HK$115 until she was finally issued an extension to permit her to remain in Hong Kong until her case was closed.[2] She was not allowed to work for any other employer; so she depended on her sister, her cousin, and others to put her up. When her employers did not turn up for the first or the second scheduled conciliation meetings (and suffered no penalty), Labour Department officials told Felicia that to pursue her case she should file it with the Labour Tribunal. A tribunal hearing was then scheduled for late September, five months later.

Belle, a volunteer at the mission, invited me to come to Felicia's hearing. I thought it would be a simple case. I naïvely assumed that Felicia had only to demonstrate that she was terminated without warning, prior notice, or pay in lieu of notice, and that she would be awarded a month's salary. Thus, one hot morning in late September, the three of us met at the Eastern District Court in Sai Wan Ho. It took me close to two hours to get there from the New Territories, and Felicia traveled over an hour to get there by tram (the cheapest mode) with Belle, who had met her at the square.

Felicia's diminutive size was emphasized by her quiet, shy, and timid demeanor. At first she had some difficulty understanding my English, but once she relaxed after the hearing, we communicated quite well. Felicia was nervous about the procedures at the tribunal. She repeatedly thanked us for coming and offering moral support. She reiterated what was in her file. All she knew was that she was terminated with no specific reason provided, and she believed that she was entitled to a month's wages in lieu of notice.

The hearing was scheduled for 9:15 A.M., so we gathered outside the assigned courtroom shortly before 9:00. As we waited, we met the Filipino translator, a young man in a sports coat and tie who greeted us warmly,

---

If cases are not resolved at that stage, they can be referred to the Labour Tribunal (HKG 1992:16, 20). Cases not resolved at the tribunal can be pursued in District Court or High Court, depending on the amount of the claim. Appeals against decisions made at the Labour Tribunal can be heard at the High Court. District or High Court decisions can be heard at the Court of Final Appeal (AMC 1992a:31–38; see also MFMW 1991:29–37). Police-related cases involve "criminal" offenses, physical or sexual assault, theft or "confiscation" of the worker's or the employer's belongings, or imprisonment of the worker in the house. With enough evidence, such cases are heard at Magistrates Court (AMC 1992a:41–47; MFMW 1991:19–21).

2. In 2006 the visa fees were raised from HK$135 to HK$160. See MFMW 2006.

then kept a "professional distance." We also met two other Filipina domestic workers. One Filipina's employer had died owing her over HK$10,000 in pay and benefits, but the deceased employer's family refused to pay her anything. This worker had already spent two years pursuing her case, and again that day, none of her deceased employer's family appeared for the hearing.

At 9:15 Felicia visibly cowered as she caught a glimpse of Mrs. Pun. We had half expected her not to come. Mrs. Pun was a large, tall, and stylish young woman, heavily made up and wearing masses of jewelry. She was accompanied by an elegant older woman whom Felicia recognized as a staff member at the agency. As we later learned, the staff member had come to serve as a "witness." Mrs. Pun frowned and nodded in Felicia's direction as Felicia looked the other way.

Shortly before 9:30 everyone was ushered by the bailiff into a large, formal-looking courtroom. Meanwhile, as we waited for the presiding officer who would serve as judge, the Chinese interpreter (an older man in a suit and tie) was taking notes and asking Felicia's employer questions about the case in Cantonese. I turned to Belle and asked her if he was allowed to do so before the case began. She said "no," and turned to the Filipino translator, who politely asked him in English to stop. The Chinese interpreter responded, "But I'm an interpreter," and the Filipino interpreter said, "So am I, and you're not supposed to ask questions about the case before it begins."

It began to seem like the cards were stacked against Felicia. Most of the whispers were in Cantonese, a language she could not understand. All the observers present were Chinese, except for the four Filipina domestic workers and me. The Chinese translator politely nodded at me, offered me his card, and asked if I was an attorney. He ignored the Filipinas. The Chinese bailiff and translator appeared friendly toward Felicia's employer and her companion from the agency, both of whom looked elegant and mature in contrast to the Filipinas who wore blue jeans and T-shirts.

The tribunal is meant to be informal and expeditious but was neither. The room and the officials appeared formal and intimidating. "Our" case was scheduled for 9:15, but the presiding officer did not arrive until 9:30. We were all instructed to rise then be seated, and not to speak during the hearing. Most observers bowed as the presiding officer entered. Then, without any explanation, he called two Chinese men to the bench—the defendant and the plaintiff for the 10:00 case. The other three cases of the morning, all involving Filipina domestic workers, were thus delayed. We waited until 10:15. Then Felicia, looking quite frightened, and Mrs. Pun, appearing cool and confident, were ordered to approach the bench.

Although the presiding officer was Chinese, he conducted the hearing in English seasoned with British legal jargon. The Filipino translator translated into Tagalog for Felicia, and the Chinese interpreter into Cantonese for Mrs. Pun. The officer turned to Felicia first and asked if she was currently employed. She answered "no." He then asked the same question in two different ways, and she became confused. He asked if she currently had a job in Hong Kong. She replied that she was living with her sister. "Answer the question," he said firmly. She repeated in a meek voice that she had no job.

After several more questions that did not seem particularly relevant to the case, the presiding officer told Felicia not to take what he was about to say as an indication that she *could not* win her case, but that she should understand that he had a copy of a letter allegedly signed by Felicia before a witness that said she had terminated her own contract. That was the first Belle and I had heard of the document. He also had a copy of a letter to Felicia from her employer accepting her resignation. The letter of termination was written in English and read roughly, "Dear Mr. and Mrs. Pun, I cannot speak English, wash, clean, cook, or do other household duties. I am no good at being a DH and therefore I have decided to terminate my contract with no claims forthcoming. . . . Sincerely, Felicia." Mrs. Pun's letter stated that she had "no objections" to Felicia's working for someone else in Hong Kong.

The judge asked Felicia if she had signed the letter. She said she had. She tried to say more, but the judge cut her off and told the translator to tell Felicia just to answer the questions. He asked why she had signed the letter. She said she was forced to. He asked how she was forced, and she explained that she didn't know, but that she was scared. He said she would have to "prove that it was signed under duress," since English law finds it very difficult to go against a written signed document. Felicia seemed confused and bewildered and asked to speak to Belle.

The presiding officer asked who Belle was. She introduced herself as a volunteer from the mission. Belle was then called to the bench and began to explain to Felicia in Tagalog that if she wanted to pursue the case she would have to prove that she had signed the letter under duress. The presiding officer suddenly became very angry and demanded that the Filipino translator repeat what she said in English. He then ordered Belle to sit down, saying that he would not tolerate anyone influencing the witnesses in his courtroom.[3] Belle returned to her seat. Felicia appeared close to tears.

The presiding officer asked Felicia if she wanted to settle the case that day or to pursue it, because he did not want to waste any more of the tribunal's time. As he translated, the Filipino interpreter looked at Felicia reassuringly and spoke slowly and calmly. Felicia answered that if possible she wanted to settle the matter that day. The presiding officer said that the employer would not agree to pay the full month's wage of HK$3,200. Would Felicia be willing to settle for less in order to close the case? Felicia answered that she would.

The presiding officer then addressed Mrs. Pun for the first time and asked if she would agree to pay half or less for the sake of closing the case.[4] Mrs. Pun answered that she would pay no sum of money because it would appear as an admission of guilt. The judge's voice was firm. He said it would not be interpreted as such, that it was a relatively small sum of money to her, that it would save everyone a great deal of time and energy, and that afterward she and Felicia could get on with their lives. He said he assumed that she had had to take time off work to come. Mrs. Pun said no, that she didn't work. The presiding officer then said (sarcastically, it seemed to me) that she therefore had all the time in the world to spend on this relatively minor case that could otherwise easily be settled with a token amount of money? She answered, "Yes . . . no . . . yes," and said she was acting "out of principle."

Under pressure to decide whether to pursue her case, Felicia looked to Belle for advice, but none was forthcoming. Finally, she said that she would. The officer abruptly announced that the next hearing would be scheduled for the second week of March 1994 (almost six months away, and over a year since Felicia's termination) and that the case was adjourned. Meanwhile, Mrs. Pun was allowed to hire a new domestic worker, but Felicia was not permitted to work. Over the next several days, Felicia spoke to another adviser at the mission who reiterated that winning her case depended on her ability to document how she was forced to sign the letter under duress. She had to decide whether it was worth waiting six months for HK$3,200 with the risk that she might still lose her case. Even if she won, Mrs. Pun might refuse to pay. Since the Labour Tribunal has no executory powers, if

---

3. Attorneys are not permitted at Labour Tribunal hearings. Union representatives or friends cannot address the tribunal but are permitted to offer support and advice (MFMW 1991:35).

4. Mrs. Pun spoke in Cantonese that was then translated into English, but it was clear from his interruptions of the translator that the presiding officer was following the Cantonese.

Felicia won, she might have to spend three or four more months in District Court with the help of Legal Aid to try to collect the awarded sum. How would she support herself in the meantime? Could her family survive so long without her income?

So far one "illegal" job had presented itself to her. A police officer wanted her to do domestic work part-time and work part-time in his karaoke bar. Felicia, however, was horrified by the behavior she witnessed at the bar. A few days after the hearing, Felicia decided that she had neither the energy nor the desire to fight, and she returned home to the Philippines. Meanwhile, Mrs. Pun received her "free replacement" from the agency. The agency profited from Felicia's fees and those of her replacement.[5] The police officer had received a week of Felicia's labor on a "free trial basis," and the Immigration Department had collected HK$345 from her for visa extensions.

Basic Conditions of the Contract

The official "Employment Contract for a Domestic Helper Recruited Outside of Hong Kong" is the only contract recognized by Hong Kong law (HK-LD 1992a, b, c, 2004; HK-ID 1993a, b, c, d, 2003, 2005). It is governed by general labor laws and by less formal policies introduced by the Labour and Immigration Departments. The contract between the "Employer" and the "Helper" is for a two-year period, although either the worker or the employer can legally terminate it at any time. It can also be renewed for additional two-year terms, if the worker and employer agree, on condition that the worker returns to the Philippines between contracts.

The contract requires that the worker be repatriated "for holidays and family-reunion" at the end of a two-year contract (HK-ID 1993a:note 5). This requirement is sometimes waived by the Immigration Department if the employer makes a convincing case that she cannot manage without the worker. The employer then must guarantee that the worker will be sent home at a later, more convenient time (for the employer), usually within the same year. Overseas contract workers are categorically excluded from applying for permanent Hong Kong residence, and the return home is meant to help ensure the impermanence of their residence. Their presence in Hong Kong can continue for only as long as their labor is deemed necessary.

---

5. Mrs. Pun was probably required to pay the new domestic worker's airfare from the Philippines, but saved more than twice that amount by not paying Felicia a month's wages.

OFFICIAL AND UNOFFICIAL EMPLOYERS

The contract stipulates that a domestic worker work for only one employer and "shall not take up, and shall not be required by the employer to take up, any other employment with any other person" (HK-ID 1993c:4b). Nevertheless, like muijai, foreign workers may be required to work for the employer's friends and relatives. Cathy was one of 2,106 new clients who came to the mission for advice or counseling during the eighteen-month period between January 1992 and June 1993. Of these clients, 109 (5 percent) complained that they were "endorsed," or required to work for an employer other than the one who had signed their contract.[6]

When a prospective employer begins the process of hiring a domestic worker, he or she is required to provide the Immigration Department with evidence of a minimum income or its equivalent in assets or savings (in 1993 the minimum was HK$150,000 per year and in 2006 HK$180,000 a year). If the prospective employer does not meet the minimum requirements, a visa will not be issued. One common situation, therefore, in which endorsement arises is when a would-be employer does not meet the income requirement. He or she may arrange for a friend or relative to sign the contract. In such cases the worker may never meet the "official" employer who signed her contract.

Jean, a twenty-two-year-old Filipina, experienced another type of endorsement, in which she was shunted from one employer to another. Instead of officially terminating Jean's contract, her employer "returned her" to Mrs. Fu, the recruitment agent. Jean had no idea where she was going when Mrs. Fu's domestic worker came to pick her up. As she left, her first employer told her not to worry, that she had "made other arrangements with Mrs. Fu." It was only later that Jean learned that her employer had located a Thai worker who agreed to work for only HK$1,000 a month. Jean did not like her second employer, who had already terminated four workers. When she complained to Mrs. Fu, she was taken to a third employer.

FOOD AND ACCOMMODATION

From the previous chapter, it should be clear that ideas about what constitutes "suitable" housing and even what constitutes a "bed" vary greatly.

---

6. A worker often has more than one complaint. When she is interviewed at the mission, she is usually asked if any other common grievances apply to her case. Information on frequency of complaints is derived from an unpublished internal report of the mission compiled in July 1993 (MFMW 1993a, b).

Of the 2,106 domestic workers surveyed at the mission, 535 (25 percent) complained that they had not been given private or adequate accommodation; 458 (22 percent) complained of insufficient food (MFMW 1993a, b). Following long working hours, inappropriate accommodation was the most common complaint among workers. About two-thirds of the respondents in the AMC survey had their own room. Of the remaining third, about 20 percent shared a room with a child and about 2 percent with an elderly woman. Over 4 percent slept "in various places in the house such as the living room, passageways, kitchen, balcony and even the toilet" (AMC 1991:53). On my first day as a volunteer at the mission I met a worker who slept on the floor under a table in the living room. Another slept on the patient examination table in her employer's medical office. Both women came to the mission with photographs they had taken to document their inadequate accommodation. Another woman came to the mission with a broken arm. She had fallen off of the tall cabinet she was forced to sleep on. Although the contract specifies that the employer must provide "suitable accommodation," immigration officers do not treat unsuitable housing as sufficient grounds for allowing a domestic worker to change employers.

By law, a domestic worker must live at her employer's home unless the Director of Immigration grants an exception. The employer is theoretically obliged to provide the worker with "suitable and furnished accommodation and food free of charge" (HK-ID 1993c:5b). As discussed in Chapter 5, if no food is provided, the employer must provide a food allowance of no less than HK$300 (US$38) per month, an amount that has not changed for more than a thirteen years. The employer must also provide "essential facilities and supplies," which include "light and water supply, toilet and bathing facilities, bed, blankets and pillows, etc" (HK-ID 1993d:6).

The 2003 version of the contract (which was in effect in 2006) is in most ways the same as the 1993 version, but it includes a "Schedule of Accommodation and Domestic Duties" (introduced in 1998) that the prospective employer must fill out and both employer and worker must sign. On this form, the employer must indicate the size of the flat, the number of persons in the household who will be "served on a regular basis," the type of accommodation and facilities provided for the worker, and the duties that the worker will be expected to perform. The 2003 employment contract expands on the issue of "suitable accommodation" from the earlier contract and states that,

> While the average size flat in Hong Kong is relatively small and the availability of [a] separate servant room is not common, the Employer should

provide the Helper with suitable accommodation and with reasonable privacy. Examples of unsuitable accommodation are: The Helper having to sleep on make-do beds in the corridor with little privacy and sharing a room with an adult/teenager of the opposite sex. (HK-ID 2003:3a)

Under accommodation, the employer must check "yes" or "no" whether the domestic worker will have a "servant room." If yes, they must indicate the size of the room; if no, they must indicate who she will share a room with, whether she will have a partitioned area, or where she will sleep. Under facilities, the employer must indicate "yes" or "no" to light and water, toilet and bathing facilities, bed, blankets or quilt, pillows, and wardrobe. If those facilities are not provided free of charge, the form states that, "application for entry visa will not normally be approved" (HK-ID 2003:B).

HOUSEHOLD WORK AND ILLEGAL WORK

Domestic workers, according to the contract, must "only perform domestic duties" for the employer (HK-ID 1993c:4a; HK-ID 2003:4a). These include "domestic cooking, household chores, baby-sitting, and child-minding" (HK-ID 1993d:4a). The 2003 version adds "looking after aged persons" and other duties (to be specified on the form by the employer). The vagueness of terms such as "household chores" or "domestic duties" means that workers can be required to mow lawns, sew, or do work for an employer's business that take place within the house. One domestic worker volunteered to help her employer make children's costumes to "donate" to schools. After making hundreds of costumes, she learned that her employer was paid for them. The Labour Department told her she had no recourse since she had done the work voluntarily within her employer's home. When the employer's home is also an office or a factory, the definition of "domestic work" becomes particularly nebulous.

In the early 1990s it was not uncommon for women to work outside their employers' homes as waitresses, shop clerks, or in factories at the employer's behest for no additional pay. During just the first four months of my research in 1993, I met "domestic" workers employed as secretaries, clothing or architectural designers, accountants, beauticians, manicurists, nurses, waitresses, dishwashers, medical technicians, cooks, salespersons, messengers, hawkers, factory workers, and researchers. The worker who slept on the medical examination table had been trained as a medical technician in the Philippines, and her duties had included conducting ultrasound examinations.

Illegal workers are often difficult for immigration officers to spot because they are outside public view and because there are several thousand Filipinos who work legally in similar occupations in Hong Kong. Many Filipinas were instructed by their employers to say that they are local residents or married to a local resident should the question ever arise. A social worker at the Catholic Centre explained that women who look "more Chinese" (some of Chinese ancestry) are more likely to be hired to do "visible" illegal work, such as hawking.

Some domestic workers were chosen because of their previous training and work experience. Of the 2,106 new clients who came to the mission between January 1992 and June 1993, 355 (17 percent) were required to do illegal work outside their employers' homes (MFMW 1993a, b). Some workers agree to do illegal work because they are coerced or because they are afraid of the alternatives. Val, for example, had worked in a shoe factory in the Philippines and was hired to do the same thing, in addition to housework, in Hong Kong. When a friend brought her to the mission one Sunday, she was exhausted nearly to the point of collapse and vowed never to return to her employer. She was advised, however, to go back once more to take photographs of the shoe factory to document the situation. Without photographs she could not prove that she had done illegal work. Her employer could claim that she was lying. Even with evidence the employer could claim that Val did the work willingly and had therefore violated her conditions of stay. The fact that Val terminated the contract, however, would lend credence to her claim that she was an unwilling accomplice. She would not gain a month's wages, since she terminated the contract, but she might gain a waiver of the required return to the Philippines. Should she locate a new employer within the two weeks (not easy to do without a good recommendation from her employer), Val would have a chance to remain in Hong Kong to process the new contract.

Sometimes domestic workers willingly do illegal work because they prefer it to household work or because they are paid more than a minimum salary. For example, Elsa happily agreed to do research and word processing for her employer. She worked very short and flexible hours, was paid more than minimum wage, and considered her work interesting and educational. A Filipina who worked as a waitress in a Thai restaurant was allowed to keep part of her tips in addition to her monthly minimum wage. Even if a domestic worker receives extra wages, she usually earns much less than a local worker would earn at the same job. A television program aired in Hong Kong in early 1993 showed how shop owners in Stanley Market hired foreign domestic workers as sales clerks because they were cheaper than local workers. Local "shop girls" at the time often earned HK$6,000–7,000 a month, not including commissions; secretaries could earn over HK$8,000 and expected reasonable hours. Domestic workers were usually paid HK$3,200 a month and could be made to work longer hours.

WHO BENEFITS?

Provisions in the contract that are presumably meant to protect the foreign worker from endorsement or illegal work may in practice be used to oppress her. If, for example, an employer requires a worker to work for someone else in a different place or doing a different job, research shows that it is the worker who is most likely to be "investigated and prosecuted, and not the employer who is the one in control of . . . and probably instigating the situation" (Boase 1991:90). According to Boase, in cases of illegal work, at least in the early 1990s, the Immigration Department invariably took no action against the employer and often took steps to prosecute or repatriate the worker (1991:88). Even when the worker reported the problem, she was often found to have breached her conditions of stay, repatriated to her country of origin, and disallowed from ever working in Hong Kong again.

In 1995, as the local unemployment rate grew, the number of publicized Immigration Department raids in Stanley Market, Worldwide Plaza, restaurants, and other locations, increased, and policies toward domestic workers caught doing illegal work grew harsher. Yet employers continued to hire foreign domestic workers to do illegal work. One possible reason was that the crackdown on part-time and illegal work was only halfhearted. The vast majority of it went unreported by either employer or domestic worker, and as long as no one complained, it was allowed to continue. As one government official suggested to me in hushed tones in 1994, foreign women who work illegally provide an important source of cheap local labor, from which many individuals, including government officials, police officers, and other civil servants, benefit. Why would they want to stop it?

Domestic workers, on the other hand, might willingly take on work that is not permitted under the conditions of their visas and contracts. Even if they enjoy the work and the extra wages, however, they are still exploited. They are paid less than locals who do the same work and their employers profit most. Domestic workers, moreover, risk unemployment, fines, imprisonment, and deportation, whereas their employers usually risk little or nothing.

As described in Chapter 2, illegal work became less common or was at least less visible and less openly talked about in 2006 than it was in the early and mid-1990s. Hong Kong's economic decline in the late 1990s through 2003 meant that more locals became available to take up low-paying, low-skilled jobs as waitresses, dishwashers, shop clerks, and as part-time domestic workers. Given the job shortages for locals, the Hong Kong government received more complaints about illegal foreign workers. The government strengthened its media campaign against illegal work, widely publicizing the possible penalties for both employers and workers.

One poster published by the Labour Department that was commonly seen in 2006 along public walkways (and in a smaller version for distribution with employment contract materials), had the image of a prison wall and window in the background. It announced boldly in Chinese and English "Employing illegal domestic helper is liable to imprisonment for 3 years." The poster provides telephone numbers to report illegal workers and a hotline for employing local domestic workers. It also states "Don't Employ illegal domestic helpers. Hiring visitors, or other people's domestic helpers to perform domestic duties, or deploying domestic helpers to perform non-domestic duties is illegal, and liable to three years' imprisonment and a fine of [HK]$350,000 upon conviction." The point about harsh punishments is somewhat undermined, however, by the examples that follow. "In March 2004, a housewife was sentenced to ten months' jail for employing a Mainland visitor as domestic helper" and "in September 2004, a restaurant owner was sentenced to four months' jail for illegally deploying her foreign domestic helper to work in her restaurant." Although it is difficult to say whether illegal work has been reduced as a result of such campaigns, it is clear that employers and workers are more reluctant to talk about illegal practices that were both common and visible a decade earlier.

Since 2003, the government has also made efforts to mount criminal charges against illegal employers. Government representatives expressed surprise and frustration that few foreign workers—even those who had won their labor claims—were willing to return to Hong Kong to serve as witnesses for criminal prosecutions. The government offered to fly them to Hong Kong from the Philippines or Indonesia and to put them up in a hotel for two or three days while they served as witnesses. As domestic workers and their advocates pointed out, however, workers had already spent valuable time pursuing their cases during which time they were not permitted to work, repeatedly had to pay to renew their visas, and depended on the support of charities. They found it disingenuous that the government would make it so difficult for domestic workers to remain in Hong Kong to pursue their own labor cases but still expect them to drop everything to return to Hong Kong to serve as witnesses months later.

WAGES AND EXPENSES

In 1975 foreign domestic workers' wages were around HK$600 a month; by 1980 they had risen to approximately HK$1,050. In 1985 the monthly wage was HK$1,800 (US$230). In the 1980s, the government set a minimum allowable wage for foreign domestic workers, and as of 2006, foreign domestic workers are still the only Hong Kong workers whose wages are governed by a legal minimum wage. The minimum wage rose steadily from HK$2,300 in 1987, to HK$2,500 in 1988, HK$2,800 in 1989, HK$3,000 in 1990, and $3,200 in 1991 (AMC 1991:45, LegCo 2003). In 1993 it was increased to HK$3,500, and in September 1994 to HK$3,750. No increase was approved in 1995. The wage reached an all-time high of HK$3,860 (US$490) in 1996 and remained at that level through 1998 (Figure 6.1). In 1999, in the wake of the Asian financial crisis, the wage was reduced to HK$3,670, and in 2003, in the wake of SARS, it was reduced again to HK$3,270. In May 2005, as Hong Kong's economy rebounded, the Labour Department raised the minimum monthly allowable wage HK$50 to HK$3,320, and in May 2006 by HK$80 to HK$3,400, still HK$460 below the 1996–98 level. In June 2007 it was raised again by HK$80.

The employment contract for foreign domestic workers states that they must be paid the minimum allowable monthly wage that is in effect at the time the contract is signed. A worker whose contract was signed after 1 September 1993 but before the next wage increase, for example, should automatically receive the monthly minimum wage of HK$3,500 which was instated that month. An increase in the minimum wage would not affect the wages of women whose contracts were signed during the previous two years, when the minimum wage was HK$3,200.

As Boase has pointed out, specified wages are meaningful to the worker only if the employer can be forced to pay them. In one case the Labour Tribunal presiding officer accepted the employer's argument that the domestic worker had agreed to work for less, even though the employment contract cannot be officially altered without the approval of the commissioner of labour (Boase 1991:90). In some cases employers have escaped paying full wages by forcing workers to sign false receipts or blank papers that are later filled in to look like receipts. In some cases reported at the mission, agencies require domestic workers to sign stacks of blank receipts before they are hired.

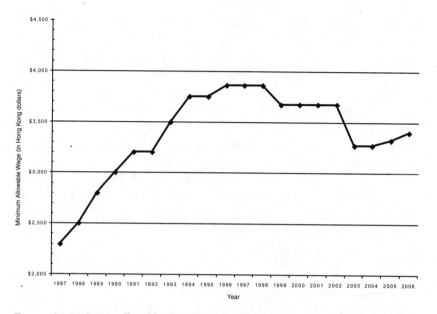

FIGURE 6.1. Minimum allowable wage for foreign domestic helpers in Hong Kong, 1987–2006. *Source:* Hong Kong Labour Department; AMC 2001; LegCo 2003.

The employer has other financial obligations to the foreign domestic worker besides the basic wage. He or she is responsible for providing free passage to and from Hong Kong upon termination or expiration of the contract. The worker is also supposed to receive a minimum daily travel allowance from the place and date of origin until arrival in Hong Kong and on her return home, assuming the most direct trip. The employer is also responsible for reimbursing the domestic worker for all the costs of preparing her documents—including visas, medical examinations, "authentication fees" paid to the consulate, and other processing fees—but only if the worker shows receipts for these expenses. Most of the domestic workers I met at the mission had paid such fees themselves and had not been reimbursed by their employers. Some were too timid to ask for reimbursement; others could not claim reimbursement because they had not received receipts.

Jean described how her sister Leah approached a Hong Kong agent, Mrs. Fu, to help find Jean a job. Leah paid Mrs. Fu HK$2,700 in agency fees (almost ten times the legal limit for Hong Kong agencies) and HK$500 for POEA processing fees.[7] The agency representative in the Philippines

7. As noted earlier, agencies are not supposed to charge a worker more than 10 percent of a month's salary.

told Jean she didn't have to pay the processing fee in the Philippines, and gave her a letter to show to the POEA. "But when I reported to POEA, I was required to pay 3,000 pesos. So I paid more than 3,000 pesos and my sister paid HK$500 for the same fee. Neither the agency nor my employer ever paid me back."

Jean was also forced to accept HK$1,000 per month less than the minimum wage. As she explained, Mrs. Fu recruited applicants "with special agreements." Workers who agreed to HK$2,200 per month were told that after two or three months their salaries would be increased. Considering the job a "stepping stone," Jean agreed to the wage of HK$2,200. When she arrived in Hong Kong, her employer accompanied her to Mrs. Fu's house. There she was asked to sign a form agreeing to the salary of HK$2,200 for the duration of the two-year contract.

> I was hesitant to sign because my sister and I thought the [legal] minimum salary would be given to me after a probation period. But I had no courage to oppose them. The first thing that flashed in my mind was that they might terminate me. I spent a lot of money in coming here and I didn't want to go back home without anything. So although it was against my will, I made a statement.

Despite the long hours, hard work (including hand washing clothes for the whole family), and sharing a bedroom, Jean was very happy for the first month. Then she received her first wages.

> When I received my first salary, my employer had deducted the HK$100 she had given me on my first day off. So I got only HK$2,100. I signed a receipt [for that amount]. A few minutes after I signed, my employer tore up the paper and asked me to sign again. I saw that $3,200 was written on the paper, so I refused to sign it. My employer said that Mrs. Fu had instructed her to do that, so although it was against my will again, I finally signed the $3,200 receipt.

Although Jean's case is extreme, underpayment of wages and other money-related grievances are not uncommon. In the mission survey, 227 (11 percent) of over 2,000 new clients over an eighteen-month period listed underpayment of wages as one of their grievances, another 88 (4 percent) complained of delayed payment, and 23 (1 percent) complained of nonpayment of wages (MFMW 1993a, b). Some of those who were underpaid had used illegal agencies. Although some illegal agencies have been closed down, others are difficult to prosecute because agents like Mrs. Fu cover their tracks with false receipts, cash payments, threats, or empty promises.

Workers who are hired without going through an agency also have problems. Connie, for example, was approached by a man who came to the Philippines in person to hire a domestic worker. This was an unusual procedure. Most employers, even those who do not go through formal agencies, hire domestic workers from a distance. The employer explained to Connie that he was quite poor and could only afford to pay her HK$1,500 (about half of the legal rate at the time), but he assured her that her work would be light since he lived alone with his wife. Later, if he could afford it and was satisfied with her work, he promised to increase her salary. By Philippine standards the pay sounded good to Connie, and she was not aware of Hong Kong's minimum wage. So, saving money on agency fees and expecting a light workload, she signed the agreement he presented. She and her employer also signed the official contract, which stipulated a wage of HK$3,200, but Connie took it as a mere formality.

After Connie arrived in Hong Kong she realized that her employer was not poor and that her workload was not going to be light. She had to clean three flats and to pack and move heavy boxes of clothing for her employer's export business. Meanwhile, Connie met other Filipinas in Statue Square on her day off and compared notes. Most of them received the official salary. She confronted her employer, who said he had consulted a lawyer and that their private contract was legally binding. Two months later Connie visited the mission. Soon after, she left her employer and filed a complaint against him at the Labour Department. The last I heard, she had been awarded her claims in the Labour Tribunal even though her employer did not appear. She then had to file for Legal Aid to try to collect the sum she had claimed. Ten months later she was working for a new employer, but had been unable to collect her award. Connie's case illustrates not only the problem with underpayment but also how workers are willing to settle for less than ideal conditions just to get a job.

Time On and Time Off

Long working hours are the single biggest complaint among domestic workers. Between January 1992 and June 1993, 747 foreign domestic workers, over two-thirds of all new clients at the mission, complained of long hours (MFMW 1993a, b). According to the AMC (2001, 2005) and

ATKI (2005) data, long working hours remain a problem a decade later. The contract says nothing about the number of hours to be worked in a day, and Labour and Immigration Department officials take essentially the same position as the employers' association: that household work cannot be measured and that work hours would be impossible to enforce. Long working hours are not officially accepted as sufficient reason to allow workers to change employers.

The contract does mention time off. Before 1997 foreign domestic workers were entitled to eleven statutory holidays a year, including the Monday after the queen's birthday. After 1997 the holidays increased to twelve and included Labor Day, China's National Day, and the anniversary of Hong Kong's reunification with China.[8] The worker is paid for these holidays if she has worked for the employer for over three months. The worker is also entitled to one "rest day" of twenty-four hours per week, chosen by the employer. The worker must be notified of the day before the beginning of the month. For the six-month period between January and June 1993, 116 (13 percent) of new clients at the mission complained that they did not receive their statutory holidays, and 26 (3 percent) complained about their rest days (MFMW 1993a, b). Margie, for example, received only irregular half days off. As mentioned earlier, the vast majority of domestic workers who were interviewed at the mission was given a curfew and rarely received twenty-four hours off.

If a domestic worker does not receive rest days or statutory holidays, the Labour Department will, at most, refer the monetary claim to the Labour Tribunal, so the worker can try to collect the payment for the holidays and rest days she worked. Employers were not penalized in such cases, only required to pay the worker for the extra days she worked. Time, however, is irreplaceable (Boase 1991:91).

Annual leave is calculated according to the time that a domestic worker has been with the same employer. The worker is entitled to seven days of paid leave for each of the first two years she works for the same employer.

8. Holidays that have continued since before 1997 include 1 January, Lunar New Year's Day, the second and third days of the Lunar New Year, Ching Ming Festival, Tuen Ng (Dragon Boat) Festival, the day after the Midautumn Festival, Chung Yeung Festival, and either Winter Solstice Festival or Christmas Day (the employer decides). Since 1997 the Monday after the queen's birthday and the British bank holiday of the last Monday in August are no longer observed. The three new holidays are on May 1 (Labor Day), July 1 (Hong Kong's establishment as a Special Administrative Region), and October 1 (National Day).

After that, the number of days per year increases by one day a year for each year she works for the same employer, reaching a maximum of fourteen days a year after nine or more years of work with the same employer. If a domestic worker is terminated because of a breach of contract, the employer is not required to pay annual leave.[9]

MEDICAL PROVISIONS

The contract requires that domestic workers submit a medical certificate to their employers. Employers are advised to take out a general health insurance policy for domestic workers, and they are required to have insurance that covers any occupational or work-related illness or injury a domestic worker might experience. Whether or not an illness or injury is attributable to her work, an employer must provide free medical and dental treatment. The worker must accept treatment "provided by any registered medical practitioner" specified by the employer. If a worker experiences illness or injury that arises "in the course of employment," then the employer must pay compensation. If a worker is sick for more than four days, she is supposed to receive "sickness allowance" (equal to two-thirds her normal pay). She is entitled to two paid sick days for each month she has worked during the first year of her contract, four days a month thereafter, and she can accumulate up to 120 sick days.

The medical coverage and benefits for domestic workers sound very reasonable. Unfortunately, there is no guarantee that domestic workers will receive those benefits because the contract provides the employer with a legal escape clause. According to the contract, if a medical practitioner certifies that a worker is not fit to work, then her employer can terminate the contract without a month's notice and without pay in lieu of notice. In other words, an employer can require a domestic worker to go to the doctor, and if the doctor certifies that she is ill and unable to work, she can be immediately terminated (Boase 1991:92, n.d.:3). The severity and duration of the illness is not specified. It appears that a worker with a forty-eight-hour flu could be dismissed without notice or benefits.[10]

---

9. Under certain circumstances, a domestic worker is also entitled to maternity leave, maternity pay, severance, and long-service pay (see AMC 1992a:20–27; HK-LD 2004; MFMW 1991:5–11).

10. Although a test case was filed addressing this matter, it was later dropped because, as her lawyer explained, the domestic worker "got tired of waiting and went home."

TERMINATION WITHOUT NOTICE

Either the employer or the worker is allowed to terminate the contract *without any explanation* provided that she or he gives a month's notice or pays a month's wage in lieu of notice. Employers often choose to pay a month's wage in lieu of notice, especially if they have another worker lined up. Workers are less likely to be able to afford to pay a month's wage, so more often they give notice. If a domestic worker does not provide the Labour and Immigration Departments with an acceptable explanation for termination, however, she must automatically return to the Philippines within two weeks of the termination date. There are no penalties for an employer who terminates the contract ahead of time. He or she is free to sign another contract even before the first domestic worker has left. The employer, furthermore, by not providing the domestic worker with a written reason for termination, jeopardizes her chances of finding a new employer. Although employers are not legally required to give workers a "release letter," those without written statements of support from their former employers often have great difficulty locating new employers and processing new contracts (see Hicks 1982).[11]

According to one report, over 80 percent of all contracts that are terminated before two years, for whatever reason, are terminated by the employer (Pascual and Tellez 1993; see also *Asiaweek* 1987:72).[12] The contract specifies several reasons why an employer can dismiss a domestic worker without notice or pay in lieu: if the worker willfully disobeys a lawful and reasonable order; misconducts himself/herself, such conduct being inconsistent with the due and faithful discharge of his/her duties; is guilty of fraud or dishonesty; is habitually neglectful in his/her duties; or is unfit for service as certified by a medical practitioner.

The question of what constitutes a "reasonable order," "misconduct," or "habitual neglect" is subject to different interpretations. Kate worked

11. In the early 1980s, the Immigration Department required a release letter to transfer a domestic worker to a new employer. The old employer declared in the letter that he/she did not object. This provision gave employers the power to decide whether a worker could transfer employment or be repatriated (Hicks 1982:4–5). Today the Immigration Department does not officially require a release letter, but it usually requires a written statement from the employer giving the date and reasons for the termination of the contract, especially if the domestic worker is petitioning for a new one.

12. According to the *Hong Kong Standard*, in a study of 356 cases of termination about one-third of them were initiated by the worker and two-thirds by the employer (Morgan 1987; MFMW 1988).

for her employer for only one month before being presented with a list of infractions for which she was terminated. Her employer had noted the exact date or time of each "incident." Under the heading "Incapacity" she read, "Spoiled soup overdone on 29/6/93 and 26/7/93" and "damaged the curtain during the work on 7/7/93." Under the heading "Disobedience," she was told, "You are reluctant to carry out the works, especially at night"; "You fail to complete the work at 8:30 p.m. on 5/7/93, at 9:30 p.m. on 16/7/93, and 7:30 a.m. on 17/7/93"; "We requested to you to buy a Chinese Newspaper according to the newspaper name we wrote to you, however, you like to buy another kind on 28/7/93."

The Burden of Proof

Specific incidents such as those cited above, which took place more than three weeks before a domestic worker was dismissed, were seriously considered in a High Court decision to reverse a Labour Tribunal ruling in favor of the domestic worker (*SCMP* 1987b). The tribunal officer had awarded the domestic worker, Ms. B, a month's pay in lieu of notice and long-service payment on the grounds that her employer had not made a case for justifiable dismissal. He had merely dismissed her without explanation. The employer then appealed to the High Court where the decision was reversed. The High Court judge reasoned that it is up to the employee to prove that the dismissal was not justified and not for the defendant employer to make out a case. The judge also stated that, "the conduct which is relied upon by an employer for dismissing an employee may be a single incident, such as one willful refusal to obey a lawful order, or it may be the cumulative effect of a series of incidents on the part of an employee" (HK-SC 1987:3). There was a detailed examination of the domestic worker's performance over several months, including her failure to sew a button on her employer's shirt, her refusal to "cease work" after being given a direct order to stop cleaning kitchen utensils, and her refusal to stop vacuuming when her employer insisted that she should go to the doctor (HK-SC 1987:5–6).

It appears that in most cases when a domestic worker is summarily dismissed without notice or payment in lieu of notice, she must prove not only that she was terminated in such a way but also that the employer "had no grounds for terminating her" (Boase n.d.:5). If she does not succeed, she is vulnerable to charges that she owes her employer a month's pay in lieu of notice. The onus of proof is on the worker.

In other countries, for instance England, where there is a concept of unfair dismissal—which does not apply in Hong Kong—the onus is on the basis that the dismissal was unfair unless the employer can show otherwise. Here in Hong Kong it is completely the reverse with the worker having to prove a negative matter, that is that the employer did not have cause. . . . From legislation which is supposedly to protect the migrants, they now have to prove themselves innocent (Boase n.d.:5).

ACCUSATIONS OF THEFT

According to Mr. Ho, Chinese amahs who worked for his family in the past voluntarily opened their bags for his mother to inspect each time they left the house on holiday. "Whenever they leave . . . their luggage was thoroughly searched. In fact, as a courtesy, they must go to their employer and say, 'this is my luggage. Now I am leaving. Would you like have a look?' to prove that they did not take anything from the house. Some good employers would say, 'No, it's okay, it's okay.' But some would say, 'Okay, open it up. Let's have a look.'" Today, domestic workers who are terminated by employers or who terminate their own contracts are advised to do the same and to have the employer sign a sheet of paper saying that they have thoroughly examined the domestic workers belongings, so as to avoid any possible accusation of theft.

Muijai were commonly accused of theft by their mistresses (Jaschok 1988:109). According to staff at the mission, the Catholic Centre, the Asian Migrant Centre, and two police officers I spoke to, accusations of theft against foreign domestic workers are common. One police inspector, who often deals with cases involving domestic workers, explained that in the vast majority of cases the accusation is unsubstantiated and involves one person's word against the other. In many cases the accusation follows a disagreement between the domestic worker and the employer or a domestic worker's expressed desire to terminate the contract. The accusation may be made to intimidate the worker or to create grounds for termination without notice. Several domestic workers I spoke with claimed that the employer's property was placed inside their luggage without their knowledge or that they were accused of taking items that their employers had given them.

When she first came to Hong Kong, Elsa heard of many cases of employers "framing" workers for theft after a disagreement. Her first employer gave her generous gifts, and she was concerned that they might be used against her. "So every time I receive [a gift] I would say, 'In the near future maybe you will say that I get it from you? That I stole it?' 'No, no, no. I'm not like that,' my employer said. 'I'm not like that.'" But once her employer did suspect Elsa of stealing money. Elsa's employer's children, aged ten and eleven, invited Elsa to come with them to shop for toys. Elsa was surprised at the amount of money they had; so she broached the subject with her coworker and cousin.

I said, "Gina, the children bought many toys! I saw HK$1,000 in their pockets!"

She said, "I wonder where they got it?"

"They said that it was given by their father."

And then my cousin said, "You know, Elsa, it's good that you told me, because our employer is already watching you because her money is lost! HK$1,000!"

So the children admitted it. They kneeled in front of me. And then my employer—well of course she is my employer and she will not say, "I'm sorry, Elsa." But the children knelt in front of me and my employer told them to say sorry to me.

MELINDA

Melinda worked for a lawyer called Mrs. Woo for over a year. During that time she cleaned the law office and sometimes helped with filing and answering the phone. Mrs. Woo often complemented her on her "Chinese appearance" and said that if anyone at the office asked why she couldn't speak Chinese, to say that she was Mrs. Woo's overseas Chinese relative. Melinda cleaned Mrs. Woo's flat and prepared meals for Mrs. Woo and her son, twenty-two, and daughter, eighteen, and she was also required to clean a second flat. Melinda was not happy with work in the office, the long hours of cleaning two flats, and the way Mrs. Woo and her children treated her. The daughter would throw money on the floor and order her to pick it up and go to the market for her. The son would stand naked at the bathroom door and order her to bring him his underpants. When she refused, he and his mother found it amusing. "What do you care?" she recalled being taunted; "you're just the maid!" Melinda began to ask her friends how she could get out of this situation.

One day Melinda's employer telephoned her to say that her contract was terminated. Mrs. Woo instructed her to come to the law office to collect her air ticket and salary in lieu of notice. When Melinda arrived at the office, a police officer arrested her on a charge of stealing money from her employer. Mrs. Woo provided her with an air ticket but claimed that she was not entitled to a month's salary since she had violated the conditions of her contract (by stealing). Melinda was taken to the police station where she was forced to spend the night. Eventually the charges were dropped for lack of evidence. She returned to Mrs. Woo's flat with a friend to get her things. Mrs. Woo was not at home, but on the advice of her friend, Melinda had Mrs. Woo's daughter check through her luggage.

Melinda then filed a case against her employer. Several days later she was arrested a second time and forced to spend another night in jail. This time Mrs. Woo had charged her with stealing stockings and underwear. Nothing was found in her possession, however, and she was let out on bail. She was instructed to return to the police station on Sunday for the final decision. That Sunday Melinda and a friend traveled from the far side of Hong Kong Island to Tuen Mun police station. It took them over two hours by bus and mass transit railway (MTR) each way and the round-trip fare cost each of them HK$50, approximately half a day's wages. When she arrived at the police station, she was told that the proper inspector was not in and that she should return on Wednesday. She came to the mission for advice, and I was elected to accompany her to the police station.

As we entered, Melinda was mistaken for Chinese and addressed in Cantonese. I explained that she did not speak Cantonese, as the person at the desk shouted down the hallway, "*Banmui* has come." A woman inspector told us to sit down. She explained that she had advised the employer to drop the charges because there was no evidence, only one person's word against another. She said that Melinda was free to go and could collect her bail money. But if Mrs. Woo made new charges, she warned, Melinda would be arrested again. I asked why she would be arrested again since it had been over two weeks since she had left her employer's house. The inspector shrugged and said that this employer was not a pleasant person. I asked whether evidence was not required to make an arrest. She nodded but did not amend her warning.

TERMINATION BY THE WORKER

The domestic worker has the right to terminate the contract without notice or payment in lieu of notice under the following conditions: if she reasonably fears physical danger by violence or disease such as was not contemplated by her contract of employment expressly or by necessary implication; if she is subjected to ill-treatment by the employer; on any other ground on which she would be entitled to terminate the contract without notice at common law. Again, the onus of proof is on her. The worker must prove that she is ill-treated or subject to danger. If the domestic worker cannot satisfactorily prove that she has reason to terminate the contract without notice, then the employer is entitled to a month's wages in lieu of notice from the worker.

Of the domestic workers at the mission over an eighteen-month period, 293 new clients (14 percent) complained of "maltreatment" including "finger wagging," rude gestures, shouting, scolding, teasing, verbal threats and abuse, withholding mail, and throwing away the domestic worker's clothing or other personal property (MFMW 1993a, b). As one worker explained, Filipinos consider a finger pointed at them or shaken in their faces extremely offensive, insulting, and patronizing. The most common names shouted at them, "dog" and "monkey," are highly offensive and bear the same derogatory and racist connotations to Filipinos as they do to Chinese. These forms of maltreatment alone, however, are not considered sufficient to justify a change of employers.

During the same eighteen-month period, 24 domestic workers (1 percent) complained of occupational hazards, 62 (3 percent) of sickness-related problems, 40 (2 percent) of sexual harassment, 33 (1.5 percent) of rape, and 162 (8 percent) of various forms of physical abuse (MFMW 1993a, b). The domestic worker who came to the mission with burn marks on her face and her upper arm explained that she had called the police, as required, in order to press charges of physical abuse. But when the officers arrived at the flat, the employer had told them in Cantonese that the worker had intentionally burned herself.

Margie described the physical abuse and maltreatment that she endured before she terminated her contract. Like 123 (6 percent) of the other new clients at the mission between January 1992 and June 1993, Margie had her documents confiscated by her employer, including her passport, Hong Kong identification card, and birth certificate, in an attempt to prevent her from leaving (MFMW 1993a, b). One day in August, Ms. Lu became incensed because Margie had put her own clothes in the washing machine. Ms. Lu threw Margie's clothes in the garbage then hit her on the head with her fist many times. In September, Ms. Lu's son hurt himself playing outside. Although Margie informed her at once, Ms. Lu "got very angry and hit me again thrice on the head. Since then every time she is angry with me she hits me." Ms. Lu began to intercept Margie's mail. Once, after being beaten, Margie cried that she wanted to leave and go back to the Philippines. Ms. Lu threatened her and persuaded her to finish the year in order to give her time to find a replacement. She forced Margie to sign two blank sheets of paper. The problems continued. In December, Ms. Lu's two children were fighting.

> The eldest child . . . was hitting her brother on the head with a stick. The boy was crying and he [clung] . . . to me. I lifted him up so the stick won't reach him. I tried stopping [her] but she won't stop. . . . [She] phoned her mother and told her . . . I hurt her. Later that afternoon, Ms. Lu arrived and started hitting me all over my body. With a slipper on her hand she hit me on my face thrice. Then she ordered me to kneel down and ask for apology and made me promise not to do it again. She even cursed my family saying that if I do it again, my four children will die. She also threatened me that if anything happens to her children, she will look for my family and will use all the ways and means to kill the rest of them. Ms. Lu made me sign a letter that I hurt [her daughter]. Afraid that she would beat me up if I refused, I signed. I then thought of leaving but Ms. Lu asked for a month's salary in lieu of notice, but since I do not have any money then, I stayed.

Eventually Margie went to the police and was brought to the hospital. The police officer who spoke to her at the hospital said that she could press charges only if she had a witness. "I was so confused at that time that my only concern is to go back home. The police closed the case."

In a famous case, a forty-seven-year-old Filipina domestic worker, a widow and mother of five children, charged her employer—a celebrated racehorse trainer, millionaire, member of the district board, and vice-chairperson of the rural committee—with five counts of indecent assault. The first time she was sexually assaulted, Anastacia had threatened to go to the police, and her employer, Chan, stopped. When she was attacked again two weeks later, she had gone to the Philippine Consulate, where staff assured her that they would contact her employer, and she had returned home feeling safer. At the trial, the consulate declared diplomatic immunity and did not testify. Anastacia's employer had attacked her twice more in the next six months.

> Fearing she would go mad after the fourth assault, she had handed Chan her one month's notice of termination. There was no choice but to wait out the month, she said, because immigration law was clear: a domestic worker abandoning her employer without a month's notice forfeited the last month's pay and, moreover, was compelled to pay the employer the equivalent of one month's salary. (Maglipon 1990:3)

Her employer refused to accept her resignation and gave his word that it would never happen again. After his fifth assault, Anastacia fled to the police with her soiled skirt and a soiled pair of her employer's pajamas, which served as the necessary physical evidence of the assault. The employer was found guilty of all five charges. The British magistrate pronounced his behavior "contemptuous of the woman's dignity." He told the man, "It gives you no credit that you subjected her to the ordeal of this trial" (Maglipon 1990:3). It would be difficult, however, to claim that the domestic worker "won" the case. When the millionaire's penalty was announced, the Filipino community was shocked. He was ordered to pay US$643 for each of the five counts. As Jo-ann Maglipon explains,

> Following Hong Kong's legal system, the criminal suit remained the attorney-general's fight in the name of the crown. Chan's fine in effect covered court expenses. Anastacia played the part of prosecution witness. Her own civil suit against him for damages and back wages was a separate fight. In this arena Chan got back [at her]. He took all of three months before offering to settle amicably with US$8,997. Then actually getting the money was another matter. Up to the time Anastacia left for Manila in August this year [1990], she had collected only US$3,213. . . . But finally she had to give up. The case had dragged out a whole one year and eight months. . . . In that entire stretch of time, she had survived solely on the kindness of friends. Back home, two of her children had to stop schooling. . . . By August, she was home. She had been away 11 years. (Maglipon 1990:4)

THE NEW CONDITIONS OF STAY

As of 2007, the "New Conditions of Stay" have been in effect for two decades. They were first introduced in April 1987 with the stated intent of protecting employers from domestic workers who "job-hop" and "moonlight." Not passed through the legislative process, the New Conditions of Stay, more commonly called the "two-week rule," are merely a policy "decided by the Governor in Council and applied by the Immigration Department," but the policy is followed by the Labour and Immigration Departments as though it were law (Boase 1991:85). Many critics have observed that the New Conditions of Stay severely penalize migrant domestic workers, restrict their ability to resist abuse, and serve as a key policy in denying them "right of abode" in Hong Kong (see AMC 1991:72–74; Boase 1989, 1991:85–94; Constable 1993:1–6; MFMW 1993c:4, 1991:25–27; Petersen and Lee 2006; United Nations Economic and Social Council 2003; Wee and Sim 2005:189–191). The main points are as follows:

> (a) Once a contract has been terminated, the foreign domestic helper must either leave within two [2] weeks or before the date of expiration of her visa

if it falls shorter than two weeks; (b) No change of employment will normally be allowed during the period of contract (two years); (c) Those who break their contracts will not be allowed to submit a new and valid contract before they leave Hong Kong; and (d) Any foreign domestic helper who breaches a condition of stay (for example working for employers not mentioned in the contract) will be returned to her country of origin and will not be allowed to take up employment again in Hong Kong. (MFMW 1991:25–26)

There are some official exceptions to these conditions. The Immigration Department can give special consideration to domestic workers who can provide evidence that their contracts were terminated because the employer was transferred to another country, died, had financial difficulties that led to his or her incapacity to pay the wage stated in the contract, or maltreated or physically or sexually assaulted the worker (MFMW 1991:26). Again, however, the burden of providing evidence of those conditions is on the worker. If an employer refuses to provide the domestic worker with documentation of such conditions, then the exception will not be granted.

PROBLEMS WITH THE TWO-WEEK RULE

The two-week rule, which requires workers to return home within two weeks of the termination of their contracts, was supposedly created to prevent domestic workers from "job hopping" (*Asiaweek* 1987:72). The government, however, has never produced figures to demonstrate the effectiveness of the rule in preventing job hopping. The vast majority of contracts that are terminated before expiration are terminated by the employer, not by the domestic worker. The rule does deter some domestic workers from leaving their employers, but in so doing, it has created severe human rights abuses.

One problem with the rule is that there is no provision to guarantee that the employer supplies the worker with return airfare, remaining wages, or other monetary claims within the two-week period. An even more serious problem is that the two-week rule encourages workers to endure poor working conditions, physical and emotional abuse, maltreatment, and illegal work. Many will not report complaints to the Labour or Immigration Departments for fear that they will be forced to return home. Returning home is especially problematic for those whose family members depend on their wages or who have not yet repaid the costs of their migration (Constable 1993:1; AMC 1991:72). Moreover, reporting abuses can plunge workers into an ordeal of conciliation meetings, Labour Tribunals, and possibly also the District Court in order to enforce tribunal awards. As my examples illustrate, this process can drag out for a year or more, and during that time the worker is not permitted to work. Government figures suggest, moreover, that an unforeseen result of the two-week rule may also be an increase in the number of foreign domestic workers who overstay their visas and become illegal workers (Wee and Sim 2005:190–91). Facing the prospect of returning home in debt, some workers prefer the risk of becoming illegal migrants.

Another problem with the two-week rule is that it places restrictions on a domestic worker that are not placed on the employer (or on other local workers). While awaiting a hearing, for example, a domestic worker is not permitted to work and is thus often completely dependent on the aid of charities. An employer's main source of income is not interrupted, nor is the employer legally denied the right to work to continue to support his or her dependents. The employer is not repeatedly required to pay fees to renew a visa in order to exercise his or her right to a fair hearing. The duration of the domestic worker's visa extension is decided "at the discretion" of the Immigration Department. Some domestic workers have, in the end, paid more to the Immigration Department to renew their visas while awaiting their hearings than the amount of wages or airfare they were trying to collect. Anastacia paid over HK$1,000 in visa extensions, and while the extensions were in effect, she, like others on a visitor's visa, was not allowed to work (Boase 1991:85–86).

Although a domestic worker is not allowed to process a new employment contract, nothing prevents the employer from hiring a new worker. Some employers begin the three- or four-month process of hiring a new worker before terminating the contract of the old one. One worker who came to the mission was grossly underpaid and was terminated by her employer without notice and without pay or airfare back to the Philippines. On her way down the stairs of her employer's flat, she encountered another Filipina who introduced herself as the new domestic worker.

A further problem is that "exceptions" to the two-week rule are made on a case-by-case basis. In 1993 the Immigration Department claimed to be very lenient in the implementation of the rule and to have granted many exceptions. By the summer of 1994, fewer exceptions were being granted. No matter how many times the rule is waived or how lenient its implementation, it remains arbitrary and capricious. As long as such a rule exists, a worker cannot be assured that her plea will be granted and that her employment in Hong Kong is secure. At any time she can be shipped home. Without the two-week rule or an equivalent policy, many domestic workers who experience abuse would simply leave the employer and change to a better one. With the two-week rule, it becomes impossible for her to do so.

JOB HOPPING

Employers, especially those with small children, want domestic workers who are reliable. Members of the employers' association claim that domestic workers should be prevented from changing jobs because of the money and time employers invest in them. As Betty Yung, chairperson of the association explained, it is extremely inconvenient for employers when a domestic worker leaves.[13] The previous situation, she said, "was not fair" to employers. "They had to wait at least three or four months for maids. Then, most helpers don't know how to cook our food, know our habits. Employers have to teach [domestic workers] how to work. After the trouble of bringing them in and teaching them, they say they have to go." Yung does not believe that the two-week rule creates problems for domestic workers. "If maids don't like their employers, they can quit and go home. After they have gone home, they can reapply to work in Hong Kong. We welcome them" (*Asiaweek* 1987:72).

Unlike local workers, foreign contract workers are constrained in their ability to change employers. No other workers in Hong Kong are prevented from "job hopping," or changing jobs if they find an employer who is willing to require fewer hours of work or to give them better pay, better accommodation, or better working conditions. In fact, one could argue that job hopping has been fundamental in promoting better working conditions and in fueling Hong Kong's economic growth. Domestic workers are obliged by the two-week rule to put the interests of their employers before their own. They cannot say to their employers, "If you can't match Ms. Wang's offer of higher pay or a full twenty-four-hour rest day, I'm leaving in a month." Nor can a woman who works sixteen hours a day simply change to a job in which she would work for only eight or ten.

WORKERS' RIGHTS AND DOCILE MIGRANTS

The United Kingdom is a signatory to most of the International Labor Organization conventions, and colonial Hong Kong was in theory also a

---

13. Employers also say that the minimum wage should not be raised at all because raising it provides incentives for domestic workers who signed at lower rates to change employers.

subscriber. Many of the basic rules and policies regarding migrant workers in Hong Kong were originally based on International Labor conventions that were explicitly designed to protect the rights of migrant workers. As Boase maintains, however, Hong Kong has "invert[ed] those principles so that instead of disciplining the employer and providing protection for the overseas worker, they are now being used to discipline the worker and to provide protection for the employer" (1991:86).

Before closing this chapter, it is important to stress that the abuses experienced by foreign domestic workers are similar to those visited on the muijai of old. Muijai worked long hours, were unpaid or underpaid, and suffered verbal and physical abuse of all sorts (Jaschok 1988:102–3). Despite the legislation that was designed to protect them, few muijai ever complained to the police or other authorities about their conditions. Maria Jaschok speculates that this reticence was due in part to the extreme distrust and "fear of authority" of the Chinese. As one Chinese informant told her, "even today (1978) Chinese do not go to police. They treat you like dirt." Jaschok observes that, "even if people were only witnesses, they feared that in the time-honoured tradition of Chinese criminal law procedures, they might end up as the accused. How much more so, I was told, did this apply to young girls" (1988:108).

Despite such similarities, the situation of foreign domestic workers is not the same as that of muijai. In Hong Kong of the 1990s and early 2000s, similar abuses often take on racist or ethnic overtones. Moreover, many such abuses were not considered legally or morally wrong in the past. Such treatment was considered the prerogative of the master or mistress inasmuch as the muijai was their "property." The situation today is not qualitatively different; the difference is one of degree. Unlike muijai, most foreign domestic workers do not believe that they are inferior to their employers, that they deserve maltreatment, or that their only recourse with regard to work-related problems is to run away. Today foreign domestic workers are taught that they have "rights" and that there are "modern" laws and policies that are designed to protect them. The majority of employers also share this view, even though, as we have seen, the current laws and policies often make little difference in terms of the sorts of abuse domestic workers face. What such continuities illustrate is not that nothing has changed, but that despite certain changes, similar abuses and forms of discipline persist.

The examples in this chapter suggest that laws and policies can be meaningless apart from the ways in which they are interpreted, applied, and carried out. The spirit of the International Labor conventions is very different from both the spirit and the letter of the law as it is practiced in Hong Kong. The ways that rules and policies are enforced and interpreted reflect deeply ingrained cultural biases that favor the rights of the employer ("master") over those of the worker ("servant"). The New Conditions of Stay and other policies contribute to the vulnerability of foreign domestic workers and place them at a serious disadvantage relative to local workers, local employers, and even "skilled" foreign professionals. Nonetheless, it is important to keep in mind that Hong Kong is still considered one of the best and most desirable destinations in Asia for foreign domestic workers. As the following chapter illustrates, domestic workers resist oppression in a wide variety of ways.

7 | RESISTANCE AND PROTEST

"Once upon a time," Sherry Ortner writes, "resistance was a relatively unambiguous category, half of the seemingly simple binary, domination versus resistance. Domination was a relatively fixed and institutionalized form of power, resistance was essentially organized opposition to power institutionalized in this way" (1995:174). Michel Foucault "drew attention to less institutionalized, more pervasive and more everyday forms of power," and James Scott "drew attention to less organized, more pervasive, and more everyday forms of resistance" (175). Ortner criticizes many studies of resistance for their "ethnographic refusal"—that is, for "thinning" culture, sanitizing local politics, and "dissolving" subjects by neglecting the wider ethnographic context in which resistance occurs. This chapter describes both organized and subtler everyday forms of resistance expressed by foreign domestic workers. I hope to convey a "thicker" sense of the ethnographic context in which resistance may or may not occur and a sense of the choices, constraints, and ambivalence experienced by domestic workers.

EXPERIENCE AND AWARENESS

In the late 1970s, after high school, Elsa and Belle got jobs in factories to help support their family. Belle sewed bras for Topform's manufacturing plant in Manila, where, despite the strong antilabor sentiments of the

Marcos period, she became a union leader, organizing protests against the triple shifts, lack of ventilation, and absence of safety standards in the factory. Elsa worked at Carter's Semiconductor, an electronics factory, where she was quickly promoted to "optical inspector." Although sympathetic toward union views, she was not willing to sacrifice the wages she contributed to her family's income. As a "manager," earning slightly more than other workers, she was reluctant to express her prolabor sentiments. In 1979 Elsa left Manila to work with her cousin Gina in Hong Kong.

Elsa and Gina's employer allowed them to divide the work as they wished. Gina did marketing and cooking, and Elsa took care of the children. They divided up the housecleaning by floors, and took turns washing the three family cars each week. Despite Gina's company and the comfortable "servant's room" that they shared in the palatial mansion, Elsa found her first six months in Hong Kong difficult. She was homesick and had difficulty adjusting to the food, the language, and the heavy demands of employers. As she explained,

> It was a difficult time. The work was new to me, and there was also a communication problem because my female employer could not speak English well, and I could not speak Chinese. Their pronunciation is not like ours; [theirs is] British and Chinese mixed together, and so you really cannot understand if you are not smart or brave enough to say, "Pardon? I cannot understand you." And by the time you ask her again, she is really irritated. She is *really* irritated! So I tried my best to try to cope up and to learn to communicate with her.

When Gina returned to the Philippines, Elsa's employers wanted her to do both jobs.

> That started the agony because I cannot cook, and they are fond of having mahjong parties. [They had them] three times a week: Friday, Saturday, and Sunday. They wouldn't allow me to take my Sundays off [only Thursdays]. The only consolation was that every time they had a very big party they would give me a tip of HK$200! . . . Normally I worked until 10 P.M., but during parties and three times a week with mahjong, I always went to sleep at 2:00 in the morning. And then I still had to get up at 6:00 sharp.

Although her employer was at times moody and critical, Elsa often found her kind and generous. If "Sir" (the husband) was away, "Ma'am" would invite her to eat with her and the children at home or at a restaurant. She also gave Elsa gifts of makeup (which Elsa did not wear) and jewelry (a gold necklace, pearl earrings, and a necklace of semiprecious stones). Elsa was patient about her employer's bad moods. "According to her I'm a very good domestic helper because I didn't mind every time she'd have a tantrum. In fact, I would always knock on her door, and take tea to her, even if she had shouted at me. That's when she began to recognize my strength and my patience." Elsa also took the initiative to learn to cook. "I decided to study cooking. I knew it would be a big benefit because I could demand any employer—any, any employer who wants to hire me! 'Cooking is a must.' That's what I said to myself. So I took the cooking class on my day off, and I'm the one who paid for it."

By the end of her contract, Elsa decided she wanted to work for a "simple family." Her first employer was very upset and asked her to name her price, but Elsa chose a new employer. Her second employer was not as wealthy as the first. The family included a couple with one child; the man was a manager for an international airline, and the woman worked at a bank. Elsa had her own room and found her employers caring and considerate. "In wintertime they would go to my room and bring along winter things—thick blankets and clothes. And if they wanted to go out for anniversaries, birthdays and things, they would always ask me to come. [Even during] my holiday and they would bring me to celebrate with them." Elsa was fond of the family, especially the child. "When I first came, she was very naughty, but she changed when I took care of her. [At first] she wouldn't greet anyone. But after six months she became very friendly with some of the Filipinas, and would say, 'Hello, aunty.'" The child's parents were especially pleased when Elsa potty trained their daughter and taught her English.

> When I first came to their place, the girl—she's already two and a half years old—was always urinating in the house so the floor is quite white. And you know, it stinks. So I trained her to ask me if she wants to urinate. . . . I wouldn't let her wear diapers. . . . I said, "If you really want to make wee wee then you have to tell aunty, and then I will give you something! You have to tell me." And I told the employer to buy her a little potty. If she tries . . . she knows she will have a gift from me. After my holiday, I gave her things—toys that she likes, a small doll, like that. I bought some books to divert her attention. I taught her English. So after one year she is really very fluent.

After eighteen months, Elsa's employers decided to emigrate to the United States. But before they left, they took Elsa and Belle on holiday with them in China. "My male employer said, 'Elsa, . . . we would like to treat you—because we like your service and the way you take good care of our daughter—so we will take you with us on our vacation in China. And don't worry about the child: *I* am the one who is responsible for her!'"

Toward the end of her second job, Elsa became more involved in community and political activities.

> Before that I was only active in the religious organizations at Saint Joseph's, but I saw that even in religious organizations there is a lot of intrigue and gossip. I don't like that, so I found another organization, where—of course intrigue and gossip you cannot avoid that—but where there is some direct service for your co-migrant workers. . . . Saint John's fellowship was forming a group; so I joined them and that is the birth of the ACFIL association [Association of Concerned Filipinas]. So I became very active there, and I could see that the work at the mission [MFMW] was good, so I told my sister that I would like to be a counselor.

Elsa's growing insight into the problems faced by domestic workers was reflected in her negotiations with her third employer. At that time the two-week rule was not in effect. So Elsa decided to stay in Hong Kong and work for a new employer on a "trial basis." She was cautious about signing the contract because the household included an old Chinese amah and a pohpoh (the mother of her male employer). Elsa explained to her woman employer, "I will work with you, but I will not sign any contract first, because I have told Sir that I have to see if I can get along with the amah and with your mother-in-law." They said, "OK, we'll try it."

The Chinese amah, who was in her early seventies and wore the traditional black pants and white blouse, did the cooking and ironing, and Elsa did the childcare and the rest of the housework. Elsa got along well with the amah. When she and the amah returned from their day off, they sometimes exchanged small gifts. As Elsa explained, the amah liked her better than previous Filipina workers because Elsa helped her when she finished her work.

Elsa expressed growing class consciousness and sympathy for the Chinese amah's work conditions. The amah

> was always complaining about our employer—about her salary, especially. . . . She had a feeling that she was being cheated. She was always checking her bank account, and it looked like there was never all that they should have been paying her. . . . Maybe they were paying her less than they were paying me. . . . She was always telling me, "You are lucky you have a contract; you have more benefits. . . ." That's why I think that most of the amahs here don't have the benefits that the Filipinas are taking. Because the employer can terminate you right away. Or maybe because they are living in Hong Kong they don't have some of the benefits that the Filipinas are getting.

Elsa described her third employer as an "educated lady" who never shouted. Yet she found her way of dealing with conflicts strange and amusing. "If she's annoyed or she wants to say something, even if she's annoyed or angry with me, she would write it in a letter! And then we would be writing letters to each other! She will write a letter . . . and put it in my room. And then I will return her letter and I have to explain my side, and I have to place it on her bathroom mirror." Their differences were usually "over petty things." The most serious disagreements involved Elsa coming home late on her rest day. But Elsa affirmed her rights:

> I hated that! She always asked me to come back early, and I always told her, "I have a twenty-four-hour holiday!" If I came back at ten, she would say, "It's quite late!" Then the next week I would get back at eleven! So whenever she said anything, I'd come back even later the next time! So one time my male employer told me, "Elsa, you have to get back early because we are worried about you. We are concerned about your safety." "No," I told him. "No! Because I have a twenty-four-hour holiday, and you must abide by it! If you are not following the contract, I am. I have been many years here in Hong Kong and I know how to take care of myself." So I always took my day off from eight [in the morning] until ten or eleven [at night]!

Elsa also successfully resolved a problem involving extradomestic work. Her employer's home, a fancy house in the Shouson Hills, had a big garden. Elsa had to mow the lawn and do the gardening. Although she disliked it, at first she did the work without complaining.

> I told myself that I have to do the gardening because I am their maid and I shouldn't complain. But one time, when I felt that the lawn mower was too heavy, I complained. I said, "I don't like to lawn-mow because it is not my job, and my skin is deteriorating because of the insect bites. And I don't like it any more." That's what I told her. "Okay, okay. We will find somebody else to do that," said the lady. They also had a fishpond out there [to clean]. And the father of my employer came to live there with his two wives, and I had to clean their rooms too! I had too much work!

After a year and a half, the Chinese amah retired and Elsa's employers expected her to take on the amah's duties in addition to her own.

> When they saw that I could tackle all the work, they thought they could save money. But I told them that it's too heavy [a workload] for me. I have to take care of the children, I have to do the cooking, the ironing, and I have to help them with their studies. . . . It was very heavy for me. So [I said], "I will give you three months to find a replacement for that amah. I don't care who you

hire as long as I have a companion." Because I can deal with anybody, especially my coworkers.

But they did not hire a replacement; so Elsa found a new employer. This job lasted only a few weeks, however, because "the American husband wanted his Chinese wife to do the housework."

Elsa worked for her fifth employer for four years, until the children got older, and her help was no longer needed. That employer allowed Elsa to volunteer at the mission as long as she finished her work first. Elsa described the employer as "very lenient for a Chinese." "She was always telling her daughters, 'you have to help your *ate* [sister] Elsa, you have to help her.' And if I was ironing the clothes, the eldest daughter would say 'Ate Elsa, you don't need to wash the dishes because you ironed the clothes. I will wash the dishes.' And she knew how to cook, too." Next Elsa worked for a Filipino couple with one daughter for two years. When I met her in 1993, she was working for a single Chinese woman from her church. As Elsa explained, "I approached *her* and said, 'I heard that you need someone to be your helper. I can help you.' And then she said, 'Yes, yes, yes!'" Elsa did not live with her employer, but shared a flat with Belle and several other Filipinas. Elsa's employer paid her share of the rent, in addition to what Elsa considered a "very handsome salary." Her employer was supportive of Elsa's volunteer work, and Elsa enjoyed helping her with her research. In exchange, her employer was teaching Elsa journalism. Belle's employer at the time was also single, and the two women shared some mutual friends from church, socialized together every so often, and considered each other friends. Her employer also allowed her to budget her own time so she could participate in outside activities. By 1995, however, they had had a falling out, and Belle was looking around for a new and very flexible employer.

Elsa and Belle have never been ashamed of their work. Even with her first job as "helper" in the Philippines, Elsa rejected the idea that she was doing shameful work. Her employers were very good to her and allowed her to attend school in the evenings. But her relatives who lived in the same compound refused to greet her. "They felt ashamed that their relative was a DH. But I didn't mind. In my mind I would say to them, 'we are not borrowing money from you! I am not a prostitute! I am not a thief! And I am earning my money in a nice way, in a nice honest way. So I don't mind if you don't greet me. As long as I am getting food in my stomach.'"

Elsa enjoys her work. "I think being a DH is quite challenging for me because I have to deal with different lands of people, and with how to get along with them. I think it's a very challenging experience. I have learned a lot." Asked how long she would continue to work in Hong Kong, she answered, "I'll keep doing it as long as I'm allowed to, for financial reasons. I told myself that if I have the opportunity to work in Hong Kong to earn [money], then I have to do it. I'm still saving money for my future because I don't know if I'll get married or remain single. But I have to be prepared financially."

EXCEPTIONS TO THE RULE

Elsa, Belle, and others have been successful in negotiating the negative features of their work and redefining their work in positive terms. They manage to arrange their time so as to pursue other interests and participate in the wider Filipino community; they gain satisfaction from the changes they have brought about in their family's standard of living and from their work at the mission, at United Filipinos in Hong Kong (UNIFIL), and with other migrant worker organizations. Their situation, however, is far from typical. Like Acosta, they had far more independence than most domestic workers I knew in the 1990s. They lived in their own apartment, where the rent was low because the building was old and there is no lift (something that would be harder to do a decade later). Both had worked for single people whom they considered friends as well as employers. They worked extremely hard, but their work was light compared to that of many women who worked for larger households. Their employers also supported and respected their social and political activities.

Both Elsa and Belle had had their share of minor problems in Hong Kong, but neither had personally experienced the "serious" problems of some of the women they counseled at the mission. Because the two-week rule did not exist during their earlier time in Hong Kong, they rarely felt "locked in" with employers they did not like. Since the introduction of the two-week rule they were fortunate, but their contacts and experience also paid off. Like Acosta, Elsa and Belle took advantage of certain illegalities. They lived outside of their employers' homes, and they worked part-time to earn extra money. Belle's last employer, like Acosta's, did not pay her a full-time salary or expect her to work full-time. Belle was satisfied with that arrangement because she could devote more time to domestic worker organizations. Acosta was satisfied with the setup because part-time work can be more lucrative. In addition to luck and good fortune, Elsa, Belle, and Acosta attributed their "success" to their assertiveness and ability to communicate with employers. Belle stressed that "one of the keys to surviving work in Hong Kong is communication. If you can communicate honestly with your employer it is much better. I haven't experienced the problems that some of the Filipinas are encountering here because, I think, I can express myself." From the start, she said to her employer, "If you have any problem with me, you tell me. I don't want you getting angry or having a long face behind my back. Even if it will hurt me, please tell me, ma'am, if you want me to do something differently. And I will tell you as well." Similarly, once her employers know that she is hardworking and responsible, Elsa felt free to negotiate with them on specific working conditions. Unlike Acosta, who had "no use for such things," Belle and Elsa were involved in worker organizations. Belle was a well-known spokesperson and advocate for foreign domestic workers' rights and actively campaigned against the two-week rule.

CATHY

Cathy (discussed in Chapter 5) is more typical of domestic workers who gradually become more assertive and politically involved as a result of their work difficulties. As she explained, despite her rigid work schedule and the strict discipline she experienced in Ms. Leung's house, she did not dare complain for several months. Ms. Leung "shouted all the time," and Cathy was scared "because I have never experienced shouting, shouting, shouting all the time before." Cathy kept reminding herself of her future plans and telling herself that if she worked harder, her situation would improve and her employer would change. She tried to work harder, to be more cheerful, and to ignore her employer's criticism. But over the next several months Ms. Leung, pressured by her own personal and financial difficulties, became increasingly antagonistic. She complained about Cathy's showers, her frequent hair washing, and her use of the phone. Finally, in March a friend referred Cathy to the mission for advice. She talked to a volunteer and began to think about her rights and her options.

One Sunday in June Cathy missed her nine o'clock curfew. Ms. Leung shouted at her and later forbade Cathy to use the washing machine or hand wash her clothes in the flat. For the first time, Cathy spoke back. Shocked, her employer slapped her and shouted angrily that her attitude had changed and that it was very bad. "Yes!" Cathy replied, "I'm changing my attitude! I'm arguing with you!" Ms. Leung then ordered her to stop washing her clothes and threw a bucket of cold water in her face. On her next day off

Cathy went to her sister's employer's house to wash her clothes. Because it took so long to wash and dry her clothes and travel back and forth, she was late again.

> When I got back home she said, "Why have you come home so late?" "Oh, I'm very sorry," I said, "because I [had to] wash my clothes at my sister's house and then I came straight here. That was in Tuen Mun." Well, she wouldn't accept my explanation. All of my explanations made her angry. [So she took] all my clean clothes and she put them on the floor, and she stepped on them. Then she splashed water in my face, and then she forced me to sleep in the living room. So I said, "I don't like [to sleep there]. I have my own room. So why can't I sleep there?" She said, "You sleep in the living room!" And I said, "I have my own room, so why should I sleep in the living room?"

The argument continued. Ms. Leung said she was sick of Cathy. Cathy responded, "I back out! I break my contract with you." Ms. Leung answered, "Before you go out you pay me 3–2!" "'How come I pay you 3–2 and you only pay me a salary of 2–3? Okay. Let's meet in immigration!' I say to her. So I go off. But she didn't give me all my things. All my dresses, shoes, all my things I didn't get."

In June Cathy filed her case against Ms. Leung; a November date five months later was set for the hearing. Cathy's grievances included underpayment, maltreatment, overwork, and illegal work. After the termination of her contract she began to volunteer at the mission, became active in UNIFIL, and supported union activities. She participated in the domestic worker demonstration that I observed in Chater Garden in August 1993.

DEMONSTRATIONS

During the British colonial period, Hong Kong locals were described as politically apathetic and they very rarely participated in political protests. Much to the disapproval of many employers, Filipina domestic workers and their protests became increasingly "high profile" beginning in the mid-1980s. According to one observer, "The Filipino maids are slowly changing their stance and tune. The Raj image of totally submissive and dutiful servants is a thing of the past. The once willing 'yes' has been replaced by a bargaining 'if'" (Flage 1987). Another observer noted, "Ten years ago, the Filipinos would have just been grateful for a job. Now they're crying 'injustice', 'give us freedom', 'give us rights'. You know how the old proverb goes, 'familiarity breeds contempt.' . . . So, let's just leave it as it has been for the last decade or so. Why stir up another hornets' nest?" (Grange 1992).

Some Sundays in the 1990s there were protests, marches, rallies, or educational drives in Central District, often sponsored and organized by the more politically active groups such as UNIFIL or the Asian Domestic Workers Union (ADWU). Rallies were organized in support of wage increases or in opposition to increased administrative fees or taxes imposed by the Philippine government, for example. Petitions are passed around demanding stricter policies against corrupt employment agencies or money-lenders or criticizing Hong Kong or Philippine government policies that are detrimental to migrant workers. Since 1987, there have been many campaigns to abolish the two-week rule.

Elsa and Belle spoke enthusiastically of one of the greatest early victories claimed by Filipino migrant organizations in Hong Kong. In 1982 the Philippine government introduced a strict policy of forced remittance known as "Executive Order 857." The law made it mandatory for Filipino domestic workers to remit 50 percent of their earnings and for other Filipino migrant workers to remit up to 70 percent of their earnings through Philippine banks (CIIR 1987:8; UNIFIL 1991). Workers who did not comply with the order would not have their passports renewed and would no longer be eligible to work overseas. In 1984 United Filipinos against Forced Remittance was formed as a loose alliance of ten domestic worker organizations in Hong Kong. In their statement to President Marcos they explained that they were opposed not to remittances but to force: "To force us to remit is a curtailment of our freedoms and an intrusion into our private affairs" (McLean 1984; CIIR 1987:8). Later that year the Philippine consul general in Hong Kong announced a 50 percent reduction of the amount, although the executive order had not been changed; and on 1 May 1985 the order was officially lifted. After denunciation of Executive Order 857 by Hong Kong organizations, similar pressure groups were formed among Filipinos in other parts of the world. Growing opposition to the Marcos government in the Philippines and criticism of the executive order by the International Labor Organization also influenced the change in policy.

After this first objective was met by the coalition of Hong Kong groups, United Filipinos against Forced Remittance was renamed United Filipinos in Hong Kong (UNIFIL), and it grew into an even larger "umbrella" organization promoting the rights of domestic workers. In 1987 UNIFIL and a number of other organizations successfully opposed a customs tax imposed by the Aquino government. In 1988 President Corazon Aquino introduced a general ban on approval of new contracts for overseas domestic workers in an attempt to "protect" them from abuse (Benitez 1988; Clad 1988; Power 1988).

The ban was then modified to apply only to domestic workers under the age of thirty-five. Domestic worker organizations in Hong Kong strongly opposed the moratorium. United Filipinos against the Ban was formed as an alliance of twenty-two domestic worker groups, which included about two-thirds of Hong Kong's domestic worker population (Fan 1988). The alliance organized letter-writing campaigns and threatened to picket Aquino's upcoming visit if the ban was not lifted. Two weeks later, the ban was lifted. A large rally was also held in 1993, when President Fidel Ramos was traveling to Beijing. Filipinos in Hong Kong urged him to address the issue of continuing to allow foreign domestic workers in Hong Kong after 1997.

The most prominent domestic worker issues during the summer of 1993 included a proposed HK$600 per month pay increase, as opposed to the HK$300 increase that the government proposed; an ongoing call to abolish the two-week rule; and an attempt to limit working hours. One Sunday in late August, as they had on many occasions over the past several years, roughly five hundred foreign domestic workers, including Cathy, Elsa, and Belle, met at Chater Garden next to Statue Square for a protest and march to Government House. Workers wore placards and waved banners announcing, "Abolish the Two-week Rule," "Solidarity Forever," "Black-list Abusive Employers," "$3,800 Now," "Enact Laws against Employers' Maid-Hopping." Leaders of the ADWU, the Hong Kong Confederation of Trade Unions (HKCTU), UNIFIL, MFMW, and other groups made speeches and led cheers and protest songs as they attempted to deliver a petition to Government House. The vast majority of the protesters were women who belonged to the ADWU or to UNIFIL; most were Filipinas, but Thais and South Asians also participated. Although the leaders were pleased with the turnout, they were disappointed with the results. The government refused to increase wages above HK$3,500 per month, the two-week rule remained in effect, and nothing was done about working hours. Moreover, as described in Chapter 8, relatively few domestic workers supported the protesters and their objectives, and even fewer supported the "strike action" the ADWU had proposed.

INDONESIAN DOMESTIC WORKER PROTESTS

In 2005 and 2006 I attended a variety of protests, rallies, and marches. The most noticeable changes from the early 1990s (aside from the fact that there were far more Hong Kong locals who staged protests around a variety of issues) were the large and visible numbers of domestic workers of many different nationalities (especially Indonesians and also some Thai) who participated in the protests and the broad spectrum of issues around which they rallied (Law 2002; Sim 2003). By the late 1990s some protests were spearheaded by organizations such as the Asian Migrant Coordinating Body (AMCB), the Coalition for Migrants Rights (CMR), and others that built on Filipino activist and NGO networks, but aimed to build coalitions of different nationalities of workers. Indonesian domestic workers joined these wider groups, but had also become highly active around their own issues as well.

In 2006 I was told by a member of ATKI (the Association of Indonesian Migrant Workers) about the first organized protest of Indonesian domestic workers that had taken place in 2001. About sixty Indonesian domestic workers had marched from Victoria Park to the Indonesian Consulate to protest the overcharging by recruitment agencies and underpayment by employers (*SCMP* 2001). So fearful were the protestors about the possible repercussions of this public action, specifically their own safety and that of their family members, that they all wore black facemasks. In 2006 they laughed about the masks. The 2001 protest was noteworthy. As Susan Blackburn writes in her historical study of Indonesian women and the state, "remarkably, some Indonesian maidservants in Hong Kong succeeded in organising themselves into an Association of Indonesian Migrant Workers, which in 2001 staged a protest rally against exploitation by employers, recruitment agencies and the Indonesian government—something which has never happened in Indonesia itself" (Blackburn 2004: 191; see also Pudjiastuti 2003; Sim 2003).[1] Today the numbers of Indonesian women who take part in such protests have grown and they show little fear of being recognized or identified. In fact, many are more than willing to pose for cameras waving banners and shouting protest slogans.

On Sunday, May 15, 2005, I attended one of two rallies held in front of the Indonesian Consulate to protest the lack of investigation into circumstances of the death of an Indonesian domestic worker. Fifty or more Indonesian domestic workers, many of them in headscarves and long gowns, waved banners and flags with the logo of the Indonesian Migrant Workers Union (IMWU) as they prayed, chanted, and delivered heartfelt speeches under the

1. Although Indonesian women's activist groups had protested in Indonesia in the 1990s against the maltreatment of Indonesian domestic workers in the Middle East (Robinson 2000), most called for a halt to such labor exportation because it was thought to diminish the status and dignity of Indonesian women (Blackburn 2004:189); at that time, few organizations called for more attention to migrant workers' rights.

scorching summer sun. Behind the barricades that had been set up by police, they displayed a "corpse" on a stretcher that was covered with an Indonesian cloth and strings of flowers. The corpse represented Suprihatin, a twenty-three-year-old Indonesian domestic worker who had recently died after falling from the nineteenth floor of the apartment building in which she worked. Protestors displayed photographs of Suprihatin, bruised and battered, as she lay in her hospital bed. Banners read "Please Help Suprihatin—Cooperate with the Police;" "Migrant Rights Are Human Rights" and "Indonesian Consulate Should Fulfill Its Responsibility as Protector of Indonesian Citizens."

The protest was primarily intended, protestors said, to exert pressure on the Indonesian government to ask the Hong Kong SAR government to reopen the police investigation. Listed on IMWU's public statement were also charges of negligence by the employment agency that Suprihatin had supposedly complained to about her employer's abuse and a call for employment agencies to take more responsibility as advocates for workers (IMWU 2005). The domestic workers explained that the circumstances of Suprihatin's death (and of a rash of similar "accidents" in Singapore) were highly suspicious. Although the media cited police and the employer who claimed it was suicide and that Suprihatin was depressed because of the tsunami in Aceh province, domestic workers who knew Suprihatin insisted that she was not depressed and that her family was not even from Aceh. Domestic workers claimed that she had complained to her friends and to staff at the employment agency about her employer and that in the hospital, shortly before she died, she indicated that it was not an accident.

As one Indonesian activist domestic worker explained in 2005, Indonesians have become emboldened in the more democratic post-Suharto period and they have become increasingly aware of workers rights, including the legality of labor organizing in Hong Kong. In large part, they credit Filipino activists for their political awakening and activism in Hong Kong (see also Piper 2005; Sim 2003). Indeed, Indonesian recruitment agency personnel are so concerned that Filipino activism and assertiveness might rub off on Indonesian workers that they warn Indonesian women in the agency run "training camps" to avoid Filipina domestic workers in Hong Kong because they are "dangerous" and "troublesome" and might cause them to lose their jobs.

GLOBAL ISSUES, LOCAL PROTESTS

In December 2005 Hong Kong was the setting for the Sixth Ministerial Conference of the World Trade Organization (WTO). Eight days of protests were held in opposition to the WTO and its role in promoting neoliberal globalization. The protests included several large colorful marches and rallies that included thousands of Filipinas, Indonesians, and other domestic workers, as well as farmers and fisherfolk from South Korea, Japan, and elsewhere who opposed the WTO-led globalization.

These protests were the culmination of over a year of planning in which domestic workers and migrant worker activists and NGO staff worked with the Hong Kong People's Alliance against the WTO (HKPA) to plan actions and educate Hong Kong locals and migrant workers about the role of the WTO in relation to globalization. As domestic workers explained, they joined the protest because they blamed the WTO and its U.S. and western European allies, as well as their own government leaders, for exacerbating the poverty and inequality in their homelands. They blamed their own governments for the commodification of migrant workers and for promoting them as a solution to local economic problems. The WTO—embodied in images of Uncle Sam—came to represent greater profits for the powerful, wealthy, and elite and greater suffering for the poor and underprivileged. The growing poverty and inequality in Indonesia, the Philippines, Thailand, India, and other parts of the "global south" meant that it had become impossible to make a living at home.[2] Small-scale farming and small businesses and industries were forced out of the market; thus many workers felt obliged to leave their families behind to earn a living. The protests articulated strong opposition to the U.S.–led war in Iraq, neocolonialism, the lack of social services in their homelands, environmental degradation caused by industrial development, and the privatization of large-scale production at the expense of small-scale farmers and producers.

On July 1, 2006, the anniversary of Hong Kong's transition from British colony to Special Administrative Region of China, despite the oppressive humidity and heat, Hong Kong people came out in force. In the morning, tens of thousands joined a parade in celebration of reunification, wearing red and waving Hong Kong and Chinese flags. In the afternoon, tens of thousands of self-ascribed prodemocracy demonstrators marched en masse. Although this protest was much smaller than the historic protest march of half a million Hong Kong people in 2003 that is credited with causing the

---

2. Domestic workers and other anti-WTO activists referred to the north-south political and economic divide (and shared interests) between the wealthy and more developed northern countries of the "global north" and poor and less developed former colonies the "global south." The division is not, strictly speaking, geographically based.

resignation of Hong Kong's chief executive, Tung Chee Hwa, the 2006 protest numbered close to forty thousand and included hundreds of Filipina, Indonesian, and Thai domestic workers who marched under the banner of the Asian Migrants Coordinating Body.[3]

Although some observers wondered why foreign workers would participate in what they viewed as a local event, those I spoke with enthusiastically supported the locals' call for universal suffrage and democratization and marched in part to express "solidarity" with local workers. Migrant workers also used the event to express their criticism of the Hong Kong government's recently increased visa fee and to demand an end to the two-week rule and to underpayment. They chanted and carried signs reading "Bring Back HK$3670" and "Abolish the Levy." They chanted enthusiastically alongside Chinese members of the HKCTU, calling for a minimum wage for all Hong Kong workers (at present foreign domestic workers are the only ones whose wage is governed by law).

Although Vivienne Wee and Amy Sim have suggested that the "fragile class solidarity" that had begun to develop between local and foreign domestic workers in the early 2000s was threatened by the imposition of the levy (2005:187), at least some local domestic workers have continued to express sympathy and solidarity rather than competition and resentment toward foreign domestic workers. In 2002 and several times since then, members of the Hong Kong Local Domestic Workers General Union (HKLDWGU) have joined foreign domestic workers in rallies and marches calling for an increase in the minimum allowable wage and opposing the previous wage cuts for foreign domestic workers. As a representative of the HKLDWGU explained to me in 2006, the Hong Kong economy has improved, and domestic workers wages should thus also be increased. When foreign domestic workers' wages are reduced, the hourly wages of local workers risk being reduced as well. If foreign workers earn more, local workers also stand to benefit.

3. An estimated 500,000 Hong Kong locals rallied in the 2003 protest opposing the proposed new PRC-backed antisedition security legislation (Article 23 of the Basic Law), and expressing their anger at Chief Executive Tung Chee Hwa's handling of the SARS crisis. The 2003 rally was credited with the defeat of Article 23 and the eventual resignation of Tung. The 2006 protest attendance was estimated at 58,000 by the organizers, at 28,000 by the Hong Kong police, and at 36,000 to 43,000 by a University of Hong Kong poll (*SCMP* July 2, 2006). Besides Filipina, Indonesian, and Thai domestic workers, South Asian migrant workers and members of the Far East Overseas Nepalese Association of Hong Kong (FEONA-HK) were also visible.

The protests described above are but a few of many that have taken place since the early 1990s. Migrant workers typically hold or participate in large rallies on the Sunday closest to International Migrants Day, International Women's Day, May Day (International Worker's Day), and many others. Cumulatively, these protests demonstrate the ever-broadening concerns of migrant workers since the early 1990s and the ever-widening coalitions of protestors. By 2006 their concerns still include issues that pertain narrowly to foreign domestic workers in Hong Kong such as calls for increasing wages, abolishing the two-week rule, opposing overcharging, underpayment, and the levy. They also include issues in their home countries, especially new legislation that has an impact on recruitment costs, remittances, and returnees. Increasingly, however, they also include wider local Hong Kong issues such as security legislation and workers' rights, and global and international issues pertaining to human rights, social welfare, and sustainable development.

The protestors themselves are far more diverse and unified than a decade earlier. Filipinos still organize to protest their own issues, such as the visit of President Gloria Macapagal-Arroyo in 2005 and the candlelight vigil against the political killings of journalists, priests, and activists in the Philippines in 2006, and Indonesians organize rallies to express their own specific criticisms of their government, such as its handling of the death of Suprihatin. But many diverse groups of foreign domestic workers (belonging to organizations that range from those based on native place ties, religious ties, sexual orientation, cultural interests, and so on), also join together in new domestic worker coalitions. These groups join in protests with local labor unions; with local domestic workers; with migrant worker unions, associations, and NGO-led groups; with local citizens, as well as with international protestors from other parts of the world (as in the anti-WTO protests).

SUBTLE FORMS OF RESISTANCE

Besides overt forms of political action such as the protests described above, there are also more subtle actions that might be interpreted as forms of resistance. As described in Chapter 1, many locals in the early to mid-1990s complained about domestic workers' use of Statue Square and other public spaces on Sundays. But despite such complaints and events that have been organized to lure them to other locations, domestic workers continue to gather in Central District by the thousands or tens of thousands (Boston 1993) and a decade later what once seemed like a controversial issue had by 2006 faded into the everyday. Even in the early 1990s, most domestic workers did not think of their presence in Central as an act of protest or resistance against their local Chinese critics. They viewed it simply as their right to be there. One domestic worker expressed the view of many when she wrote, in response to an editorial recommending that domestic workers take a ferry to Lantau on Sundays: "That [suggestion] is absurd. Central, as its name suggests, is the centre for all manner of activities. Is there a place on Lantau where we can attend a concert, watch a film, shop, have our hair done, or, most importantly, attend Mass?" (Palaghicon 1992).

Yet, in a Gandhian sense, we might identify the presence of these workers in the square in the face of 1990s opposition as a protest. After six days of obeying their employers, on the seventh day the workers please themselves. They refuse to move from their peaceful "sit-in." Despite the accusation that foreign workers "do private things in public places," they continue to do so, and they gain strength and solidarity from their communal activities. In slightly less conspicuous corners of Central women continue to apply makeup, give each other manicures, pedicures, permanents, or massages. Elly, a hairdresser back home, sets up shop on the steps of the same government building week after week. She charges HK$20 for a haircut, less than a quarter of the going rate at local salons. Her customers take a number and then sit and chat while waiting their turn. The monetary exchange is done very subtly. No Chinese, and only the rare westerner, will patronize Elly's "salon." Elderly Chinese stop and gawk at what they consider yet another low-class public display of private grooming. Elly and her entourage have had to develop a "thick skin." They are used to brushing off the condescending attitudes of passersby. In return they crack jokes and poke fun at the bald old Chinese man who stares and points disapprovingly. In a language he cannot understand, they say, "He only wishes he had hair to cut!" and more aggressively, "The only cut he will get is with a razor!" The Filipinas then all break into loud peals of laughter, and the Chinese onlookers turn away, mumbling and frowning to one another.

Down the hill in the square, although banks and post offices are closed, domestic workers do business. Especially common by 2005 is the sale of the ubiquitous international telephone calling cards. Women also buy (and sell) stamps, change money, and send remittances or gifts home. Packages are weighed on small scales that are circulated, and the cost of transport is quickly calculated by a formula that most have committed to memory. Then a friend, relative, or friend of a friend from a nearby town in the

Philippines, returning home on holiday, agrees to transport the package to the Philippines for the cost of excess baggage. Such efficient transactions are facilitated by common knowledge of which parts of the square are meeting places for people from particular regions of the Philippines.

Throughout the 1990s in the square, almost right under the eye of the Urban Services patrols, an assortment of illegal transactions took place.[4] Acosta's friend Saluda sold Filipino magazines; Julietta sold postage stamps, airmail envelopes, and aerograms; and Edna sold jewelry that she kept concealed in a large purse. Other women wandered around with large, lightweight "carry-on" bags. Inside what might easily be mistaken for an ordinary piece of luggage is a smorgasbord of Philippine food for sale. Other "caterers" set up shop alongside ice cream and soft drink stands. In the summer of 2004, however, a domestic worker was arrested for selling a box lunch in the square. Following this arrest, monetary transactions of various sorts were still going on in and around the square, but they became much more subtle than they had been a decade earlier.

Filipinos are not the only ones who hawk or conduct business. Indian men and Chinese of all ages subtly sell sheets, towels, toys, electronic gadgets, or socks and children's shoes. Some hawkers move rapidly about the area, concealed by the crowds that gather around them, constantly keeping an eye out for blue uniforms. Less cautious illegal hawkers casually set out mats or sheets and display their wares. If stopped by patrols for illegal hawking, domestic workers may claim they are just showing recent purchases to their friends, and the surrounding shoppers willingly go along with the charade. Caught selling food, as Carolyn French (1986a) notes, they will suddenly burst into a chorus of "Happy Birthday," instantly transforming the cluster of customers into one of many birthday parties that take place in the square.

Mobile photographers in the square—mainly Filipinos—charge nominal fees for "studio portraits" that play an important—if subtle—role in transforming the lackluster image of humble maids. Filipinas often appear in the square decked out in all their finery. They pose for portraits alone or with friends, townmates, or relatives on the bridge next to the fountain or in other scenic spots. Each photographer has his own base where, later in the day after the film is processed, customers go to look through photo albums to claim their purchases.

---

4. Until 1999, the Urban Services were responsible for controlling and registering hawkers (vendors). After 1999, the Urban Services Department was replaced by the Food and Environmental Hygiene Department.

These photographs, along with letters and audiotapes, make up an important part of the communication network with relatives back home. Photographs also help to create and perpetuate the image that life in Hong Kong is happy and glamorous. As a twenty-two-year-old domestic worker told me, when she was in the Philippines she and her friends saw photographs of their sisters and townmates posing in the square, against the backdrop of striking modern buildings, "looking very pale, beautiful, stylish, and very fat." She sighed as she explained that such images made them want to come to Hong Kong and experience its pleasures firsthand. Her own experience has been far from glamorous, but she has not told her family about her difficulties, and she continues to send them cheerful letters and photographs as "evidence" of her well-being.

Activities in the square stand in striking contrast to the rest of the week's activities. Photographs, letters, Philippine newspapers, romance novels, movie magazines, horoscopes, and comic books are borrowed and shared. Some women drink beer or sing and dance as young Filipinos and South Asian men linger about. Prayer sessions, preaching, evangelism, and the accompanying requests for cash donations known as "love money" are not uncommon. Some domestic workers spend the day playing cards, gambling, or window shopping in the fancy nearby shopping centers. In the early 1990s, workers who were not allowed to use their employers' telephones waited patiently in long lines at telephone booths in the square. A decade later the lines are much shorter. Although most Filipinas now have cell phones (which they can surreptitiously use to send text messages or make phone calls even while they work) some still prefer to use the phone booths and calling cards to call overseas.

Members of one of the hundreds of different Filipino associations (organized on the basis of native town or region, dialect, or other common interests) hold meetings or celebrations in corners of the square or Chater Garden. Most of these organizations are socially oriented, but others have explicitly political intentions. On special occasions they reserve one of the nearby local church halls for beauty contests, talent shows, elegant fashion shows, cultural performances, and other types of philanthropic fund-raising. They may collect money for social events (such as monthly birthday dinners), for a new schoolhouse or church for the community back home, or for aid to those left homeless by floods, typhoons, earthquakes, or catastrophes such as the Mount Pinatubo eruption. Such activities provide important occasions for women to dress up, enjoy themselves, show off artistic or musical talents, and become someone other than "Mrs. Liu's maid."

After working alone in the employer's home all week, on Sunday in Central foreign workers gain strength in numbers. They reestablish and express other facets of their identity, if only for a few hours. As they share news from home, they are no longer "DHs" but wives, mothers, aunts, sisters, townmates, and schoolmates. Their activities transform them into beauty contest winners, volleyball champions, and philanthropists. For a few hours once a week they are better able to ignore common insults, to stand their ground, or to respond in kind. On Sunday, unlike other days of the week, when a Chinese man on the tram gives a group of Filipinas a dirty look because they are laughing too loud or when an old woman recoils because a Filipina domestic worker's shoulder has rubbed against hers, the domestic worker may be the one to utter the common Cantonese insult *"chisin"* (crazy), which is often followed by peals of approving laughter from her companions.

On Sundays domestic workers are also consumers. Shops, street markets, and supermarkets in Central are packed with shoppers, as women buy the necessary toiletries, snacks for the day, and weekly food items. In the street markets, tucked away in Central's alleyways, hawkers who sell shoes, clothing, imitation designer handbags, watches, and toys at reasonable prices, are mobbed by domestic workers looking for necessities, bargains, and gifts for loved ones far away. Across the road from the street stalls is Worldwide Plaza, an arcade filled with shops—many of which employ Filipinas—selling food, music, movies, movie magazines, newspapers, and other products imported from the Philippines. Some Filipinas resent the attitudes they may encounter at shops and restaurants, and on Sundays they are more likely to defend themselves. Edwina recounted a time when she was buying apples at a supermarket. The clerk asked her how many apples she was buying and the price. Edwina told the clerk that it was *her* job. A Chinese man in line said, "You Filipina maids have no right to complain about anything in Hong Kong." Edwina asked to speak to the manager, who was sent for, and who apologized to her politely.

Some of the less expensive fast-food restaurants of Central District, such as McDonald's, Deli France, Oliver's Deli, Cafe de Coral, and also the Philippine favorite, Jollibee, do a roaring business from domestic workers who meet there on Sundays. For a change, Filipinas are the ones being served rather than serving. Rejecting the deference expected of "maids on their day off," some domestic workers assert their rights. If they think that scowling teenage clerks or waiters do not give them prompt and polite service, they may tell them off, remind them that they are paying customers, or ask to speak to the manager. Nora Dulatre wrote a letter to the *South China Morning Post* about the "rude behavior" she and other Filipinas received from staff at the McDonald's in Central (1992b). Perhaps in recognition of the business he stood to loose, the "Operations Manager" promptly responded with a letter to the paper assuring Ms. Dulatre that McDonald's is dedicated to delivering "fast, friendly service" and that the management team would be "actively addressing" her complaints (Tong 1992). Jaschok has noted that on Sundays, unlike other days of the week, napkins and condiments that are usually "self-serve" in fast food restaurants are strictly distributed to each customer individually. In protest, one Filipina with whom I ate at McDonald's, ignoring the scowl on the server's face, always made a point of requesting extra ketchup and napkins.[5]

Since the mid-1990s, Victoria Park, just a few kilometers away from Central in Causeway Bay, has become the main location where Indonesian domestic workers congregate in the thousands on their day off. The activities that go on there are similar to those in Statue Square, but the park is much bigger and surrounded by a major shopping district, so many locals and tourists go there as well. Even at first glance the clusters of domestic workers in Victoria Park appear noticeably different from those in Statue Square. Many of the Indonesian women proudly wear white, pastel, or patterned headscarves, and some also wear long elegant gowns that they might not be permitted to wear in their employer's home. In the paved region of the park there are dozens of small photographic businesses set up in small stalls on Sundays, catering to domestic workers' fantasies of glamour, leisure activities, romance, and escape. The clientele, almost entirely Indonesian domestic workers, have their photographs taken posing against backdrops ranging from the Eiffel Tower, European castles, and mansions with swimming pools, to scenes of Autumn trees and psychedelic fantasy lands. Other stalls specialize in turning existing snapshots or wallet-sized photographs into poster-sized images of men and women in traditional Indonesian costumes and wedding scenes. Unlike Statue Square, Victoria Park has a large grassy area where domestic workers' organizations rent stages and speaker systems to host musical and dance performances, religious programs, and fund-raising activities. As they had done following the tsunami that struck Aceh in December 2004, Indonesian domestic worker organizations banded

5. According to James Watson, napkins and condiments are often handed out individually at many McDonald's throughout Hong Kong during busy times, even at those not frequented by Filipinas (personal communication, November 1995). It is noteworthy, nonetheless, that Filipinas "resist" this treatment and interpret it as aimed at them.

together again in June 2006 to organize a fund-raising event to benefit the victims of the May 27, 2006, Yogyakarta earthquake.

CONTROLLING EMPLOYERS

Employers are a common topic of conversation among domestic workers on their day off. Women compare them, air grievances about them, and supply advice. Maria's employer underpays her; what should she do? Sunita's employer makes her work in the market as well as in her mother's house; should she just put up with it until her contract is completed, or should she write to the Labour Department? Corazon is forced to work from six in the morning until midnight and her health is suffering. Susannah's employer has terminated her contract for no apparent reason, and she now has less than two weeks to find a new one. Sunny's employer is flirting with her again, and Lilia—see how thin her cheeks are now—is not getting enough food. Fely has a good employer, but she is leaving for the United States. Ask your employer if she knows anyone who might hire her.

Legal and financial problems are commonly discussed. Anna has given her passport to a loan shark and is unable to retrieve it before her visa expires; Mary's employer has confiscated her ID card; Joanna's sister still hasn't paid her back. Women are directed to the mission, the Catholic Centre, Helpers for Domestic Helpers, Christian Action, ATKI's mobile counseling group in Victoria Park, or to one of several other places where they can get legal help and advice. Others are satisfied, or at least temporarily comforted, by the sympathy they receive or the knowledge that others may be even worse off. And others, as a last resort, write down the name of a local employment agency that claims it can find "very good" new employers for "DHs" who are not "finish contract."

One Sunday in 1993 a friend of Acosta's told a group of us, including two recent arrivals to Hong Kong, a joke about "Maria, the Stupid DH." Maria repeatedly misinterprets her employer's instructions to "fry" the chicken and instead thinks her employer says to "fly" the chicken; so she throws it out the window and has nothing to eat. Then Maria's contract is terminated. The reason Maria gives to the Immigration Department for her termination is "starvation." Acosta commented on this popular joke and took the opportunity to share her own experiences and offer advice.

This is what happened to me before! [My employer said], "Eat yourself. Fly the chicken." . . . "Why should I eat myself!?" Because some Chinese their English is not very good. I ran to the telephone. "What do they mean I have to eat by myself?!" "No, you have to get the chicken in your refrigerator, and you have to eat it." . . . Because the *r* in Chinese sounds like an *l*.

As she continued to think about the joke, Acosta went on: "After several days she [Maria] was terminated. You see, this is the problem. Even if you are not a very talented person and you become a domestic helper, if you cannot communicate with them, and you cannot understand the point of exactly what they say to you, you may get upset, you may not answer them." Acosta was appalled that starvation was the reason for termination. She turned to me to make sure I understood.

> That means she's not eating! Impossible if *I'm* Maria! You should buy your own food. If [employers] are very selfish—that is what I always advise. When someone complains to me, "Oh, my employer she never feeds me. I'm starving. My employer, she never gives me food," I say to them, "You want to stay in Hong Kong? You want money? Then you have to buy your own food." If she says, "I don't have the money," [then I say,] "I'll lend you HK$100—you can buy food. There. *And you HAVE TO teach your employer not to be selfish. Put your food in the kitchen so that she will feel embarrassed, and she can buy for you!"* Yes, I always advise this. One of my friends really liked my advice. Another one of them was so boring she had to go back to the Philippines. She told me, "Oh, never mind. In the Philippines I can eat plenty of food." "Oh? You don't want money?" I told her, "Then you don't need to come here anymore."

After a young new arrival complained about the food her employer gave her, Acosta told her how she had persuaded her first Chinese employer to give her a food allowance.

> I said to them, "I don't like your food. If possible, could you give me my food allowance, please?" You have to talk to them, nicely. The couple is quite nice about it, but the pohpoh is bad—but I don't care about the pohpoh because she's not the one who pays me. The lady signed the contract, and she said to the husband, "Give it to Acosta, so she can work." So they gave me HK$300 a month—and the wife said, "Come here Acosta. I will give you HK$300. Okay? You can buy whatever food you like, and you can cook it. Oil, salt, pepper, rice, you can get free here. With this HK$300 you can buy your vegetables, meat or fishy." "And what will I do with this, ma'am? I mean, where can I cook?" I asked. "In the kitchen, of course. You can't cook in the bathroom! You can cook here, where else? Okay. But the drinks—you can have some of our drinks if you like. And the bread, I'll always buy you fresh bread in the morning. . . ." The HK$300 nearly doubled my salary because my salary is HK$500 [a month back then] you see? It's so nice.

Acosta explained how she intentionally left the food she bought for herself out where her employers would see it.

> So you know what she's doing, the pohpoh? She is embarrassed about every-thing I put there! . . . She said, "No, no, no. I know what you're buying." They gave her plenty of money for food too; so when she was out buying [food for herself] she bought food for me too! That marks the beginning of the time when she was very nice to me.

Thus Acosta recommended appealing to the employers' pride and to "embarrass" them into providing either food or food allowance.

Acosta also explained how she successfully resisted "dress codes" and asserted her right to "dress up" when she was at work. Unlike many domestic workers, she does not wear what she refers to as the "DH uniform"—blue jeans and T-shirts. She wears skirts that reach above her knees, blouses, earrings, and some makeup. She does this in part, she explained, to allay suspicion that she is doing aerobics and so that people will take her for a "professional" or a local resident running errands in town. Her dressing up, however, has irritated some of her employers.

> The first time I went to the house I was dressed up like this. I have to work far away [from where I live], and I don't want to look like a beggar. I pity myself sometimes too, because when I'm not in Hong Kong I always wear decent clothes. So I continued to do that here. . . . [When I got to the house] the woman employer asked, "Where are you going?"
> I said, "What? I am coming here. It's my time to work."
> "Oh. You look like you are going to the disco."
> When she said that, I felt very embarrassed. Then she pointed at my lips and said, "What for?" because I had put on a dark color. They don't like that. One of her friends had introduced me, and the trouble was that her friend did not tell her that I wear makeup. She said to me, "Maybe you have already got a boyfriend?" And my ears look like the typhoon is coming! I don't know, I couldn't control myself! I had to answer back. You know what I said? I said, "Excuse me, missus—" [Acosta looks down at the ground and tries to strike a subservient pose] "Excuse me, Mary, what did you say to me? Repeat. I'm going to the disco because you see that I'm dressed up and you see I put some color on my lips? Oh, excuse me. Don't you know that it's winter and I don't want to crack my lips? And with the money that you pay me I can't afford to buy proper lipstick—even any kind of lipstick. I don't want to crack my lips. I want to have lovely lips! You know?"
> "But you're only a maid!" She said that! Wow! This lady I didn't like. This lady talked bad. But because she knew my situation [doing part-time work], I didn't want to get in trouble.

Acosta then talked to the Chinese friend who had introduced her to Mary. Mary had already complained to her about Acosta, saying, "She's only a maid; she doesn't have to use makeup!" So Acosta decided to level with Mary.

> I went back to her house. "If you don't want me to look like this, you better find another one [domestic worker], because I can't stand myself walking in the street looking bad. . . ."
>
> She said, "Ah, take off your dress, dress up, whatever you want then. You are working here."
>
> "Yes," I said, "I always follow your regulations. . . . If I'm not taking good care of your house, then . . . you can complain. But when it's my dress you don't like, then *you* have to mind your own ways."

Domestic workers have figured out different ways to control their employers and manipulate the rules. As described in Chapter 5, some workers warn their employers about medical expenses they might incur if they are forced to bathe immediately after ironing. Elsa recommends taking a "fake" bath in the evening: run the water and wet the towel to "fool" the employer, then take another in the morning, after the employer has left the house. An article in the popular domestic worker magazine *Tinig Filipino* suggests other "tips or rather tricks" for domestic workers:

> To pacify irate employers because you went home after curfew hour is to tell them that the MTR [mass transit railway] was congested and the line to the ticket counter was a mile long. . . . To get rid of the head-cracking nags of your "Pohpoh" is to get the walkman, use the headphones and dance to the music while working. . . . To stop your friends from calling you on early mornings while your employers are still around is to imitate your employer's voice and tell them to get lost. (Miguel 1992)

LANGUAGE, JOKES, AND HUMOR

Public displays of loud uninhibited laughter, like tears and anger, are not unusual in Statue Square. And like nail clipping and hair cutting, such behavior is also subject to criticism from Chinese observers. Loud, uncontrolled laughter not only helps to relieve tension but also expresses freedom from the rules and regulations of the workplace. At seven o'clock each Sunday evening, one group of friends in Chater Garden is transformed into the "Joking Circle." At seven, like clockwork, these women cease all other discussion and turn instead to "jokes and funny stories." As we shall see, some jokes told by Filipinas are explicitly critical of employers and symbolically reverse the roles of employer and domestic worker. Other jokes reflect certain "funny" aspects of life in Hong Kong, and others, like the "stupid DH" joke, provide an entrée that permits women to comment on their experiences and offer advice. Even though the subject matter and content of certain jokes reflect or seem to reinforce the status quo, the laughter they evoke in the context of the square can itself be interpreted as an expression of subtle but stubborn resistance.

Many jokes reflect topics that are central to domestic workers' lives: affairs and marital problems, life in Hong Kong, and difficulties with employers. In one popular joke, a man is about to desert his wife (an overseas worker) for another woman.

> HUSBAND: Goodbye, mother of five!
> WIFE: Goodbye, father of two! (see Layosa and Luminarias 1992:67)

Some jokes reflect life in Hong Kong outside the employer's home. Several involve the motif of thrift. The thriftier she is, the more money a worker can remit home.

> In a restaurant:
> WAITER: May I help you? How many are you?
> DH 1: We're four.
> WAITER: Smoking or nonsmoking?
> DH 2: Whichever is cheaper. (Quezon 1991; see also Gervacio 1991b)

The newness and unfamiliarity of Hong Kong is also a common topic of jokes. Acosta told a joke about a domestic worker from a rural part of the Philippines who arrived at the Hong Kong airport.

> No one is there to meet her so she gets back in line at the ticket counter. The person at the counter says, "Your ticket was coming to Hong Kong, right?" She answers, "Yes, but no one was here to meet me." So she asks directions to the domestic airport. He tells her that there is no domestic airport in Hong Kong. She answers, "I have to go to the domestic airport because I am a domestic helper."

As Acosta explained, "Some workers are ignorant. They come from the village; they don't know how to speak English. So [after] only five days in Hong Kong and maybe they have to terminate and go back to the Philippines."

Another joke reflects the domestic worker's ignorance about double-decker buses. Maria has just arrived in Hong Kong and is asked to accompany her employer on the bus. They go up to the upper deck. When the bus starts to move, Maria stands up abruptly.

EMPLOYER: What's the matter?
MARIA: Ma'am, we have to go down.
EMPLOYER: Why? (with astonishment).
MARIA: Ma'am there's no driver here! (J. Mariano 1992:23)

Such jokes make light of the difficulties of adjusting to Hong Kong life, and they also remind women how far they have come in learning to cope and adapt.

Jokes may temporarily reverse the pattern of dominance and subservience between employer and worker or between local Chinese and overseas workers and reveal a "hidden transcript" (Scott 1990). One popular joke/prank I was told about at the mission involves a substitution of the Tagalog word *unggoy*, which means "monkey," for the Cantonese word *m'goi*, which can be translated as "please," "thank you," or "excuse me." This joke is played in a variety of contexts. In a restaurant, for example, a domestic worker might call out to the Chinese waiter: "Unggoy, unggoy!" The waiter is likely to interpret this as a polite but poorly pronounced attempt to get his attention by saying, "Excuse me" or "Please." The Filipina, meanwhile, has succeeded in getting the waiter to answer to the epithet "monkey." Alternatively, a group of Filipinas who decide to elbow their way to the front of the line at the MTR station in typical Hong Kong Chinese fashion, might call out, "Unggoy! Unggoy!"—thus making a mockery of everyone in the crowd. This joke is also used on Chinese employers when a worker thanks her employer for her wage or excuses herself for accidentally brushing up against her chair or for coming home late on her day off. The joker asserts her ability to outwit and thus claim symbolic superiority over an employer or local Chinese, if even for just a moment. That the employer or waiter is unaware of the insult does not diminish the worker's pleasure in outwitting that person.[6]

The following joke, depending on how it is interpreted, creates either the illusion of equality between domestic worker and employer or a reversal of their roles. In either case, the humor arises mainly from the knowledge that

6. Folk speech is also used to communicate about employers without their knowledge. On the phone or in the presence of a woman employer, for example, a worker may refer to her employer as *nanay* (mommy), or *bruha* (witch), or *kulasa* (a slang term for wife). Male employers may be referred to as *tatay* (father).

the domestic worker does not "know her place" and behave in the way her employer expects.

> *LADY EMPLOYER:* We'll have breakfast tomorrow morning at exactly 8:00 A.M.
>
> *MAID:* All right Ma'am. But if I'm not downstairs on time, do start without me. (Layosa 1991b)

The joke "So you're a member of the family too?" (see Chapter 5) also raises the question of the domestic worker's status vis-à-vis her employer's family and provides a critical commentary on the covert ways employers attempt to subordinate domestic workers.

Chinese employers' mispronunciation of English is a common subject for jokes. Several take the form of a "quiz" that demonstrates the special skill of a domestic worker in interpreting the employer's poor English (e.g., Begonia 1990:41; Salda 1993:48).[7] The humor of the following miscommunication is compounded by the sensitivity of the topic. Employers fear that domestic workers might abuse their children, and domestic workers fear false accusations that might bring termination.

> One morning, my boss rang me up and asked if his little son was still crying.
>
> *BOSS:* Maria, is my little son still crying?
>
> *MARIA:* He is still crying a little bit [pronounced "beet"], sir.
>
> *BOSS:* No, no, no! Don't beat him! (Layosa and Luminarias 1992:61)

Many jokes deal with cooking, preparing chickens, and with domestic workers eating alone. Perhaps chickens are popular because, as Elsa suggests, Filipinos are revolted by meat that is "undercooked" or steamed with "the blood left in it" by Chinese. As demonstrated in Acosta's anecdote mentioned above ("Eat yourself. Fly the chicken."), chicken jokes also poke fun at Chinese employers' English.

> Maria's employers are going out for dinner.
>
> *SIR:* (In broken English). Maria, come—eat outside.
>
> *MARIA:* Sir, you mean you're going out to dinner?
>
> *SIR:* Yes, come . . . you like?

---

7. Another employer is mocked for referring to eggs cooked "sunny side up" as eggs "fried like the sun" (Gervacio 1991a:32).

MARIA: Thank you, sir. But I prefer to eat here.

SIR: All right. Just cook yourself! ("Vicky" 1992).[8]

Some jokes raise the question of whether the ultimate fault is with the employer who cannot give clear instructions or with the domestic worker who takes instructions too literally. These jokes also point to the difficulty and the futility of trying to please some employers. Sally's employer tells her to follow the washing instructions on the label of clothes very carefully. When Sally gives her employer the pink blouse she asks for, her employer says

EMPLOYER: Sally, why my blouse is still damp?

SALLY: Ma'am, I just followed the washing instructions.

EMPLOYER: Why, what is the instruction?

SALLY: It says, "wash and wear!" (J. dela Cruz 1992:109)

In a similar joke, the employer asks Liza to "dress the chicken." Liza takes the instructions literally and dresses the chicken in one of her employer's dresses (Aquino 1993).

THE ROMANCE OF RESISTANCE

The "member of the family" joke criticizes the exploitation of domestic workers. Other jokes criticize domestic workers who are too docile and subservient. And yet others (such as *unggoy*) create a temporary role reversal between local Chinese and overseas workers. Although certain jokes are critical of the oppression experienced by workers, the subject matter of these jokes, on the whole, cannot be said to express a powerful form of resistance. Many jokes are ambiguous: They teach domestic workers neither to resist and disobey their employers nor to be submissive and subordinate. Rather, they serve as commentaries, as "joking imitations" of employers, or as "stories" workers tell about themselves (Basso 1979; Geertz 1973). In other words, they are as important for what they *say* as for what they do.

8. In another version of this joke, the domestic worker is portrayed as naïve or gullible, but at the same time moral and self-righteous. The employer says, "Hello, Lita. We are not coming home for dinner. So you better cook yourself and eat yourself." The domestic worker replies, "Ma'am, but that's double murder!" (Begonia 1990; Layosa and Luminarias 1992:91–92).

Many domestic worker jokes are based on actual work experiences that are so sad that they are funny. Jokes, furthermore, are a particularly appropriate and effective genre through which to comment on experience, for by definition they involve a reversal, an exaggeration, or an unexpected "twist" on reality, which creates their humor. For many women, the entire experience of domestic work in Hong Kong sometimes seems a cruel joke, a distortion of their old lives and their previous social status and identity. The most ordinary and unself-conscious behaviors—when to bathe, what and how to eat, for example—are thrown into doubt by an employer's expectations and different cultural norms. Yet life in Hong Kong also involves humor and other pleasures, and jokes effectively express both aspects of a worker's experiences.

This chapter has considered some of the ways that domestic workers use overt and more subtle forms of protest to assert their rights. They use "confrontation, chicanery, or cajolery" to "establish their own limits within a particular household" (Dill 1988:37–43), and they use "craftiness," "confrontation," and "quitting" as important methods to preserve personal dignity (Coley 1981:253–69). Over the years they have been increasingly successful at establishing cross-ethnic coalitions. Nevertheless, we must heed warnings not to romanticize resistance (Abu-Lughod 1990; Ortner 1995). The overall "success" of Filipina domestic workers in improving the structure of domestic work or the reputation of domestic workers has been limited. The rules and policies that control domestic workers, especially the two-week rule and the policies regarding full-time, live-in work, remain serious impediments and a constant source of frustration. Attempts to create more positive images of domestic workers, furthermore, are undermined not only by the opposing negative views of the public at large but also, as discussed in the following chapter, by domestic workers themselves.

8 | DOCILITY AND SELF-DISCIPLINE

Previous chapters have highlighted some ways that employment agencies, employers, and governments attempt to mold women into docile and obedient workers, and some ways that domestic workers and prospective domestic workers are implicated in the disciplining process, wittingly or not. We have also seen how domestic workers attempt to resist certain types of control, through political and legal avenues, public demonstrations, or subtler forms of protest. This chapter describes some of the ways that domestic workers impose discipline on themselves and thus helps us steer clear of either romanticizing resistance or, at the opposite extreme, portraying Filipina domestic workers as passive, oppressed victims.

This chapter asks why women like Dally and Cathy tolerate work-related problems for so long, why Linda would interpret her employer's strict regulations as signs of concern, and why Filipinas fight for the right to continue to work as domestic workers in Hong Kong, even after they have experienced maltreatment and abuse. I have already alluded to economic factors that are involved in their decisions: Women have debts to pay and families to support. Another factor is that life in Hong Kong not only offers hard work and difficulty but also pleasure, freedom, and independence. There are other less obvious factors as well. In particular, the Filipino and other domestic worker communities often encourage women to tolerate difficulties for the sake of their families, to change themselves rather than the system, and to discipline themselves for the sake of national pride.

DALLY

Dally is a cheerful twenty-three-year-old whom I met at the mission and later interviewed at the shelter where she was staying. She was shy and nervous when I asked if I could turn on the tape recorder and begin the interview. "I decided to come to Hong Kong to help my parents' financial problems, and I also want money, to earn some money for myself," she began. "I finished college in the Philippines. I studied education. I have only one cousin in Hong Kong. She helped me to escape from my employers' house." Dally giggled nervously and stopped. Rosa, a domestic worker in her early forties who was also staying at the shelter, interrupted, "She is so nervous, sister! Turn it off." She pointed to the tape recorder. Rosa then brought me a letter that Dally had been composing to submit to the Labour and Immigration Departments. Dally suggested that I read the letter out loud into the tape recorder. I began:

> Date of arrival in Hong Kong: April 1993; date that work began: April 2, 1993; date of termination: September 1, 1993; salary stipulated in contract: HK$3,200.

"Did you receive your salary?" I asked.
"Only two months' salary, sister" Dally answered.
I continued reading the letter:

> I came from Pangasinan to work in Hong Kong as a domestic worker under the employ of Mrs. Koo. There were five in the family: Husband and wife, two children, and an elderly woman [the wife's mother]. Since it is my first time working abroad, I wanted to work to the best of my ability and to complete my two-year term. On my first day there, she taught me what to do. . . . I woke up at 5:30 A.M. and started working at 6:00 A.M. I hand washed all the clothes. I prepared the sheets and towels for the washing machine, but . . . they did not like . . . me to operate or open the washing machine. So I didn't know how to operate it. I finish my work at 10:30 or 11:30 P.M., and after that I go to bed to rest. When there are many things to do I sleep at 12:00. I also do car cleaning. Ever since I work there, when they go out they always lock me in the kitchen.

I paused and looked up at Dally. She was trembling. "They locked you in?" I asked.

"Yes, sister. From the beginning, sister. But I cannot complain."

Rosa interjected, "Chinese people are very, very bold."

Dally began, "In the beginning I thought it was okay because they did not know me. [I thought] that if they knew me better, if I work hard [they would stop]. I thought they would only do it for a little while. But they always did it."

"Were you their first domestic worker?" I asked.

"No, sister. Many, many [others were] terminated. Only one finished a two-year contract."

"And *she* was crazy!" Rosa interjected.

The conversation stopped, and I continued reading the letter aloud:

So I do my work, very rushed every day because every day they go out early. So I am like a prisoner of their house.

"You spent all day in the kitchen?" I asked. She nodded. "What did you do there all day?"

"[There were] many, many things to wash. Dishes, and they all put the washing there. I washed their slippers every day, and their nightshirts, and clothes. Even if we put some things in the washing machine, there are still many clothes to hand wash. Only the sheets and the towels go in the machine."

"Was the old lady at home during the day?" I asked.

"Yes sister, but she went out to take her granddaughter to school . . . and she always locked the door when she goes."

The letter continued:

On my first month there my employer did not give me a holiday; so I waited. Although I tried to be a good servant, I noticed that the old employer is very demanding and frequently scolds me. Every time she is angry at me about everything that I do. How can I concentrate on my work?

Last May when my employer gave my salary, she deducted HK$500 [to pay] for one pair of chopsticks. I don't have the receipt because she doesn't like to give it to me.

"One pair of chopsticks cost that much? Were they gold?" I asked in jest.

"No, sister. Ivory chopsticks. She said that she did not buy the sticks in— what do you call that, a street market—she bought them in a high-class department store."

"Did you break them?" I asked.

"No, sister. I don't know. Maybe I wrapped them up and threw them away by mistake."

The letter continued:

Last July 8, 1993, my employer gave me $3,000 in June. She told me that she would give me the balance that night. But she wrote on her receipt the amount of $3,200. . . . I was waiting for the rest of the money, but to my dismay she never gave it. Last July my employer said she did not want me to go out any more. She told me that I will have all the holidays I want when she releases me. She said last July 15th that she will release me on August 15th. So I am waiting for that date, but when that date [arrives] my employer doesn't release me. So I try again to get my salary and to have a weekly holiday. But still she doesn't like to give it.

"So for over a month you had no day off?"
"No, sister."
Rosa rolled her eyes.

She said to me that when I go out I cannot come back any more; so I am afraid to go out. Then the following month still I have no salary, holiday, statutory holiday, and I am locked in the kitchen. I also found out that they did not give me my letters.

"How did you know she had them?"
"I see them there. I noticed it on the dining table, and I say to her, 'Ma'am, I will get my letter.' She said, 'You will get it in the evening, or tomorrow. You better work hard so that I will give it to you.' So I worked hard. But when I worked later on that night—when I washed the plates—I made noise, and she said, 'Better be careful when you wash our dishes. They're very expensive. I brought them from Japan.' Then she said, 'So I'll give it [the letter] to you tomorrow.' But then she never gave them. Even five days later."
Rosa shared her own experience, "Even my employer, she tore up my letters. So I have all my letters come to my cousin's address."

So I found a way to contact my cousin to ask for her help. Last August 28 I saw a Filipina cleaning the windows from my kitchen window. I asked for help and she granted it to me. I wrote a letter to my cousin, and together with my passport and DH contract, dropped it out of the window. So the Filipina called my cousin. . . . I wrote to my cousin about the problems with my employer: that she always locks me in the kitchen and that I have no salary and no holiday. Last August 30, when I'm fixing their room, my employer asked me to get my identity card and to give it to her, but I refused. So when I didn't give my identity card to her, she said that she will get it from my bag. I could not believe that she could do that, but she went to my room and got the ID card. Last September 1, I again asked my employer to give me my salary, but still she doesn't.

My cousin was very worried about my situation there in my employer's house. So she [explained] the situation to her employer and asked for her advice. . . . Her employer accompanied her to the Labour Department and to the Immigration Department, but the immigration person told her to get the police. So last September 1, at about 4 P.M. they came to my employer's house. But no one was around to open the door when they rang the bell. I was the only one in the house, but how can I open the door if they lock me in the kitchen? They waited outside for twenty minutes. Then the old woman arrived with her granddaughter. The police asked the old woman if they have a Filipina maid. She denied it. So the police turned back to her granddaughter and asked if that picture in my passport is their maid. So the little girl answers, "Yes, that's Dally. She is in the kitchen." The little girl opens the kitchen and called me so I come out. I see my cousin and many police, so I cry and cry because I think I am safe already. Then the policeman talks to the old woman. She called her daughter, my employer, and she came and talked to the police in Chinese. Then the police interviewed me about what happened and about the wrong things that they have done to me. So my cousin, together with the police, get me.

I asked my employer to check my things, and after they checked, I packed. So I went to my cousin's employer's house. On the following day I reported to the Labour and Immigration Departments. They gave me my schedule for conciliation.

"When is the conciliation?" I asked.

"September 16, sister, 11:30 A.M."

"And then if your employer doesn't come?"

"Then we go to the Labour Tribunal. But if she agrees to pay my claims, then it will be finished, and I will try to process a new contract."

I asked her how she put up with such treatment for six months. "I tried my best to—I tried to live there for six months, sister, because I thought of my debts in the Philippines. I thought, of my family. I thought even if they treat me like that, I will do my best to work again. But they were never satisfied with my work."

"How much did you have to pay in the Philippines?"

"Thirty-five thousand pesos to an agency. I had to borrow it from my aunty. So even if they treated me badly, I wanted to stay there so I can pay her back. But she always shouted at me, 'Oh, Dally, you're so very dirty. This one, this one, very dirty!' So, never mind, I thought. I will sacrifice myself for my parents, for my brother and sisters. I am the one who helps the family because my brother is in college. I pay his tuition and allowance. And the next [sibling] is in high school. I have older brothers and sisters, but they are already married. I am the eldest with no husband; so I am the bread earner."

"Sometimes, sister," she paused, "I'm scared. I want to go back to the Philippines, but sometimes," her voice trailed off, "I like to work here in Hong Kong. And if possible . . . I will still work again. I know that God is always with us. Maybe the first time I worked in Hong Kong he tested me to see if I can manage, if I can handle my problems. Maybe my second employer will be very kind to me. Not a dragon."

"Nothing is impossible," Rosa added. "We prefer to get a very good employer the second time!" Maria, who had just joined us, added, "For me it was also bad the second time." Rosa said, "Anything is possible if you pray hard enough." Maria shook her head, "Praying isn't enough."

INVOKING NATIONAL PRIDE

Some of the most striking examples of self-discipline are illustrated in *Tinig Filipino*, a popular magazine published in the early and mid-1990s in Hong Kong by and about Filipino domestic workers. In the 1990s I often saw the magazine passed around in Statue Square on Sundays, and it reached tens of thousands of readers each month.[1] Many articles from *Tinig Filipino* reflected and encouraged passivity, compliance, and similar sorts of discipline as imposed by employers, agencies, and governments. *Tinig Filipino*'s content—including articles, short stories, jokes, letters, opinions, "cleaning tips," and suggestions for how to deal with employers—was written mostly by domestic workers. It covered migrant-related news, occasional articles about UNIFIL activities or workers' legal rights, and lists of places where workers could go for shelter or legal advice. It was mainly designed to help workers cope with loneliness, homesickness, and work-related problems. Advice often took the form of pop psychology, urging workers to change

---

1. By the late 1990s *Tinig Filipino* was no longer in existence. There were several new monthly or bimonthly newspapers geared toward Filipina domestic workers that competed for the same niche but were distributed free in Central District and places where Filipinas congregated. These include *The Sun* (which was established in the mid-1990s) and *Hongkong News* (Williams 2002). *The Sun* and *Hongkong News* have some similar content as *Tinig Filipino* but include a wider spectrum of news events and political issues that relate to migrant domestic workers, and much less editorializing and advice. They are supported solely by advertisers who sell products such as loans, remittances, phone cards, cargo and shipping, and employment opportunities to the Hong Kong Filipino migrant worker clientele.

their attitudes and diffuse their negative feelings about employers or work. Many articles aimed to boost domestic workers' national pride, self-esteem, and sense of professionalism. Much of the advice suggests workers should find satisfaction "from within," rather than address the conditions of their oppression. Although reassuring on an individual level, such advice provides only temporary "coping" mechanisms and helps mask the unequal and exploitative nature of domestic work.

As illustrated in *Tinig Filipino*, much of the discipline that Filipinas impose on their compatriots is done in the name of national pride. Compatriots remind one another that they represent the Philippines and should behave in ways that reflect well on their homeland. It is their responsibility to oppose Chinese stereotypes about Filipino drinking, gambling, poverty, backwardness, loose sexual morals, gossiping, loitering, and littering. In response to criticisms in the local newspapers, Aquarius Fe writes, "Let us do something . . . to prevent the Hong Kong people from having the negative impression that we Filipinos . . . are dirty and uncooperative" (1990:32). In a letter to the editor, Edith Autor reiterates Fe's points and writes that this is the time and the season "to prove to the Hong Kong community that we Filipinos are people with value, honor and dignity. . . . That we are hardworking and honest . . . that we do not make too much unnecessary noise . . . that we do not literally litter' ourselves in the corridors or in the passageways" (1991).[2]

June Laggawan Sannad expresses similar disgust at the behavior of a Filipina on a bus who

> sat with legs up and feet at the window. Just imagine, a lady sitting with legs up and feet at the window of a public transportation! Although she was wearing jeans, for me it was improper to sit the way she did. . . . Let us not be so selfish by behaving in any way we want. . . . Let us bear in mind that . . . we do not only carry our own name but the whole name of [all] Filipinos and that our misbehavior effects the reputation of the whole Filipino community. To the lady concerned, I'm sorry but I think we should discipline ourselves next time. (Sannad 1993)

Vady Madamba cautions readers, "Remember, avoiding discotheques and pub houses doesn't only keep us from temptation and suspicious

---

2. Vickei Dorde asks her compatriots, "Where are your manners?" and describes a variety of disturbing scenarios: Filipinas drinking and playing cards in public, fighting over men, not paying back loans, not waiting their turn in lines, making too much noise. She asks, "Are we that desperate that we no longer show decency in public anymore?" (1992).

eyes but it may earn us—the whole Filipino community—good reputation from our hosts" (1991). Oly Rueda stresses the moral responsibility of domestic workers to their "race" despite their "lowly" position in Hong Kong.

> Reading these commentaries [in the Hong Kong newspapers] has urged me to call upon every Filipino helper to belie those criticisms by preserving the epitome of a dainty and demure image as well as indulging in activities geared towards the enrichment of our Philippine culture. . . .
>
> If we still have . . . the feelings of a true Filipino, let us join hands to prove to the whole world that Filipino maids still have moral values though how lowly we are in this foreign land. Let us help the government of our host country in its drive to maintain a clean environment. Let everyone of us develop a sense of responsibility by avoiding litter[ing] around. But foremost, let us realize that whatever misbehavior we show in our sojourn is a disgrace and a shame to the whole Filipino race. (Rueda 1992)

Evangeline C. Ragus describes her response to her employer's view of the Philippine government and economy:

> Hearing all our country's flaws being enumerated by a Chinese made me feel so ashamed. . . . Furthermore, with millions of Filipinos being out of the country, the image of the Philippines and its citizens has worsened. In Hong Kong, other than being "kung-yans" [*gungyahn* (workers)] during working hours, the Filipinos are the squatters, litterers, gamblers, hawkers at the Square, etc. (1992)

Ragus pleads with fellow Filipinos to behave in ways that will make them "proud to be a Filipino anytime, any place," even though "the immediate past and the present could make you hesitate." She concludes her letter by asking whether "DH" should stand for "Doctor of Humanities" or "Danger to Humanity."

APPEALS TO PERSONAL PRIDE

Appeals are also made to workers' sense of personal pride and individual responsibility. Examples relating to Statue Square and domestic workers' physical appearance illustrate the point. *Tinig Filipino* publishers and staff helped organize new sites where domestic workers could go on Sundays. The magazine sponsored festivals and sports events in an attempt to decongest Central District, and several articles and letters encouraged workers to clean up the square and to spend their Sundays outside of the district.

Benita, a Filipina in her mid-thirties, sold copies of *Tinig Filipino* in the square once a month, but otherwise she refused to go there. She was critical of those who go there to "waste time and gossip," create "a bad image for Filipinos," or "get into trouble" (see Escoda 1989:33).[3] Instead, she spent her spare time with women who are involved with sports events and entertainment organized or cosponsored by *Tinig Filipino*. Benita highly admired Linda Layosa, who was once a domestic worker and then became the magazine's full-time editor. She agreed with many of Layosa's views.

Keeping things clean, in public and at home, is a central topic of one article by Layosa. She admonishes readers for their lack of *malasakit* (concern) for the "host country" and for employers. She cites the garbage domestic workers leave in the square and the waste of water and electricity in employers' homes as examples. She urges workers to "prove to our employers that we have concern for them. And that we don't only work for the sake of money, but because we care for the household" (1991a:23–24). Many contributors to *Tinig Filipino* echo the same view, urging domestic workers to develop better self-discipline. "In our employer's house, we do our best to make it tidy and clean. So, why not discipline ourselves once we are in the square or other public places so that we will not receive criticisms always?" (Dulatre 1992a).

The magazine also offered advice about personal cleanliness, grooming, clothing, and appearance. Some advice included "beauty and makeup tips," but much of it coincided remarkably well with employers' ideals. Emphasis was placed on modesty and personal cleanliness. One worker suggested dressing to avoid looking "loose" or provocative or so as to attract male attention. Alternatively, women were warned against dressing too much like a "T-bird" (lesbian).

> Staying clean is a lady's best asset. And since our employers want us to be clean always, especially when we are taking care of a baby, thus, we should take interest in our personal appearance. This does not mean that we should wear the latest fashion in town, like those attractive clothes we see in the department store. As long as our clothes are clean and suitable to the occasion, it doesn't matter whether they are new or not. . . . Since hands are used for handling things, they should be kept clean and if possible, let's keep our

3. A forty-five-year-old domestic worker told Jaschok that she avoids the square because she feels "dirty, confined, exposed to hostile eyes, [and] self-conscious" when she is there (1993:33).

fingernails short. Also avoid applying nail polish during working days, especially when you are in charge of cooking. The nail polish may peel off and it
may easily fall into the food. (Jacinto 1991)

Like employers' rules described earlier, this article discusses the importance of clean feet, lack of body odor, and keeping teeth clean. Another
letter, which received much support from readers, implored domestic
workers not to wear "sexy" clothes. Annabelle Basabica writes, "Could
you expect a man to act like a saint when you are garbed in sexy clothes?"
(1993; see also Chang and Groves 2000; Groves and Chang 2002).

ATTITUDES

These and other articles in *Tinig Filipino* promote and teach "the proper
attitude" for a "DH." They encourage domestic workers to maintain a positive outlook and to control any anger they may feel toward their employers.
The ideal attitude for a domestic worker, most articles insist, is passive and
acquiescent. The solution proposed in such articles is always an inward one,
a personal one, and is not directed at creating or implementing wider social
change. Simplistic solutions as learning "patience," "love," "contentment,"
"devotion," or "positive thinking" are advocated. The first step is for the
domestic worker to take responsibility and realize that *she* may be the problem. One domestic worker writes, "On my first contract, I took my job for
granted. My employers were not happy and commented about it. I went to
my room and thought seriously about my situation. I realized the problem
was not my work nor my employers. I was the problem. When I changed my
attitude and my behavior, things began to get better" (T. de la Cruz 1992).

When employers seem unreasonable, such articles maintain, it is the
worker's responsibility to try to understand the situation. In an article
titled "Can You Read Your Boss?" Layosa encouraged workers to study the
employer's "hidden feelings," to try to recognize the employer's "words of
precaution," to study "his movements or body language." Her advice is to
"accept criticisms from your employer. Once he frankly criticizes you, don't
think that he is just throwing to you whatever worry he has. Similarly, do
not immediately think that you are right and your employer is wrong. It
would help you better if, after he has given you some lashing words, try to
analyze the situation objectively and honestly. In this way you will be able
to see your real mistakes" (Layosa 1992a).

Layosa assumes that it is the domestic worker who is in the wrong and
that the employer's anger has a just cause. Along similar lines, the article

"Because of Love" encourages workers to learn to love their employers, no matter how bad they may be. The author criticizes fellow workers,

> If you only came here to work and you're just after money and never winning your employers' trust and confidence, then, there's something wrong with you. . . . Loving our employers is not that easy. Loving them takes a lot of time and effort . . . They may be the meanest boss, very inconsiderate, too meticulous, fault-finder, and strict but then, we have to learn to dance with them. . . . My secret in winning their confidence? Simple! I always have a ready smile. . . . I maintain my patience and above all, I always seek the Lord's guidance. (Jose 1992)

Positive thinking is another simple solution. Layosa "suffered a lot of heartaches, loneliness, humiliation, and all sorts of negative feelings" during her first year as a domestic worker, but she has "overcome all of these easily by thinking positively" (1990b:27). Another worker suggests that "contentment" holds the key (Gelacio 1989:20); another that "patience" is "the key to success" (Marie '89 1989:24). Susie Sapo Silvestre recommends "optimism" and writes, "We should learn how to accept and love our work no matter how humble it is. What we need is more patience, hard work, sacrifice and determination" (1992). According to Janet Maniego, "The road to success takes . . . [a] vital quality called patience" (1993). Yet another article contends that failure always comes before success and that the key ingredient is "persistence" (Tenorio 1993). Toto Campano provides a slightly more complex formula, with five hints for attaining success: be diligent, do not procrastinate, be happy always, be thrifty, and be devoted to your work (1993; see also Blanco 1993).

None of these articles even hinted that an employer might take any responsibility for the situation or, indeed, might be to blame for the worker's difficulties. Domestic workers often believe and remind each other that their individual weaknesses are the cause of any difficulties they encounter or cannot overcome.[4]

RELIGION, TOLERANCE, AND PASSIVITY

Many letters and articles in *Tinig Filipino* express resignation, helplessness, and passivity. Before she became the editor of the magazine, Layosa wrote, "I am not as lucky as some of you who follow the terms and conditions

---

4. This attitude is similar to what Richard Sennett and Jonathan Cobb (1973) have described as "hidden injuries of class."

of the contract to the letter. My employers have their own version of working conditions which I am helpless to change and which I have to follow" (1990b:30). In another column she writes,

> There is no use finding fault with our employers. The best thing is how we can find a remedy so as to positively divert our emotions in order to avoid conflicts and to enhance harmony inside the household. Since we are subordinates, the best thing is for us to give way to our employers' moods and tantrums. After all, they own their homes and it is the only place where they can be themselves. (1990c)

Sheila D. Torrefranca, a domestic worker with a college degree in sociology, advocates the epitome of passivity. According to Torrefranca, the *worst* thing for a worker to do in response to unfair criticism is to defend herself.

> By reacting negatively or even heatedly to criticism we make it easy for our employers to antagonize us more. The more resistance we show the harder the employer will pound on the issue and make life very unpleasant for us. . . . If you care about yourself you have two choices to approach and cope with criticism—the POSITIVE approach, if you don't have the heart to live in constant slanging match with your employer . . . or the NEGATIVE way if you prefer to live in misery. (1992)

Ma. Teresa W. Francisco writes of her friend "Dina," who became furious when her employers asked her to paint the flat while they were away on vacation. The author shared Dina's view that this work was "intended for men," but she advises fellow workers not to get angry but to treat the work as a learning experience. "I just treat those 'unusual' assignments my boss gives me as learning experiences that will enrich my life. . . . I also regard those experiences as different subjects as when I was in school. . . . My only wish now is to 'graduate' with a pocketful of good and useful knowledge and worthy diploma to be brought home when I decide to settle down. I encourage you, my classmates to feel the same" (1993).

  Like Dally, domestic workers also advocate religious solutions to their difficulties as a substitute for attempting to enact change. A domestic worker in a bad situation writes, "What I did then was to keep praying to our Almighty God that He will change the attitude of my employer because I really believe that only God can change their attitude towards me" (Marie '89 1989:21). Layosa also invokes the Bible to justify suffering and as a promise of otherworldly rewards. She consoles readers with the biblical passage "You, servants, must submit to your masters and show them complete respect. . . . If you endure suffering even when you have done right, God will bless you for it" (1990c). "Mommie Jingco," a missionary who wrote a regular column on religion, uses the Bible to glorify the role of "servants" and to justify the subservience that they owe to their "masters."

> What is wrong with being a domestic helper anyway, or shall I use the word servant or muchacha? From Christ's point of view these are the people who will become great because they humble themselves to serve others. It was Christ [who] promoted servanthood.
>
> . . . Here are some tips to remember from the Scriptures: . . . Servants be obedient to those who are masters according to the flesh, with fear and trembling as to Christ; not with eye service, as men pleasers, but as bond servants of Christ doing the will of God from the heart, with goodwill doing service, as to the Lord, and not to men, knowing that whatever anyone does, he will receive the same from the Lord, whether he is slave or free. Ephesians 6:5–7. ("Mommie Jingco" 1991)

Prayer is also invoked as an aid in controlling negative feelings toward employers. "When my employer gets angry with me all I do is pray," writes Vivian E. Saremo: "Lord, I am angry or my boss is angry with me. Pardon us for what fault I have done and for what fault he has done" (1993). Another writer identifies many negative popular stereotypes about Filipinos and advocates religion and prayer as the appropriate response.

> Their impression about us is very bad. . . . Are we Filipinos, lazy, idiots, stupid, dishonest, evil necessity, environmental nuisance and many more to tell? These are all written, published in the local newspaper and can even be heard from the local people's lips. Do you know how humiliating is this? This is a big embarrassment to us! We are in a very awful position. Indeed, we are degraded, humiliated and discriminated against. . . . Be proud then to be a Filipino. Let's prove that we are not here to disgrace our country but to work and earn money . . . let's lift our hands to God, for God is mightier than anything. Through Him, we can find assurance, guidance and care. (Padua 1991)

REMEMBER WHY WE ARE HERE

When they feel lonely or have difficulties, workers remind one another to remember why they came to Hong Kong in the first place. When things get tough, workers tell each other not to complain or give up but to remember their families. Many letters and articles remind readers that they came to

Hong Kong "for the sake of our loved ones" (Gelacio 1989:20), and therefore they should not give up, no matter how difficult their experiences. "I came to Hong Kong as a domestic helper, so however hard it was to cope with the treatment, I had to struggle for my goal: for financial stability and to give a better life for my family. Through patience and determination I was able to finish my two-year contract with my first employer" (Espinosa 1991). Layosa wrote: "We chose to be here, we acted on our own free will, so we must do whatever it takes to make ourselves better while we do our menial jobs here in this foreign land" (1990b:27).

Although she does not seem to share Layosa's notion of "free will," Mommie Jingco does share her view of the reason why workers migrate. "Filipinos did not choose to leave their families to be domestic helpers. In fact many are struggling to be called domestic helpers, especially when they are treated rudely by their employers. It is not easy to take the fact that [a] few years back [at] home they are employers with two or three domestic helpers but now they are helpers of another nationality. But they have to take this because they want to help their families and our country" (1991). Encouraging fellow domestic workers to stay and make the most of their situation, Silvestre writes,

> Nobody forced us to go out of our country. We left our families of our own free will—ready to face whatever consequences we may encounter. . . . We are here for specific goals—to earn money and to improve our living standards. . . . There are those whose lives are nightmares, yet they are determined to go through because they all have aspirations in life. We have plans for ourselves and for our family. Our dream is at stake so, no matter how hard our work is, we still choose to stay. (1992)

Other workers place more emphasis on the economic reward. "Basically, we are here in Hong Kong to look for a greener pasture, to uplift our lives and to earn money. We have taken the risk to work abroad just to fulfill this purpose" (Padua 1991). A monthly column on "success stories" also emphasizes the economic rewards of overseas work (Gonzales 1993).[5] "Pelican" encourages domestic workers to appreciate their work because of the good they can do for their own families and especially for their employers' families. She comments on the difficulties of adjusting to a life that is so different from the one she envisioned when she was a university student—the

---

5. See also the poem "I Am Your Job," which advises workers to appreciate their work (M. Mariano 1991).

rudeness of employers, the cruelty of employers' children, the constant criticism, the lack of communication, and the constant label *chisin* (crazy). She urges workers not to give up. "By your example the children are now less violent and a bit courteous. . . . Your popo has forgotten her bad habits. . . . The couple seldom argue nowadays. . . . You still have much to do for that family. God has put you there for a purpose and you have responded rightly. As a DH you are His instrument. . . . You are working as a DH—a Doctor of Humanities for a humane race" ("Pelican" 1992d).

FORM AND CONTENT

Both the form and the content of domestic workers' letters and articles in *Tinig Filipino* resemble rules from employers and agencies. Layosa suggested that workers "keep a timetable" and "carefully plan and schedule" personal activities (1990d). In her condemnation of what she calls "Filipino time" (running late), Layosa's comments bear a remarkable similarity to those of M. S. Chow, who considers the "general attitude to work and carefree lifestyle" of Filipinas "incompatible with the hardworking ethics and serious attitude of the Chinese" (1987). Layosa promotes eradicating the notion of "Filipino time" because "it is destroying us. . . . We do not need training for punctuality. Only self-discipline and common sense. . . . In order to avoid this disappointing and shameful thing we should cast off from our minds the notorious connotation of Filipino time, instead, let's change it to this 'Filipino time is the most exact time'" (1990d, and see 1990b:27).

In some cases, domestic workers seem to imitate the lists of rules and regulations distributed to them by employers and agencies. One worker offers seven suggestions on "How to Be a Good Domestic Helper."

1. Be sincere. Learn to care, respect, and love the family members, especially their kids.
2. Be a hardworking maid. Do your responsibilities/obligations without being told all the time.
3. Have a pleasant personality. A smile can do a lot of wonders. Politeness can cure bad moods. Patience is a sign of maturity and a rewarding asset of life.
4. Learn to adapt to our employers' ways and culture.
5. Learning our employers' language is also an important factor especially if an old person is staying with the family and also when we go to the market.

6. Be simple. I remember my lady boss commenting before: Do not wear make-up during working hours. We should dress up neatly and accordingly, but we should be neat especially if we are dealing with children.

7. Learn to show concern for your employers' belongings. Treat the house as your own. (Espinosa 1991)[6]

Another worker sent in "The Eight Beatitudes of a Domestic Helper" (Nicolas 1992).[7] An article called "10 Simple Habits for Our Lives" advises workers to run their employers' homes "like a business." It thus aims to "professionalize" the status of "helpers" and to promote the worker's sense that her work is professional regardless of whether others look down on it. It also imposes the same sort of discipline employers themselves often demand.

1. Practice discipline in day-to-day maintenance (e.g., Don't leave dishes in the sink; dispose of newspapers and junk mail daily).

2. Make "Do it now" your motto for small jobs (e.g., Empty dishwasher when the cycle finishes; water a wilting plant right away.)

3. Do the little things ahead of time (e.g., Plan for dinner in the morning; tidy the house before bedtime.)

4. Don't get sidetracked (e.g., If you've planned to wash curtains one day, don't stop until the job is complete.)

5. Make a list of household management tasks, (e.g., Pick a different day to change sheets; do laundry; plan menus and be consistent.)

6. Manage your employer's house like a business (e.g., Plan your housekeeping around your schedule.)

7. Be vigilant. Watch for 10 minute slots when you can get something done, (e.g., Keep small mending jobs, like cleaning one refrigerator shelf.)

8. Make a list of all heavy-duty jobs like washing windows and cleaning woodwork. Divide these jobs into 30 minute tasks and add one task to your routine each week.

6. An article called "Don'ts When Working Abroad" includes similar rules (Tagoylo 1991). The *Tinig Filipino* reader, however, is not likely to realize that Tagoylo is the manager of an employment agency in Hong Kong.

7. This includes: "Blessed is the domestic helper who knows where she is working and how she is working there; . . . who works patiently, hard and honestly; . . . who considers her job an opportunity for service . . . who is willing to sacrifice her personal time and pleasure by working harder to make her family happy."

9. List all jobs that can be delegated, then delegate them, (e.g., Schedule a time each month for kids to straighten their games and toys.)
10. Evaluate your overall performance from time to time. Ask yourself:
"What were the trouble spots?" (Sanchez 1993)

Unlike the "professionalization" of household work that is "liberating" in
the cases described by Leslie Salzinger (1991) and Mary Romero (1992),
this sort of professionalization is not liberating, nor does it improve work
conditions. Government regulations prevent Filipinas from turning household work into a "business" by organizing work teams, working for multiple
employers, or charging by the job or by the hour. In their attempts to professionalize their occupation, Filipina domestic workers actively promote
ever more rigid forms of discipline. Professionalization, in this case, means
adhering to stricter timetables and adopting more efficient and "modern"
work methods (e.g., Sanchez 1993). Similar to Taylorism or "scientific
management" imposed on industrial workers, the "professionalization" of
household work entails "techniques that dictate precisely how each task is
to be performed in order to obtain the highest level of productivity within a
strict time economy"; the "fragmentation of skills into simple procedures";
and "the stripping away of individual judgment (separation of conception
and execution)" (A. Ong 1991:289).

This professionalization may improve a worker's relationship with her
employers if, as a result of it, the employers are more satisfied with her
work. It may also increase a domestic worker's sense of personal "satisfaction," but it cannot transform the wider negative reputation household work
bears in Hong Kong. Nor does it allow women to organize themselves into
teams or "businesses" or to create more time to spend with their families or
to demand higher wages for their labor. If Filipina domestic workers complete their work sooner, they may simply find that more work is assigned.
They cannot go home and spend more time with their children or earn a
higher wage by taking on additional part-time work.

A number of articles in *Tinig Filipino* actively promote greater pride in
domestic work and contest demeaning stereotypes by creating an analogy
between domestic workers and university students. Statue Square is referred
to as a "university" where workers go to attain a "BSDW" (Bachelor of Science in Domestic Work) or a "DH" (Doctorate in Humanities) ("Pelican"
1992; Sanchez 1993; Vincente 1991a, b). Such articles attempt to equate
domestic work with higher-status occupations and to foster contentment
in an essentially exploitative situation. A domestic worker's "knowledge"

does not easily translate into power. The more difficult the "tests" (ordeals) that a domestic worker "passes" (survives), the more oppressed she may be. Despite suggestions to the contrary, the "DH" contract is not a "transcript," and she does not receive a "degree" when she finishes. This discourse may be aimed at transforming demeaning aspects of domestic work, but in so doing, it also imposes discipline and docility.

It may be tempting to interpret attempts to "professionalize" the occupation as forms of "cultural struggle"; that is, as a struggle "over cultural meanings, values, and goals" as opposed to a "class struggle" (A. Ong 1991:281). But to interpret this phenomenon as a form of struggle (or as resistance) is to miss an important point: The type of professionalism promoted by Filipinas would generate the ideal domestic worker desired by employers and agencies. The "professional" domestic worker is, in essence, docile, willingly submits herself to work discipline, and therefore conforms closely to the employers' and agencies' "ideal." With the ideas of docility and self-discipline in mind, let us look again at the protest of August 1993.

ANTIPATHY TOWARD PROTEST

Alongside the protest in Chater Garden, which began early in the afternoon on the last Sunday of August 1993, was the usual crowd of domestic workers who congregated in the square and the garden for their day off. Acosta briefly passed through the square to greet some friends on her way to do "aerobics." Like Acosta, most of the women in the garden ignored the protestors or watched them with amusement or curiosity. They hardly glanced at the informational flyers, or they placed them on the damp concrete of the garden wall and sat on them to prevent their clothes from getting soiled. A few women said they might keep the phone number and give the union a call later on if they had problems with their employers. But most of the onlookers were uninterested or wanted nothing to do with the protest. They shied away from the television and newspaper cameras covering the event. One woman was frightened at the possibility that her employer might see her on the evening news and associate her with the demonstration; she and her friends quickly moved to a more remote area of the garden. Benita did not even pass through the square that day because she knew the protest would be taking place there.

On Monday I asked Acosta what she thought of the protest and whether she would ever consider joining the union. She explained that once several years before she had thought about joining, but her employer issued her a memorandum telling her that she did not approve of the union; so she decided against it. "The union is doing good, but for the employer it's not good," she explained. "In my opinion, if an employer is already good, there is no need to force them to give me more. . . . But some people want a raise in salary because they work until two in the morning. They are supposed to be the ones who get a higher salary. But if employers are good to you and you don't have to work too hard, why do you need more salary?"

Like Acosta, many domestic workers were not in favor of the salary increase. Even though it had been two years since the previous raise and the increase of HK$600 per month being proposed by the ADWU would barely keep up with the rate of inflation, many domestic workers shared their employers' view: Employers are the ones who shoulder the burden of inflated costs, since they are required to provide room and board to domestic workers. Like their employers, furthermore, domestic workers maintained that by Philippine standards and compared with other parts of Asia, their wages were excellent. Even though union members forcefully pointed out that domestic workers *are* affected by inflation (both in Hong Kong and in the Philippines), that employers' salaries had increased to meet inflation over the past two years, and that pegging Hong Kong wages to prices or wages in the Philippines is ridiculous, many domestic workers were unwilling to risk protesting for higher wages. They would rather not "rock the boat" and insisted that "a bird in the hand is worth two or more in the bush." "It's this sort of attitude," one domestic worker commented of the protests, "that gives us Filipina maids a bad name."

Comments about the protest published in *Tinig Filipino* indicated that many domestic workers did not understand the problem with the two-week rule or the reason why ADWU, UNIFIL, and other organizations opposed it (BMP 1993). Some workers thought the two-week period ought merely be extended to three weeks or a month to allow more time "to look for a new employer." They missed the point that the two-week period was never intended to provide time to locate new employers. Furthermore, cases of unfair termination are not settled in two weeks, or even two months. As activists have been trying to explain since the rule was first introduced in 1987, the main problem is that workers whose contracts are terminated, some after only a few hours or a few days, are required to go back to their home country, reprocess their papers, repay fees, and wait approximately four months before they can work for another employer. This procedure leaves domestic workers highly vulnerable.

Many of the workers quoted in *Tinig Filipino* opposed the pay increase: "If we keep on asking for wage increases, many Chinese employers will not be able to afford us and they might just decide to get help from other countries" (BMP 1993:8). And like members of the employers' association, workers were wary of limiting working hours: How can it be done? Would employers still hire us? Employers with babies need us on call twenty-four hours a day. If we aren't willing to do the job, others will replace us.

There were also disagreements between members of the ADWU and other groups. In contrast to the ADWU's official stance, many politically active domestic workers were satisfied with the government's proposed HK$300 a month salary increase. Some thought the union should have placed more emphasis on the two-week rule and less on the issue of wages, but they felt a commitment to participate in the protest and the march to Government House. Both Elsa and Belle took part in the protest and afterward expressed frustration at the apathy and passivity of many of their fellow domestic workers. As Elsa explained after the protest:

> I am really very depressed and sorry. Because most of the Filipinos here, if they are in good condition with their employer, it seems that they don't mind what will happen. . . . And if we are giving leaflets to educate them they will say, "Can we earn with that? Can we earn with that?" And they will not read it; they will throw it away. And you know, we are trying to help them. And it just seems that they don't have any interest. And if they have experienced problems, they don't know where to go to, or they don't know how to solve the problems—especially labor and immigration related problems.

As representatives of UNIFIL and the ADWU explained, sometimes after domestic workers have experienced difficulties and received help from the union or the mission or another organization, then they become involved, aware, and concerned. "Passivity" and "activism" do not simply characterize two different types of domestic worker. At a certain time or in a certain context, a domestic worker may approach her problems in differ-ent ways. The "passive" worker, moreover, is not necessarily unaware of the problems of domestic work. Like Acosta, she may simply feel that her time in Hong Kong is limited, and therefore she will earn money while she can and then move on.

ACCOMMODATION

Compared with the multitude of studies of resistance, accommoda-tion has received little attention. In a noteworthy section of an article on women industrial workers, Aihwa Ong describes how, "at some industrial sites, factory women seemed overwhelmed by the needs of their families," and this concern "restrain[ed] their capacity to participate in sustained social action" (1991:297). Other women avoided production politics "not by resisting control at work but by 'graduating' from industrial employment altogether" (298). These explanations also hold true for domestic workers. Many are afraid to resist or to assert their rights because they do not want to risk the loss of income used to support their families back home. Many, like Dally, hope merely to "endure" or "survive" what they consider a degrading and demeaning occupation in order to earn their ticket out. Some hope to start a business back home, to invest in land, or to build a house in the Philippines, so that their lives will be easier later on. Yet others hope to meet a man who will rescue them from economic hardships.

Emotional support from friends and relatives back home, religious faith, Sunday pleasures, and a constant focus on future goals help domestic workers survive and put up with the day-to-day hardships of their work. As Shellee Colen says of West Indian domestic workers, "Their determination to achieve their goals for themselves and their children keeps them going. It is buoyed by letters from home saying 'we're praying for you' and 'if it wasn't for you we wouldn't make it'" (1986:64).

Such factors are important to consider, but the issue of accommodation, acquiescence, or passivity should not be so easily dismissed. As I have maintained, another dimension of accommodation can be equated with Foucault's notion of self-discipline. As we have seen, some forms of domestic worker discipline are self-imposed, and discipline can also be a source of "pleasure," as discussed further in Chapter 9. In attempting to challenge hegemonic representations, domestic workers often advocate certain forms of discipline. Like Bedouin women who willingly adopt the veil (Abu-Lughod 1986, 1990) and yet simultaneously resist certain forms of control, Filipina domestic workers actively promote "professionalization" in an attempt to create a more positive image of their occupation. The image of the disciplined domestic worker they promote is remarkably similar, although not identical, to that of employers and agencies.

Like industrial workers in Malaysia and Taiwan (A. Ong 1987; Kung 1983) and like domestic workers in the United States (Colen 1986; Dill 1988), instead of agitating for radical change, many domestic workers express a desire to be treated with "empathy," with greater personal or moral consideration, and with fairness (A. Ong 1991:299–300). Such consideration is not something most domestic workers think they can demand; it is something they believe they must earn by complying with the rules.

9 | PLEASURE AND POWER

Had this book ended with a critique of institutionalized forms of power and their oppressive effect, it would have overlooked the importance of domestic workers' efforts to resist their oppression. To regard these women simply or solely as oppressed by those "with power" is to ignore the subtler and more complex forms of power, discipline, and resistance in their everyday lives.

There is a tendency to view the situation of domestic workers in Hong Kong in terms of broad patterns of transnational labor migration. It is easy to conclude that foreign domestic workers, recruited from powerless sectors of the Philippine or Indonesian population, are simply and easily exploited by agents, employers, and governments and relegated to the lowliest of occupations. Several studies indicate, however, that Filipina domestic workers are *not* generally from the poorest and least educated sectors of Philippine society (AMC 1991; French 1986a). Moreover, although subject to wider global political and economic patterns over which they have little control, foreign domestic workers do not view themselves as passive pawns, although they often feel unempowered, subordinated, and subservient. For every domestic worker who expresses a sense of being propelled by circumstances, there are others who stress their choice in going to Hong Kong, in selecting a particular recruitment agency, and in remaining with or accepting a particular employer. They do so, in many cases, not because they are literally forced to but because they "choose to" for the sake of their parents, their children, their families, the adventure of life in Hong Kong, and their own future. This perception of the situation, however, is but one of many possible constructions of reality.

I have tried to show that no matter how "accommodating" domestic workers may at times appear, they are not completely passive. Even the most downtrodden slaves and prisoners exhibit some "resistance," even if only in the form of accommodation to their masters' or captors' demands for the sake of survival (Scott 1990). Some theoretical perspectives emphasize workers as willing and active agents; others, as oppressed victims of unscrupulous agencies and governments. But foreign domestic workers, on the whole, cannot be described either as passive pawns of exploitation or as active subjects who successfully resist control and discipline.

Many of the negative images associated with foreign domestic workers and many of the harshest forms of discipline they endure resemble those experienced by muijai ninety years ago. Yet, however useful such historical precedents are to help understand the maltreatment of foreign domestic workers in Hong Kong today, history does not provide a full explanation. The experiences of foreign workers are significantly different from those of muijai. Today rules, laws, and policies exist that both restrict and empower foreign workers in different ways. And many of the negative images of foreign domestic workers have taken on new racial overtones that did not apply to amahs and muijai.

Foreign domestic workers in Hong Kong, I contend, are not simply subject to institutionalized power (see also Abu-Lughod 1990; Foucault 1978:95–96; Groves and Chang 2002; Haynes and Prakash 1991; A. Ong 1991; Ortner 1995). Rather, they are implicated in a field of discursive power in which they both contest and contribute to alternative versions of reality. Domestic workers express humor and use secret languages that their employers do not understand; they have ways of circumventing the employer's rules; and they even practice subtle forms of "sabotage" of their work (cf. Scott 1985). Although many of these forms of resistance take place on a discursive level, they provide a domestic worker with at least a temporary sense of satisfaction, pleasure, or empowerment.

Discursive forms of resistance—unlike strikes, rallies, or public demonstrations—often go unrecognized by employers. Bilingual jokes that equate Chinese employers with monkeys, for example, do little to alter the structural relationship between employer and domestic worker, or even the worker's perception of it, especially since the employer interprets such disparaging remarks as an expression of politeness or a sign of accommodation. Through such behavior, like other forms of deference behavior, a domestic worker expresses both an understanding and a critique of the existing power structure, but she simultaneously conforms to her employer's desires.

In most cases scholars insist that deference behaviors are "protective disguises" that enable workers to "conform to employers' expectations and shield their real feelings" (Cock 1980:7–8, 103; Rollins 1985:168–70). "Uncle Tom" performances, Judith Rollins says, do not mean that workers view their subordinate position as acceptable, necessary, or natural, as some have suggested (e.g., Newby 1979).[1] Following Hortense Powdermaker (1943:750–58), Rollins views the domestic workers' "meek, humble, and unaggressive" demeanor as a "culturally approved adaptation to a powerless situation." The African American domestic worker who "Uncle Toms"

> *derives pleasure* from the performance. This "unaggressive aggressiveness" yields two kinds of psychological rewards: appeasement of guilt and a sense of superiority. If she is a Christian . . . she believes it is sinful to hate; acting meekly, even lovingly, relieves her of the guilt she feels for these "conscious and unconscious feelings of hostility and aggression toward white people." Additionally, this role may make the domestic feel superior in these ways: hers will be the final victory in the hereafter; she is demonstrating that she is spiritually superior to her employer; and she *enjoys* the success of being able to fool whites. (Rollins 1985:169, emphasis added)

Like Jacklyn Cock (1980:7–8), Rollins stresses that the deferential performance *does not* lessen the performer's sense of exploitation (250) and that it is "a performance of the powerless that pleases those who keep them without power" (251). Such performances exist, according to Rollins, because they are required or rewarded by employers and because they provide psychological rewards (170). As James C. Scott notes, deferential behaviors that are turned on and off at will are intentional and should not be read as indications that the performers believe themselves to be inferior (1990:23–36). As one of Powdermaker's informants told her, "When I'm around them [whites], I act like they are more than I am. I don't think they are, but they do" (Powdermaker 1943:754).

---

1. Like Rollins, Jacklyn Cock argues that South African domestic workers "do not accept the legitimacy of their own subordination in the social order. On the contrary, they have a high consciousness of exploitation; . . . and considerable insight into the structures which maintain their subordination" (1980:7–8).

Deferential behaviors clearly illustrate the problem with examining power simply on the level of social relations or of viewing resistance as overtly transformative. According to Scott, however, deference behaviors may be rewarding: "What may look from above like the extraction of a required performance can easily look from below like the artful manipulation of deference and flattery to achieve its own ends" (1990:34). Although an awareness of deference behaviors alters our understanding of the formulation of power, it does not alter the *apparent* structure of the relationship between employer and worker. The employer continues to view the worker as subordinate, and the worker confirms her lower status by her behavior, although she may derive pleasure from her ability to fool her employer.

Another way to view deferential behavior is as both resistance, in the sense of cultural critique from which the performer derives pleasure, and as accommodation or acquiescence, in the sense that the behavior complies with the employer's objectives. Deferential behavior can be said to raise the question of the "naturalness" of a domestic worker's presumed inferiority. It thus transforms her status or at the very least points to a disjuncture between the power and identity the employer thinks she or he has vis-à-vis the worker and the worker's own view of reality.[2] Yet deferential behavior is also a form of accommodation inasmuch as it outwardly conforms to the employer's desires.

Although it is understood that more overt forms of protest can lead to social change, the efficacy of subtle behavioral or discursive forms of resistance to effect change is less clear. As Aihwa Ong (1991) maintains in regard to women factory workers in Malaysia and Taiwan, discursive forms of resistance may indeed transform a situation. Factory workers have often contested "hegemonic categories of human worth" and have attempted, in Allan Pred's words, "to seize language for their own purposes," engaging in "symbolic struggles over social position, identity and self-determination" (1990:46–47). They have thus found voices to "validate their actual experiences, breaking the flow of meanings imposed on them, and thus directly defining their own lives" (A. Ong 1991:300). Third World women factory workers have created "oppositional tactics" and "alternative interpretations and images" (296) to the discourses

2. This is like the retelling of their history by outcaste Bhuinyas in eastern India, which Prakash (1990, 1991) says renders their subordinate status "cultural" rather than "natural" and thus contests the dominant view of their identity. Yet unlike the narratives that reconstruct Bhuinya history and identity, yet fall short of questioning their subordination vis-à-vis higher castes, deferential behavior transforms the domestic worker's status.

produced by transnational companies, which "disassemble" women workers, "reassemble" them as commodities, and define them as "low grade" and "docile" (293).

I suggest that foreign domestic workers may have found voices to validate their own experiences but that their overall success in transforming either the public meanings or the conditions associated with their work has not been overwhelming. One reason is that domestic workers often try to live up to their employers' ideals rather than to contest them. They frequently strive to become "ideal workers" who resemble the hegemonic image of the Chinese amah as a "superior servant."

As we have seen, many Filipinas spend their free time participating in activities that help them to "forget" that they are maids. Rather than focus their energy on union activities or on attempts to transform their work, many prefer "less political" Filipino clubs and organizations. Birthday parties, organized outings, and picnics are entertaining and give domestic workers something fun to look forward to during the work week. They seek ways to "escape" the negative aspects of their occupation. Glamorous beauty contests, elegant cultural performances, and highly structured and publicized sports competitions organized by church and community groups also serve as a means to contest negative stereotypes. Such activities convey an image that is the antithesis of poor, backward, uncultured, promiscuous, and immoral maids. Thus, even while women "do something different," or seek pleasure and excitement to escape the stigma of their occupation for a few hours, they may also be contesting certain negative images.

Moreover, like industrial workers and domestic workers in other regions of the world, many foreign domestic workers in Hong Kong express a desire to be treated with dignity by their employers and by the wider public (Coley 1981; A. Ong 1991:296–300). Yet as we have seen, they whisper admonitions to compatriots and coworkers, imploring them to work harder, to complain less, and to behave better. Their everyday forms of resistance are geared toward surviving the situation with their sense of humanity intact. They rarely undermine or alter the underlying structural conflicts of domestic work in Hong Kong because unlike factory work, domestic work is performed in the isolation of the individual household at the behest of many different employers. Alternative discourses about domestic work are expressed most strongly on Sundays, away from employers' homes. On the shop floor, factory workers share the same conditions and are directly exposed to their coworkers protests, but domestic workers are isolated from their coworkers and their individual forms of protest appear diffused and fragmented when recollected on Sundays.[3]

Even in some striking and important instances when domestic workers' activism has brought about change—as in Filipina opposition to forced remittance and to the ban on new contracts—the degree of change reflects the limits imposed by self-discipline. In their opposition to Philippine Executive Order 857 on forced remittance, for example, Filipina domestic worker organizations demanded that the amount of the forced remittance be reduced to 25 or 30 percent but not that the order be revoked. Only with the persistent encouragement of Agapito Aquino (Benigno Aquino's younger brother) and the growing opposition to Marcos in the Philippines did the demands escalate. The Marcos opposition had much to gain from the support of overseas workers. Workers scored a victory, but within limits. They gained a greater choice of how and how much money to remit, and they could avoid the 10 percent cut that the Philippine government took on remittances sent through official Philippine bank channels, but the need to work overseas in the first place and the need to remit money remained relatively unaffected.

The protest against President Aquino's ban on approval of new contracts for Filipino domestic workers in 1988 is even more to the point. Although it was designed to prevent abuse of overseas domestic workers, it was these very workers who opposed it as infringing on their freedom to choose their work. They might, for example, have supported the ban and linked revocation to the repeal of the two-week rule. Had they done so, or perhaps enacted a supportive strike, they might have lost their jobs altogether. Chinese employers would have viewed Filipinas as ungrateful, unappreciative, and unworthy, and they might have replaced them with workers of other nationalities who would "appreciate" employment. Instead of using the ban to promote better work conditions, Filipina domestic workers demanded that Aquino allow them to continue to work in Hong Kong. In the end Hong Kong was exempted from the ban without any concessions, on the basis of its "good record"—a good record that domestic workers were not willing to contest.[4]

3. As Foucault has written, "Solitude is the primary condition of total submission" (1979:237).

4. Similar opposition was expressed by domestic workers to the "protective bans" and age limits proposed by the Philippine government as a result of the execution of Flor Contemplacion in Singapore and the sentencing of Sarah Balabagan in the United Arab Emirates in 1995. As noted at the end of Chapter 4, in January and February 2007, Filipino domestic workers and activists in Hong Kong and Manila marched in protest of certain aspects of

In the 1980s and early 1990s, domestic workers' conditions in Hong Kong improved in terms of salary and in terms of Philippine government controls on remittances and customs taxes, in large part because of worker activism. But domestic work continued to be viewed as a lowly and demeaning occupation, and the louder the voices of protest, the stronger the criticisms of Filipinas became. Abuse cases continued to increase in the early 1990s, and both the Hong Kong government and employers maintained a high level of control over domestic workers through the two-week rule. As employers were quick to forecast and as domestic workers constantly warned one another, wage demands cannot be too high, or workers will price themselves out of the market. Conditions cannot be too good or employers will cease to hire them.

In fact, domestic worker salaries could have increased by HK$600 a month in 1993 without any significant or discernible decrease in the number of jobs. Even with the HK$300 per month salary hike, the number of foreign domestic workers in Hong Kong increased by over ten thousand in 1994 and another ten thousand in 1995. Yet the majority of domestic workers, well acquainted with women who would work in Hong Kong for much less than the stipulated minimum wage, were not willing to risk their jobs. Thus higher salary demands were undermined by economic insecurity and by the powerful discourse of domestic workers who called for passivity, docility, and a heightened sense of gratitude, personal appreciation, and politeness toward their Hong Kong "hosts."

Efforts to professionalize and upgrade the image of domestic work have not been very successful. Throughout the 1980s and 1990s the popular image of Filipina domestic workers became increasingly critical and derogatory. Criticism of their work, personal habits, and morals were increasingly heard. In the following decade, however, even as Hong Kong's economy weakened and the government promoted retraining programs for local

---

the new POEA guidelines pertaining to Household Service Workers (HSW). The Philippine government promoted the new guidelines as beneficial to overseas workers, but many domestic workers and worker advocates considered them yet another indication of the government's disregard for overseas workers' real interests. Following the outburst of criticism from workers and activists, the POEA agreed to reduce the proposed minimum age of HSWs from twenty-five to twenty-three. Whereas many activists supported the proposed universal minimum wage for overseas HSWs at US$400 per month, Hong Kong workers were more ambivalent since this was below the 2006 FDH minimum wage of HK$3,400 (US$436). The point in the new guidelines that infuriated domestic workers and advocates most was the requirement for mandatory cultural and language training. Protestors viewed this as yet another form of "government extortion" and another way to "milk the maids" (APMM 2007; UNIFIL 2007).

women, the overall numbers of foreign domestic workers continues to increase. The Hong Kong public, moreover, continues to consider overseas women workers—by virtue of their economic status, their ethnic/national identity, and their gender—most appropriate to perform degrading, yet necessary full-time and live-in household work and caring for children, the elderly, and the disabled.

One main factor that undermines political activism among foreign domestic workers in Hong Kong is the fear of being replaced by cheaper and more docile workers from elsewhere. In the mid-1990s, President Ramos received repeated verbal assurances from the Chinese government that Filipina domestic workers would be allowed to remain in Hong Kong after reunification in 1997, but at the time such assurances meant little. From the vantage point of the mid 1990s, it seemed that if Filipinas were to remain in Hong Kong in the twenty-first century, they would still be maids—proud domestic workers with "good" working conditions perhaps, but still living away from home and still outsiders working for the local elite. In urging Ramos to be assertive, domestic workers were ultimately asking not for equality but for the right to continue to be "domestic helpers" in a foreign land. If they were to be replaced by cheaper or more docile workers in the years to come (as has been the case with Indonesian workers), then the smaller battles they won in Hong Kong might have few long-lasting effects. That is why in the mid-1990s Filipinas like Elsa, Belle, and Acosta wanted to earn while they could and then get out. From the pre-1997 perspective it seemed that upcoming political changes might demonstrate just how little power foreign workers and their organizations really had.

The problem is not that foreign domestic workers lack class consciousness or an awareness of the historical context in which they live and work. Many Filipinos are all too aware of previous migrations, of the problems with the Philippine economy, and of the global patterns that propel them in unforeseen directions. They do not hesitate to criticize the Philippine government for failing to boost the economy in order to create more jobs at home. The problem is that despite the important improvements that domestic workers' organizations have helped bring about, the overall structural position of domestic workers remains relatively unchanged. They still work overseas at jobs that Hong Kong locals have rejected and for which their training and abilities overqualify them. Filipinas and other foreign domestic workers are, in essence, struggling for the right to continue to do menial work under exploitative conditions.

From my mid-1990s vantage point, I concluded that after Hong Kong, perhaps it will be Europe or Canada for the younger domestic workers like Dally and Cathy, or perhaps Taiwan or Singapore for those like Elsa and Acosta who prefer to remain closer to home. There they will encounter slightly different rules and regulations—in Singapore mandatory pregnancy tests every six months, in Canada higher educational requirements—but the game is the same: work hard, earn money, and remit it home. Domestic workers seemed aware of some of the structures of power, but their protests did not seem to touch or address the more pervasive local and global structures. By and large, resistance remained on a discursive level, expressed quietly and as a form of personal release.

Lila Abu-Lughod has posed the question of how to account for situations in which people appear both to resist and to support systems of power "without resorting to analytic concepts of false consciousness, which dismisses their own understanding of their situation, or impression management, which makes of them cynical manipulators" (1990:47). Domestic workers who accommodate to the demands of their work or "put on" deferential behavior for their employers are not simply "cynical manipulators." They are both exerting power and simultaneously being dominated by it. This understanding of a domestic worker's behavior, whether consciously deferential or unconscious but "necessarily conditioned by hegemony," forces us to alter our view of the larger picture of power (cf. Haynes and Prakash 1991:11).

The forms of discipline that domestic workers appear to "buy into" are not an indication of "false consciousness" or cultural "coercion" and "oppression." Women strive to become "superior" domestic workers for their own reasons as well. As Abu-Lughod, following Foucault, suggests, "Power is something that works not just negatively, by denying, restricting, prohibiting, or repressing, but also positively, by producing forms of pleasure, systems of knowledge, goods, and discourses" (1990:42). Following this line of reasoning, we can begin to see how Filipina domestic workers derive pleasure, or at least some satisfaction, from attempts to organize their work better and maximize their productivity, to get along better with employers, and to "professionalize" their image, even at the cost of becoming ever more obedient and hardworking. Their work, after all, is what allows them to remain in Hong Kong, a wealthy and modern cosmopolitan place that excites their imaginations while extracting their labor.

AFTERWORD

In 2007, I am struck by what has changed and by what has remained the same for foreign domestic workers in Hong Kong. In the earlier version of this book I wrote, "as long as the local economy remains strong . . . foreign domestic workers will face little competition from local workers." I also suggested that Filipinas might be replaced by "cheaper or more docile workers from another country" or by "mainland Chinese workers." At the time few had properly anticipated the Asian financial crisis and the global economic downturn, or the impact of SARS on Hong Kong's economy. As we have seen, however, despite the Hong Kong government's active promotion of local domestic workers, so far they pose little threat to the livelihood of foreign domestic workers because they fill a different niche. Local workers are unlikely to become full-time or live-in workers. Their employers, moreover, do not want or need or cannot afford the help of full-time domestic workers. As long as there are employers who require the labor of live-in workers and as long as local women are unwilling to fill that role, the market for full-time and live-in foreign workers will continue.

Nor have mainland Chinese women entered the market in any significant way. Given the challenge they would pose to Hong Kong's immigration policy, this is unlikely to happen in the near future. But other foreign women who are viewed as "cheaper and more docile" than Filipinas have indeed increased in number. The number of Indonesian domestic workers (rather than Thai women as many predicted in 1994) has grown exponentially since my earlier research. In 2006 they constitute almost half of Hong Kong's foreign domestic workers. Filipinas still constitute over half of Hong Kong's foreign domestic workers (their figures remaining well over a hundred thousand), but overall their numbers have dropped to close to their 1994 levels after reaching a peak of over 150,000 in 2001.[5] Several surveys of Indonesian domestic workers suggest, moreover, that Indonesians

5. As I noted in the first edition and in a later article, 1997 prompted some Filipina domestic workers, such as Elsa and Belle, to finally make the decision to return home. Belle left Hong Kong in 1996. She got married, had a child, and later started a small telecommunications business for migrant workers. Elsa went to work for a migrant worker NGO in Manila. Both of their younger sisters became domestic workers in Italy. Others, like Jane—who has since become a grandmother—have gone on to work as caregivers in Canada. Molly moved to Macao when her employer relocated there, and Fely remarried and moved to Canada with her Canadian husband (see Constable 1999 and 2003b).

overwhelmingly suffer from severe underpayment of wages, overcharging of employment fees, and a variety of other abuses.

Another thing that has not changed is the disadvantaged status of foreign domestic workers as temporary migrants. Despite two decades of persistent and vigorous protest against the New Conditions of Stay, the two-week rule is still in effect and still serves as a marker of the lack of rights and privileges accorded to immigrant workers relative to both local workers and foreign "professionals" in Hong Kong. Foreign domestic workers are welcome to come to Hong Kong to care for the young, the elderly, and the disabled within the intimate spaces of the home, and they are welcome to clean and cook and partake in physical and emotional labor that is essential to reproduce the lifestyle of Hong Kong's middle class, but they are prohibited from becoming permanent residents of Hong Kong, to retire there and enjoy its benefits or social services, or to bring their family members there with them. Nor are they free to change employers without first returning home. The two-week rule, as discussed in Chapter 6, compounds the vulnerability of foreign domestic workers because if they are laid off, they must return home within two weeks—usually for several months—before they can come back to work again. Many prefer to put up with poor or illegal working conditions rather than suffer the financial hardship of pursuing legal action or returning home.

The decrease in the minimum wage and the government-imposed levy for retraining local domestic workers were changes I had not anticipated in 1997. Whereas the minimum wage for foreign domestic workers increased fairly steadily from 1986 to 1996, since the mid-1990s the increases became few and far between and the government imposed two substantial wage decreases in 1999 and 2003 (see Figure 6.1). From 2003 until 2006, despite the Hong Kong government's claims of economic recovery, the minimum allowable wage is still lower than it was a decade earlier, and it remains well below the 1996–98 peak of $3,860. Whereas in 1993 domestic workers rallied to demand a HK$600 per month increase to match inflation, and many were sorely disappointed to receive only HK$300, by 2006 standards HK$300 seems generous. Activists continue to make powerful arguments for increasing the wage and for making the process for determining the minimum wage more transparent (AMCB 2004).

Yet despite such discouraging news, there are also some reasons for optimism, and today I am far more optimistic about the situation than I was a decade ago. Surveys and anecdotal evidence both show that although many of the same problems and abuses exist in Hong Kong today, Filipina domestic workers in 2006 are much better off than they were ten or fifteen years ago, and they are better off than other nationalities of foreign domestic workers. Whereas 58 percent of Filipinas received the minimum wage in 1986, 99 percent received it in 2001, compared with 52 percent of Indonesians and 91 percent of Thais (Wee and Sim 2004: 20–21; AMC 2001; French 1986a). Filipinas are most likely to receive the legal wage (or higher), and they are also far more likely to get four rest days a month than Indonesians. According to the breakdown of the nationalities of residents of domestic shelters, Filipinas are also less likely to suffer from various forms of physical and emotional abuse than Indonesians. And although the numbers of Filipina workers have declined from their peak, over 100,000 Filipina domestic workers remain in Hong Kong, and the vast majority of their employers abide by the legal conditions of their contracts.

In contrast to older views of migrant workers as passive, powerless victims of globalization, many recent studies have attended to both subtle and overt expressions of empowerment and agency. In the case of foreign domestic workers in Hong Kong, the growing importance of collective action is especially evident. Scholars have identified several factors that have helped to empower Filipina domestic workers individually and collectively (Wee and Sim 2004; Yamanaka and Piper 2005). In a comparison of the gains for Filipinas relative to the problems faced by Indonesian domestic workers in Hong Kong, Wee and Sim (2004:13–14) make four important observations:

1. The Philippine government has done a better job of regulating and overseeing recruitment practices than the Indonesian government.
2. Filipinas have a higher rate of education and literacy than Indonesians in general and are far more likely to be literate in English, thus enabling them to read employment contracts and Hong Kong government polices pertaining to foreign workers.
3. Civil society is more extensive and developed in the Philippines than in Indonesia, and there are many more Philippine NGOs and advocacy groups concerned with the welfare of migrant workers (see also Law 2002; Piper 2005; Sim 2003; Yamanaka and Piper 2005).
4. Labor migration from the Philippines is a long-term phenomenon (becoming common in the late 1970s), whereas the main increase in Indonesian labor migration began only after 1997, during the Asian financial crisis (2004:14).

The long-term process of Filipino labor migration has helped to facilitate the development of greater knowledge and more extensive informal and formal networks. Mobile phones—ubiquitous among Filipinas by 2005—have also played an important role in facilitating (often subtle) communication and support networks. Over the past decade and a half, Filipinas have gained a greater ability to control the complex and challenging processes of recruitment and employment.

Many of the lessons that Filipina workers and activists have learned over the years are also beneficial to other nationalities of foreign domestic workers. The majority of women who go to the mission (now tellingly renamed the Mission for Migrant Workers) and to the mission-run domestic shelter are Indonesian. In ever-growing numbers, Indonesian domestic workers have begun to seek assistance and to assert their rights. Indonesian domestic workers' associations, organizations, and labor unions are growing and multiplying. Indonesian workers' participation in rallies and marches is visibly increasing and becoming more enthusiastic and creative as well.

As other scholars have noted, the alliances between different nationalities of domestic workers and even between foreign workers and local ones—fragile though they may be at times—are noteworthy and also cause for optimism (Law 2002; Piper 2005; Wee and Sim 2004, 2005). Local workers may at times blame foreign workers for "stealing their rice bowl," but some have nonetheless supported foreign domestic workers' demands for wage increases, and they have expressed support and solidarity toward foreign workers who have suffered abuse and injury. Moreover, many different nationalities of migrant workers (not only domestic workers), come together on an increasingly regular basis to support rallies that are organized by the Asian Migrant Coordinating Body, the Coalition for Migrant Rights, the Hong Kong Confederation of Trade Unions, and many other groups. These groups point to the importance of migrant NGOs in promoting migrant rights, and in labor unions in beginning to recognize the shared interests of local and migrant workers.

Given the proliferation of migrant worker organizations in Hong Kong over the years, it would be naïve to expect that they would always agree on issues (e.g., APMM 2005; Sim 2003). Divisions between Filipino organizations risk being remapped onto Indonesian affiliate groups, thus potentially threatening what would otherwise constitute a united front of migrant workers. It is therefore especially striking and encouraging that Filipinas who are employed in Hong Kong do not express hostility, resentment, or competition toward Indonesian workers. Filipinas—to my surprise in 2005 and 2006—did not regard Indonesians as poaching on their own or their compatriots' employment opportunities. On the contrary, Indonesians are regarded as fellow migrant workers who face similar challenges and who can potentially benefit from the knowledge and experience of Filipino predecessors. Filipinas and Indonesians (as well as other foreign and local workers) all stand to benefit from improved work conditions. If all foreign workers recognize and assert their legal rights, there will be no underclass of subservient workers for exploitative or abusive employers to turn to.

Filipino domestic worker activists have clearly influenced other nationalities of workers in Hong Kong. They have also influenced Philippine national politics. Former domestic workers who were members or officers of UNIFIL have gone on to found the Migrante political party in the Philippines and to work for activist organizations and NGOs in the Philippines. In July 2006 close to four hundred Filipinas from a wide spectrum of organizations—ranging from normally conservative and apolitical religious groups to activist groups—numbering ninety-eight groups in all, participated in a daylong summit. The summit included a speech by a former domestic worker and the chairperson of the activist organization Migrante International on the impact of globalization on Philippine government policies and migration. The participants unanimously passed resolutions that would be presented during President Gloria Macapagal-Arroyo's July 2006 State of the Nation address. These resolutions ranged from improving the work conditions in Hong Kong and the conditions for migrant returnees to opposing the rash of murders of leftist activists, journalists, politicians, and clergy in the Philippines in 2006.

As was blatantly apparent at the anti-WTO protest in December 2005, the local and international networks of current and former domestic worker activists and NGO staff continue to grow, creating networks with labor activists and union members across the globe. Although politically active domestic workers and union members constitute but a tiny percentage of domestic workers overall, the issues that they care about are much broader and more far-reaching than a decade ago. As the number of domestic worker–related organizations and NGOs in Hong Kong have burgeoned and multiplied, some organizations have relocated staff or created new branches and affiliates in South Korea, Japan, Taiwan, and Macau. NGO staff members and domestic worker activists and worker advocates are now increasingly involved in conducting research, forming transnational networks, and attempting to define and influence policy making.

In the twenty-first century, foreign domestic workers in Hong Kong still constitute a small piece of a growing global pattern of gendered migration and inequality. Women from the poorer regions of the world continue to leave their homes and families behind to work as temporary migrants in the wealthier regions of the world, and they continue to do the less desirable work that will benefit the more privileged and the elite. Although, as I have shown, the situation in Hong Kong is not ideal, it is nonetheless far better than in many other places, and it continues to be a most favored destination for migrant workers. This is due in part to legal policies and employment protections that exist (at least in theory) in Hong Kong. But it is also due to the painstaking and persistent efforts of domestic workers and domestic worker activists to assert migrant workers' rights.

REFERENCES

Abu-Lughod, Lila. 1986. *Veiled Sentiments: Honor and Poetry in a Bedouin Society.* Berkeley: University of California Press.

——. 1990. The Romance of Resistance: Tracing Transformations of Power through Bedouin Women. *American Ethnologist* 17(1):41–55.

Adams, Kathleen M., and Sara Dickey, eds. 2000. *Home and Hegemony: Domestic Service and Identity Politics in South and Southeast Asia.* Ann Arbor: University of Michigan Press.

Aguilar, Filomeno V., Jr. 1983. The Agrarian Proletariat in the Rice-Growing Areas of the Philippines. *Philippine Studies* 31(3):338–66.

Anderson, Bridget. 2000. *Doing the Dirty Work? The Global Politics of Domestic Labour.* London: Zed Press.

Andres, A. 1984. Conditions, Problems, Prospects, and Policy Issues of Overseas Employment: The Case of the Filipino Domestic Helpers in Hong Kong and Japan. *Jōchi Ajia-gaku: Journal of Sophia Asian Studies* 2. Institute of Asian Cultures, Sophia University, Tokyo.

Appadurai, Arjun. 1991. Global Ethnoscapes: Notes and Queries for a Transnational Anthropology. *Recapturing Anthropology: Working in the Present,* ed. Richard Fox, 191–210. Santa Fe, N.M.: School of American Research Press.

Aquino, Febe Grace. 1993. Chicken in Dress. *TF* (October):49.

Arellano, Teddy P. 1992. Statue Square a "Home away from Home." *SCMP* 14 October.

Armstrong, M. Jocelyn. 1990. Female Household Workers in Industrializing Malaysia. *At Work in Homes: Household Workers in World Perspective,* ed. Roger Sanjek and Shellee Colen, 146–63. American Ethnological Society Monograph Series 3. Washington, D.C.: American Ethnological Society.

Asato, Wako. 2004. Negotiating Spaces in the Labor Market: Foreign and Local Domestic Workers in Hong Kong. *Asian and Pacific Migration Journal* 13(2):255–74.

Asian Migrant Centre (AMC). 1991. *Foreign Domestic Workers in Hong Kong: A Baseline Study*. Hong Kong: Asian Migrant Workers Centre.

———. 1992a. *Foreign Domestic Helpers in Hong Kong: Assistance Manual*. Hong Kong: AMC.

———. 1992b. Foreign Domestic Workers, Needed but out of Sight—A Dilemma. *Asian Migrant Forum* 5:24.

———. 1992c. Philippines: Making the Export of Labor Really Temporary. *Asian Migrant Forum* 6:19–20.

———. 2001. *Baseline Research on Gender and Racial Discrimination Towards Filipino, Indonesian and Thai Domestic Helpers in Hong Kong*. Hong Kong: AMC, ADWU, Forum of Filipino Reintegration and Savings Groups, IMWU, and Thai Women's Association.

———. 2004. *Asian Migrant Yearbook 2004: Migration Facts, Analysis and Issues in 2003*. Hong Kong: AMC and Migrant Forum in Asia.

———. 2005. *Underpayment: Systematic Extortion of Indonesian Migrant Workers in Hong Kong. An In Depth Study of Indonesian Labor Migration in Hong Kong*. Hong Kong: AMC.

Asia Pacific Mission for Migrant Filipinos. 1991. Factors, Trends, and Prospects Affecting Labour Outmigration. *APMMF News Digest* 5(1):25–27.

Asia Pacific Mission for Migrants (APMM). 2005. On the Opposing Views on the Wage Struggle of Foreign Domestic Workers in Hong Kong. 17 March. Available at http://www.apmigrants.org/papers/07.htm. Accessed August 17, 2006.

———. 2007. New POEA Training Scheme: A New Racket for Extortion, a New Burden for Filipino Domestic Workers. 16 January. Available at http://www.apmigrants.org/papers/12.htm. Accessed February 22, 2007.

Asiaweek. 1987. Hongkong's Maid's Debate. *Asiaweek* 10 May, 72.

Asis, Maruja M. B. 2003. Asian Women Migrants: Going the Distance, But Not Far Enough. *Migration Information Source*. March 1, 2003. Available at http://www.migrationinformation.org/Feature/print.cfm?ID=103. Accessed June 1, 2006.

Asis, Maruja M. B., Shirlena Huang, and Brenda S. A. Yeoh. 2004. When the Light of the Home Is Abroad: Unskilled Female Migration and the Filipino Family. *Singapore Journal of Tropical Geography* 25(2):198–214.

Association of Indonesian Migrant Workers in Hong Kong (ATKI). 2001. The Condition of Indonesian Migrant Workers in Hong Kong. Hong Kong: ATKI.

———. 2005. Second Survey on the Conditions of Indonesian Migrant Workers in Hong Kong. Hong Kong: ATKI.

Atkinson, Julie. 1992. Clean Your Own Backyards First. *SCMP* 18 September.

Autor, Edith. 1991. There Is a Season . . . *TF* (August):4.

Bakan, Abigail B., and Daiva Stasiulis. 1995. Making the Match: Domestic Placement Agencies and the Racialization of Women's Household Work. *Signs* 20(2):303–35.

Baker, Hugh. 1966. The Five Great Clans of the New Territories. *Journal of the Hong Kong Branch of the Royal Asiatic Society* 6:25–47.

———. 1968. *A Chinese Lineage Village: Sheung Shui*. London: Frank Cass.

Basabica, Annabelle. 1993. The Way We Wear in Summer. *TF* (May):37.

Basso, Keith. 1979. *Portraits of "the Whiteman": Linguistic Play and Cultural Symbols among the Western Apache.* New York: Cambridge University Press.

Batha, Emma, and Victoria Finlay. 1994. Woman Appeals against Conviction for Branding: Stripping Maid Naked. *SCMP* 24 June.

Begonia, Angie R. 1990. Double Murder. *TF* (April):41.

Benitez, Mary Ann. 1988. Ban on Filipino Maids Tougher Than Expected. *SCMP* 28 January.

Bickers, Robert A., and Jeffrey N. Wasserstrom. 1995. Shanghai's "Dogs and Chinese Not Admitted" Sign: Legend, History, and Contemporary Symbol. *China Quarterly* 142 (June): 444–66.

Blackburn, Susan. 2004. *Women and the State in Modern Indonesia.* Cambridge: Cambridge University Press.

Blanco, Gina E. 1993. When Everything Else Fails . . . Try Hard Work. *TF* (June):22.

BMP. 1993. On Salary Increase, Rest Hour at Iba Pa. *TF* (October):8–10.

Boase, Melville. 1989. The Two-Weeks Rule for Foreign Domestic Helper. *HK Staff* 13 July, 24 August.

——. 1991. The Two-Weeks Rule in the Context of the Legal Position of Foreign Domestic Helpers (FDHs). *Serving One Another: Report of the Consultation on the Mission and Ministry to Filipino Migrant Workers in Hong Kong,* app. 10:85–94. Hong Kong: Christian Conference of Asia, Urban Rural Mission.

——. n.d. Migrant Workers—Government Policies as Seen to Work in Practice. Unpublished speech. MFMW Files.

Boon, James A. 1974. Anthropology and Nannies. *Man* 9:137–40.

Boserup, Ester. 1970. *Woman's Role in Economic Development.* New York: St. Martin's Press.

Boston, Vonnie. 1993. Filipinos Looking Forward to Sunday Market. *SCMP* 15 April.

Bourdieu, Pierre. 1977. *Outline of a Theory of Practice.* Cambridge: Cambridge University Press.

Brandes, Stanley. 1980. *Metaphors of Masculinity: Sex and Status in Andalusian Folklore.* Philadelphia: University of Pennsylvania Press.

Briones, L. M. 1985. Roots of the Present Crisis; Internal and External Forces Crucial in the Crisis. *Foreign Capital and the Philippine Crisis,* ed. Rosalinda Pineda-Ofreneo, 2–7, 25–29. Quezon City: University of the Philippines Press.

Calagione, John, Doris Francis, and Daniel Nugent, eds. 1992. *Workers' Expressions: Beyond Accommodation and Resistance.* New York: State University of New York Press.

Campano, Toto. 1993. Do You Want to Be Successful? *TF* (January):25.

Carino, Benjamin V. 1987. The Philippines and Southeast Asia: Historical Roots and Contemporary Linkages. *Pacific Bridges: The New Immigration from Asia and the Pacific Islands,* ed. J. T. Fawcett and B. V. Carino, 305–25. New York: Center for Migration Studies.

Catholic Institute for International Relations (CIIR). 1987. *The Labour Trade: Filipino Migrant Workers around the World.* London: CIIR.

Chan, Mimi, and Helen Kwok. 1990 [1985], *A Study of Lexical Borrowing from Chinese into English with Special Reference to Hong Kong.* Hong Kong University: Centre of Asian Studies.

Chan, Raymond. 1992. Potential for Unique Flea Market. *SCMP* 18 September.

Chaney, Elsa M., and Maria Garcia Castro, eds. 1989. *Muchachas No More: Household Workers in Latin America and the Caribbean.* Philadelphia: Temple University Press.

Chang, Kimberly A., and Julian M. Groves. 2000. Neither "Saints nor Prostitutes": Sexual Discourse in the Filipina Domestic Worker Community in Hong Kong. *Women's Studies International Forum* 23(1):73–87.

Chaplin, David. 1978. Domestic Service and Industrialization. *Comparative Studies in Sociology* 1:97–127.

Cheng, Ada S.-J. 2003. Rethinking Globalization of Domestic Service: Foreign Domestics, State Control, and the Politics of Identity in Taiwan. *Gender and Society* 17(2):166–86.

——. 2006. *Serving the Household and the Nation: Filipina Domestics and the Politics of Identity in Taiwan.* Lanham, MD: Rowman and Littlefield.

Cheng, Irene. 1976. *Clara Ho Tung: A Hong Kong Lady, Her Family, and Her Times.* Shatin, New Territories, Hong Kong: Chinese University of Hong Kong.

Childress, Alice. 1986. *Like One of the Family: Conversations from a Domestic's Life.* Boston: Beacon Press.

Chin, Christine B. N. 1998. *In Service and Servitude: Foreign Female Domestic Workers and the Malaysian "Modernity" Project.* New York: Columbia University Press.

Chong, M. S. 1985. Filipina Maids Are Spoiled . . . *SCMP* 18 June.

Chow, M. S. 1987. The Rising Tide against Domestics. *HKS* 11 May.

Chu, Victor. 1982. Saga of Filipina Maids. *HKS* 17 June.

Chugh, Sanjay. 1992. Appalled by Car-Park Suggestion. *SCMP* 21 September.

Chun, Sally (with the Hong Kong Domestic Workers General Union). 2004. Local Domestic Helpers in Hong Kong: A Vulnerable and Dispensable Lot? Hong Kong: Committee for Asian Women. Available at http://caw.jinbo.net/popups/articleswindow.php?id-39. Accessed August 15, 2006.

Clad, James. 1988. A Domestic Problem: Filipino Maids Oppose a Ban on Working Abroad. *Far Eastern Economic Review* 17 March, 18–19.

Cock, Jacklyn. 1980. *Maids and Madams: A Study in the Politics of Exploitation.* Johannesburg: Ravan Press.

Cohen, Myron. 1976. *House United, Housed Divided: The Chinese Family in Taiwan.* New York: Columbia University Press.

Colen, Shellee. 1986. "With Respect and Feelings": Voices of West Indian Child Care and Domestic Workers in New York City. *All American Women: Lives That Divide, Ties That Bind*, ed. Johnetta Cole, 46–70. New York: Free Press.

——. 1989. "Just a Little Respect": West Indian Domestic Workers in New York City. *Muchachas No More: Household Workers in Latin America and the Caribbean*, ed. Elsa M. Chaney and Maria Garcia Castro, 171–94. Philadelphia: Temple University Press.

——. 1990. "Housekeeping" for the Green Card: West Indian Household Workers, the State, and Stratified Reproduction in New York. *At Work in Homes: Household Workers in World Perspective*, ed. Roger Sanjek and Shellee Colen, 89–118. American Ethnological Society Monograph Series 3. Washington, D.C.: American Ethnological Society.

Colen, Shellee, and Roger Sanjek. 1990a. At Work in Homes, I: Directions. *At Work in Homes: Household Workers in World Perspective*, ed. Roger Sanjek and Shellee

Colen, 1–13. American Ethnological Society Monograph Series 3. Washington, D.C.: American Ethnological Society.

———. 1990b. At Work in Homes, II: Directions. *At Work in Homes: Household Workers in World Perspective*, ed. Roger Sanjek and Shellee Colen, 176–88. American Ethnological Society Monograph Series 3. Washington, D.C.: American Ethnological Society.

Coley, Soroya Moore. 1981. *And Still I Rise: An Exploratory Study of Contemporary Private Black Household Workers*. Ph.D. diss., Bryn Mawr College.

Constable, Nicole. 1993. Human Rights and the New Conditions of Stay. *Migrant Focus* 1(1):1–6.

———. 1994. *Christian Souls and Chinese Spirits: A Hakka Community in Hong Kong*. Berkeley: University of California Press.

———. 1996. Jealousy, Chastity, and Abuse: Chinese Maids and Foreign Helpers in Hong Kong. *Modern China* 22(4):448–79.

———. 1997. Sexuality and Discipline among Filipina Domestic Workers in Hong Kong. *American Ethnologist* 24(3):539–58.

———. 1999. At Home but Not at Home: Filipina Narratives of Ambivalent Returns. *Cultural Anthropology* 14(2):203–28.

———. 2000. Dolls, T-Birds, and Ideal Workers: The Negotiation of Filipino Identity in Hong Kong. *Home and Hegemony: Domestic Service and Identity Politics in South and Southeast Asia*, ed. Kathleen Adams and Sara Dickey, 221–47. Ann Arbor: University of Michigan Press.

———. 2003a. *Romance on a Global Stage: Pen Pals, Virtual Ethnography, and "Mail Order" Marriages*. Berkeley: University of California Press.

———. 2003b. A Transnational Perspective on Divorce and Marriage: Filipina Wives and Workers. *Identities: Global Studies in Culture and Power* 10:163–80.

———. 2006. Brides, Maids, and Prostitutes: Reflections on the Study of "Trafficked" Women. *Portal: Journal of Multidisciplinary International Studies* 3(2). Available at http://epress.lib.uts.edu.au/ojs/index.php/portal.

Coser, Lewis. 1973. Servants: The Obsolescence of an Occupational Role. *Social Forces* 52:31–40.

Custodio, G. 1978. Socioeconomic Profile of Landless Agricultural Labourers. Paper presented at the Workshop on Landless Workers, PCARR, Los Baños, Philippines, 8 December.

da Costa, Felipa. 1972. Amahs Aren't What They Used to Be. Hong Kong University, Hong Kong Special Collection, Political Science Clippings, 14.3(1).

dela Cruz, Julia. 1992. Wash and Wear. *Sapang Pagyuko Kawayan: A Collection of Jokes from Filipino Overseas Workers*, ed. Linda R. Layosa and Laura P. Luminarias, 109. Hong Kong: AsiaPacific.

de la Cruz, Tina. 1992. A Time to Change. *TF* (April):33.

Dill, Bonnie Thornton. 1980. The Means to Put My Children Through: Child-Rearing Goals and Strategies among Black Female Domestic Servants. *The Black Woman*, ed. LaFrances Rogers-Rose, 107–23. Beverly Hills: Sage.

———. 1988. "Making Your Job Good Yourself: Domestic Work and the Construction of Personal Dignity. *Women and the Politics of Empowerment*, ed. Ann Bookman and Sandra Morgen, 33–52. Philadelphia: Temple University Press.

——. 1994 [1979]. *Across the Boundaries of Race and Class: An Exploration of the Relationship between Work and Family among Black Female Domestic Servants.* New York: Garland.

Donnithorne, Audrey. 1992. Let Them Stay. *SCMP* 17 September.

Dorde, Vickei. 1992. Where Are Your Manners? *TF* (December):32.

Drummond, Lee. 1978. The Transatlantic Nanny: Notes on a Comparative Semiotics of the Family in English-Speaking Societies. *American Ethnologist* 5(1):30–43.

Dudden, Faye. 1983. *Serving Women: Household Service in Nineteenth-Century America.* Middleton, Conn.: Wesleyan University Press.

Dulatre, Nora. 1992a. "Ningas-Cogon" Lives On . . . *TF* (September):16.

——. 1992b. Happy Workers. *SCMP* 2 November.

Dumont, Jean-Paul. 2000. Always Home, Never Home: Visayan Helpers and Identities. *Home and Hegemony: Domestic Service and Identity Politics in South and Southeast Asia*, ed. Kathleen Adams and Sara Dickey, 119–35. Ann Arbor: University of Michigan Press.

Ebrey, Patricia. 1986. Concubines in Sung China. *Journal of Family History* 11:1–24.

Ehrenreich, Barbara, and Arlie Russell Hochschild, eds. 2003. *Global Woman: Nannies, Maids, and Sex Workers in the New Economy.* New York: Holt, Metropolitan Books.

Elliott, Elsie. 1981. Amend Laws on Filipina Maids. *SCMP* 29 September.

Endacott, G. B. 1958. *A History of Hong Kong.* London: Oxford University Press.

Escoda, Isabel T. 1989. *Letters from Hong Kong: Viewing the Colony through Philippine Eyes.* Manila: Bookmark Press.

Espinosa, Leonor. 1991. How to Be a Good Domestic Helper. *TF* (September):9.

Fairchilds, Cissie. 1984. *Domestic Enemies: Servants and Their Masters in Old Regime France.* Baltimore: Johns Hopkins University Press.

Fan Cheuk-wan. 1988. Maids Unite to Battle Manila Ban. *HKS* 28 February.

Fawcett, James T., Siew-Ean Khoo, and Peter C. Smith, eds. 1984. *Women in the Cities of Asia: Migration and Urban Adaptation.* Boulder, Colo.: Westview Press.

Fe, Aquarius. 1990. To Whom It May Concern . . . *TF* (March):32–33.

Finlay, Victoria. 1994. Second Base Earmarked for Maids. *SCMP* 24 June.

Flage, Percy. 1987. Filipina Maids Show Growing Discontent. *HKS* 5 April.

Forestier, Katherine. 1991. Picking up the Threads. *SCMP* 5 November.

Foucault, Michel. 1978. *The History of Sexuality. Vol. 1: An Introduction.* New York: Random House.

——. 1979. *Discipline and Punish: The Birth of the Prison.* New York: Vintage Books. French edition 1975.

——. 1985. *The History of Sexuality. Vol. 2: The Uses of Pleasure.* New York: Random House.

Francisco, Ma. Theresa W. 1993. Coming to Terms with Our Jobs. *TF* (June):43.

Free, Brett. 1993. "Ethnic Cleansing" Label Thrown at Objectors to Filipino Maids. *HKS* 14 January.

Freedman, Maurice, ed. 1970. *Family and Kinship in Chinese Society.* Stanford: Stanford University Press.

French, Carolyn. 1986a. *Filipina Domestic Workers in Hong Kong.* Ph.D. diss., University of Surrey.

——. 1986b. Filipina Domestic Workers in Hong Kong: A Preliminary Survey. Chinese University of Hong Kong, Centre for Hong Kong Studies, Occasional Papers 11.

Gaff, Jennifer. 1983. *The Maid's Manual*. Hong Kong: Redcoat Investments.

Gaitskell, Deborah, Judy Kimble, Moira Maconachie, and Elaine Unterhalter. 1983–84. Class, Race, and Gender: Domestic Workers in South Africa. *Review of African Political Economy* 27/28:86–106.

Gamburd, Michele R. 2000. *The Kitchen Spoon's Handle: Transnationalism and Sri Lanka's Migrant Housemaids*. Ithaca: Cornell University Press.

Gathorne-Hardy, Jonathan. 1972. *The Rise and Fall of the British Nanny*. London: Hodder and Stoughton.

Gaventa, John. 1980. *Power and Powerlessness: Quiescence and Rebellion in an Appalachian Valley*. Urbana: University of Illinois Press.

Gaw, Kenneth. 1991. *Superior Servants: The Legendary Amahs of the Far East*. Singapore: Oxford University Press.

Geertz, Clifford. 1973. Deep Play: Notes on the Balinese Cockfight. *The Interpretation of Cultures*, 412–53. New York: Basic Books.

Gelacio, Merlita Lucero. 1989. Don't Give Up. *TF* (December):20–21.

Gervacio, Emy. 1991a. Egg for Breakfast. *TF* (April):32.

——. 1991b. At the Barber Shop. *TF* (December):90.

Gilbert, Andy. 1995. Outrage at the Freeze on Maids' Pay. *SCMP* 26 September.

Giles, Tony. 1992. Filipino Domestics Have No Alternative Venue. *SCMP* 14 September.

Giles, Wenona. 1992. Gender Inequality and Resistance: The Case of Portuguese Women in London. *Anthropology Quarterly* 65(2):67–79.

Gill, Lesley. 1994. *Precarious Dependencies: Gender, Class, and Domestic Service in Bolivia*. New York: Columbia University Press.

Ginsburg, Faye D., and Rayna Rapp, eds. 1995. *Conceiving the New World Order: The Global Politics of Reproduction*. Berkeley: University of California Press.

Glenn, Evelyn Nakano. 1986. *Issei, Nisei, War Bride: Three Generations of Japanese American Women in Domestic Service*. Philadelphia: Temple University Press.

Gonzales, Mercy D. 1993. Hardwork, Patience, and Faith Equals Success. *TF* (February):23.

Gramsci, Antonio. 1971. *Selections from the Prison Notebooks*. New York: International.

Grange, Shiela. 1992. Domestics—Just Leave Things as They Are. *SCMP* 17 October.

Granger, David. 1992. What Choices Do Filipino Maids Have? *SCMP* 8 October.

Groves, Julian M., and Kimberly A. Chang. 2002. Romancing Resistance and Resisting Romance: Ethnography and the Construction of Power in the Filipina Domestic Worker Community in Hong Kong. *Filipinos in Global Migrations: At Home in the World?* ed. Filomeno V. Aguilar, Jr., 316–43. Quezon City, Philippines: Philippine Migration Research Network and Philippine Social Science Council.

Hansen, Karen Tranberg. 1989. *Distant Companions: Servants and Employers in Zambia, 1900–1985*. Ithaca: Cornell University Press.

——. 1990. Part of the Household Inventory: Men Servants in Zambia. *At Work in Homes: Household Workers in World Perspective*, ed. Roger Sanjek and Shellee Colen, 119–45. American Ethnological Society Monograph Series 3. Washington D.C.: American Ethnological Society.

——. 1992. *African Encounters with Domesticity*. New Brunswick, N.J.: Rutgers University Press.

Hardie, Alison. 1992. Domestics Can't Stay at "Home." *SCMP* 22 September.

Haynes, Douglas, and Gyan Prakash. 1991. Introduction: The Entanglement of Power and Resistance. *Contesting Power: Resistance and Everyday Social Relations in South Asia*, ed. Douglas Haynes and Gyan Prakash, 1–22. Berkeley: University of California Press.

Hecht, Jean. 1956. *The Domestic Servant Class in Eighteenth-Century England*. London: Routledge and Kegan Paul.

Hicks, Andrew. 1981. Filipina Maids Get a Bad Deal. *SCMP* 1 July.

——. 1982. Filipina Domestic Workers in Hong Kong. Unpublished Report. Hong Kong University Special Collections.

——. 1983. Waiting for Word on Policy Review over Admission of Foreign Domestics. *SCMP* 6 January.

Ho It Chong. 1958. The Cantonese Domestic Amah: A Study of a Small Occupational Group of Chinese Women. Research Paper, University of Malaya [Singapore].

Hondagneu-Sotelo, Pierette. 2001. *Doméstica: Immigrant Workers Cleaning and Caring in the Shadows of Affluence*. Berkeley: University of California Press.

Hong Kong Census and Statistics Department. 1990. *Social Data Collected by the General Household Survey*. Special Topics Report 6. Hong Kong: Census and Statistics Department.

——. 1991. *Hong Kong Social and Economic Trends, 1980–1990*. Hong Kong: Census and Statistics Department.

——. 1993. *Hong Kong—25 Years' Development Presented in Statistical Data and Graphics (1967–1992)*. Hong Kong: Census and Statistics Department.

——. 2001. Thematic Household Survey Report No. 5. August. Hong Kong: Census and Statistics Department.

Hong Kong Government (HKG). 1992. Labour Tribunal Ordinance (Cap. 25). Hong Kong: Government Printer.

Hong Kong Immigration Department. 1993a. Guidance Notes for Application for Renewal of Contract/Change of Employment by Overseas Domestic Helper in Hong Kong. Hong Kong: Immigration Department.

——. 1993b. Guidance Notes for Application for Entry to Hong Kong to Work as Domestic Helper. Hong Kong: Immigration Department.

——. 1993c. Employment Contract (for a Domestic Helper Recruited from Outside of Hong Kong). Hong Kong: Immigration Department.

——. 1993d. Explanatory Notes: Employment Contract for a Domestic Helper Recruited from Outside Hong Kong. Hong Kong: Immigration Department.

——. 2003. Employment Contract (For a Domestic Helper Recruited from Abroad). Hong Kong SAR: Immigration Department of the Government of the Hong Kong Special Administrative Region.

——. 2005. Guidebook for the Employment of Domestic Helpers from Abroad. Hong Kong SAR: Immigration Department of the Government of the Hong Kong Special Administrative Region.

Hong Kong Institute of Household Management (HKIHM). n.d. Hong Kong Institute of Household Management. Manila. Hong Kong University Foreign Domestic Helper Project Files.

Hong Kong Labour Department. 1992a. Labour and Employment in Hong Kong. July 1992.

———. 1992b. Guidance Notes on the Employment Ordinance (Cap. 57) and the Employment Contract for Foreign Domestic Helper. Hong Kong: Government Printer.

———. 1992c. A Concise Guide to the Employment Ordinance (Cap. 57). Hong Kong: Government Printer.

———. 2004. Practical Guide for Employment of Foreign Domestic Helpers—What Foreign Domestic Helpers and Their Employers Should Know. Hong Kong SAR: Labour Department.

Hongkong Standard. 1986. Hongkong's No Maid-for-Measure Answer. *HKS* 28 October.

———. 1988. Filipinas Are the Favourite Workers. *HKS* 7 February.

———. 1992a. Maids Make a Mess at Post Office. *HKS* 23 May.

———. 1992b. Filipino Area Gets Reprieve. *HKS* 18 September.

———. 1993. Maids Not a Social Problem. *HKS* 6 May.

Hong Kong Supreme Court (HK-SC). 1987. In the Supreme Court of Hong Kong: Labour Tribunal Appeal 44/87. Unpublished record.

Hong Kong Trade Development Council. 2004. Dissecting Hong Kong's Unemployment Problem. 1 February. Available at http://tpwebapp.tdctrade.com/print/print.asp?url=http://www.tdtrade.com.econforum/boc/boc040201.htm. Accessed May 5, 2006.

Horn, Pamela. 1975. *The Rise and Fall of the Victorian Servant.* New York: St. Martin's Press.

Huang, Shirlena, and Brenda S. A. Yeoh. 1996. Ties That Bind: State Policy and Migrant Female Domestic Helpers in Singapore. *Geoforum* 27(4):279–93.

Huang, Shirlena, Brenda S. A. Yeoh, and Noor Abdul Rahman, eds. 2005. *Asian Women as Transnational Domestic Workers.* Singapore: Marshall Cavendish Academic.

Hugo, Graeme. 2002. Indonesia's Labor Looks Abroad. *Migration Information Source.* Available at http://www.migrationinformation.org/Profiles/print.cfm?ID=53. Accessed June 1, 2006.

———. 2005. Indonesian International Domestic Workers: Contemporary Developments and Issues. *Asian Women as Transnational Domestic Workers*, ed. Shirlena Huang, Brenda S. A. Yeoh, and Noor Abdul Rahman, 54–91, Singapore: Marshall Cavendish Academic.

Hui, Shirley. 1986. Umelco Backs Ban on Chinese Maids. *HKS* 7 March.

Hunt, A. R. 1992. Statue Square Is for Everyone. *SCMP* 21 September.

Indonesian Migrant Workers Union. 2005. Indonesian Consulate Should Fulfill Its Responsibility as Protector of Indonesian Citizens. 15 May 2005. Available at http://www.mfasia.org/mfaStatements/Statement14–IMWU-Kothiko.html. Accessed August 20, 2006.

International Organization for Migration. 2005. *World Migration: Costs and Benefits of International Migration 2005.* Vol. 3, IOM World Migration Report Series. Geneva: International Organization for Migration.

Jacinto, Maritess. 1991. Personal Cleanliness. *TF* (September):25.

Jaschok, Maria. 1988. *Concubines and Bondservants: The Social History of a Chinese Custom.* Hong Kong: Oxford University Press.

——. 1993. "A Public Nuisance": Reflections on the Occupation of City Spaces by Filipina Domestic Helpers in Hong Kong. Paper presented at the International Conference on Africa and Asia, Hong Kong, August 24.

Jose, Lanie Mathias. 1992. Because of Love. *TF* (February):8.

Kaibigan. 1984. A Comment on Philippine Conditions. Unpublished Report, Manila.

Kaplan, Elaine. 1987. "I Don't Do No Windows": Competition between Domestic Worker and Housewife. *Competition: A Feminist Taboo?* ed. Valerie Miner and Helen E. Logino, 92–105. New York: Feminist Press.

Katarungan, Elsa. 1993. Most Maids Keep Quiet. *SCMP* 14 May.

Katzman, David. 1978. *Seven Days a Week: Women and Domestic Work in Industrializing America.* New York: Oxford University Press.

Keezhangatte, James J. 2004. Indian Household Workers in Hong Kong: Emerging Themes on Migration and Social Relationships. *E-Journal of Hong Kong Cultural and Social Studies* 3(June). Available at http://www.hku.hk/hkcsp/ccex/ehksss01/frame.htm?mid=o&smid=1&ssmid=2. Accessed August 12, 2006.

——. 2005. *Transnational Migration, Resilience, and Family Relationships: Indian Household Workers in Hong Kong.* Ph.D. diss., University of Hong Kong.

Kung, Lydia. 1983. *Factory Women in Taiwan.* Ann Arbor: University of Michigan Press.

Laguerre, Michel S. 1990. Household Workers in Urban Martinique. *At Work in Homes: Household Workers in World Perspective,* ed. Roger Sanjek and Shellee Colen, 164–75. American Ethnological Society Monograph Series 3. Washington D.C.: American Ethnological Society.

Lai, G. 1993. Letter. *SCMP* 26 July.

Lam, A. 1993. Most Overseas Helpers Inefficient. *SCMP* 23 August.

Lamphere, Louise. 1987. *From Working Daughters to Working Mothers: Immigrant Women in a New England Industrial Community.* Ithaca: Cornell University Press.

Lan, Pei-Chia. 2003. Among Women: Migrant Domestics and their Taiwanese Employers Across Generations. *Global Woman: Nannies, Maids, and Sex Workers in the New Economy,* ed. Barbara Ehrenreich and Arlie Russell Hochschild, 169–89. New York: Holt, Metropolitan Books.

——. 2005. Surrogate Family, Disposable Labour, and Stratified Others: Transnational Domestic Workers in Taiwan. *Asian Women as Transnational Domestic Workers,* ed. Shirlena Huang, Brenda S. A. Yeoh, and Noor Abdul Rahman, 210–32. Singapore: Marshall Cavendish Academic.

——. 2006. *Global Cinderellas: Migrant Domestics and Newly Rich Employers in Taiwan.* Durham: Duke University Press.

Law, Lisa. 2002. Sites of Transnational Activism: Filipino Non-government organizations in Hong Kong. *Gender Politics in the Asia-Pacific Region,* ed. Brenda S. A. Yeoh, P. Teo, and Shirlena Huang, 205–22, London: Routledge.

Layosa, Linda R. 1990a. Come to Think of It . . . *TF* (January):19.

——. 1990b. Come to Think of It . . . *TF* (April):27–30.

——. 1990c. Don't Find Fault . . . Find a Remedy. *TF* (July–August): 15.

——. 1990d. Come to Think of It . . . *TF* (November–December):33.

——. 1991a. Malasakit . . . A Vanishing Trait? *TF* (February):22–24.

——. 1991b. Maid in Hong Kong. *TF* (December):91.

——. 1992a. Can You Read Your Boss? *TF* (January):12.

Layosa, Linda, and Laura P. Luminarias, eds. 1992. *Sapang Pagyuko Kawayan: A Collection of Jokes from Filipino Overseas Workers.* Hong Kong: AsiaPacific.

Leahy, Patricia. 1990. *Female Migrant Labour in Asia—A Case Study of Filipino Domestic Workers in Hong Kong.* M.A. thesis, University of Hong Kong.

Lee, P. K. 1992. Expats Do Not Understand Practical Problems. *SCMP* 2 October.

——. 1993a. Maids Now in Airport. *SCMP* 27 January.

——. 1993b. Tax on Maids Is Workable. *SCMP* 9 February.

Legislative Council (LegCo). 2003. LegCo Panel on Manpower. Adjustment of Minimum Allowable Wage (MAW) of Foreign Domestic Helpers (FDHs). LC Paper No. CB(2)1515/02–03(01). Hong Kong.

Lim, Elizabeth. 1983. Loopholes in Domestic Deals. *SCMP* 12 January.

Loveband, Anne. 2004. Positioning the Product: Indonesian Migrant Women Workers in Contemporary Taiwan. *Journal of Contemporary Asia* 34(3):336–49.

Madamba, Vady. 1991. Discotheque and Pubhouses: Let Us Avoid Them. *TF* (December):65.

——. 1992. Provide Filipinos with a Park. *SCMP* 15 September.

——. 1993. On Friday Afternoon at the Statue Square. *Diwaliwan* 1(5):56.

Maglipon, Jo-ann Q. 1990. *The Filipino Migrant: Braving the Exile.* Hong Kong: MFMW.

Maniego, Janet. 1993. Patience Is the Key. *TF* (February):21.

Margold, Jane. 1995. Narratives of Masculinity and Transnational Migration: Filipino Workers in the Middle East. *Bewitching Women, Pious Men: Gender and Body Politics in Southeast Asia,* ed. Aihwa Ong and Michael Peletz, 274–98. Berkeley: University of California Press.

Mariano, Jocelyn. 1992. No Driver. *Sapang Pagyuko Kawayan: A Collection of Jokes from Filipino Overseas Workers,* ed. Linda R. Layosa and Laura P. Luminarias, 23. Hong Kong: AsiaPacific.

Mariano, Mila. 1991. I Am Your Job. *TF* (December):20.

"Marie '89." 1989. My Personal Experience. *TF* (December):21–24.

Marshall, Bob. 1992. More Cleansing? *SCMP* 22 September.

Martin, Emily. 1987. *The Woman in the Body: A Cultural Analysis of Reproduction.* Boston: Beacon Press.

——. 1994. *Flexible Bodies: Tracking Immunity in American Culture from the Days of Polio to the Days of AIDS.* Boston: Beacon Press.

Maza, Sarah. 1983. *The Uses of Loyalty: Domestic Service in Eighteenth-Century France.* Princeton: Princeton University Press.

McBride, Theresa. 1976. *The Domestic Revolution: The Modernization of Household-Service in Eighteenth-Century France, 1820–1920.* New York: Holmes and Meier.

McDermott, Joseph. 1981. Bondservants in the T'ai-hu Basin during the Late Ming: A Case of Mistaken Identities. *Journal of Asian Studies* 40:675–701.

McKay, Deirdre. 2003. Filipinas in Canada—De-skilling as a Push toward Marriage. *Wife or Worker? Asian Women and Migration,* ed. Nicole Piper and Mina Roces, 23–51. New York: Rowman and Littlefield.

——. 2005. Success Stories? Filipina Domestic Workers in Canada. *Asian Women as Transnational Domestic Workers,* ed. Shirlena Huang, Brenda S. A. Yeoh, and Noor Abdul Rahman, 305–38. Singapore: Marshall Cavendish Academic.

McLean, John. 1984. Marcos Urged to End Remitting Rule. *SCMP* 21 November.

Mercer, F. W. 1992. Other Meeting Places Available. *SCMP* 21 September.

Meskill, Johanna. 1979. *A Chinese Pioneer Family: The Lins of Wu-Feng, Taiwan, 1729–1895*. Princeton: Princeton University Press.

Miguel, Adoracion. 1992. How To . . . *TF* (December):24.

Mission for Filipino Migrant Workers (MFMW). 1988. A Short Survey of Filipino Domestic Helpers in Hongkong. *Kaibigan Migration Folio* 1 (December): 19–23.

——. 1988–94. Client Files.

——. 1989–91. *Tinig Mula Sa Ibayong Dagat*. Hong Kong: MFMW.

——. 1991. *Know Your Rights: A Legal Guide for Foreign Domestic Helpers*. Hong Kong: MFMW.

——. 1992–93. News Clipping Files.

——. 1993a. Report, 1 January–30 June.

——. 1993b. Report on New Clients. July.

——. 1993c. *Migrant Focus* 1(1):4.

——. 1995. POEA Memorandum Circular 41. *Migrant Focus* 2(1):1.

—— 2006. The Price (Hike) of Being a Foreign Domestic Worker. *Migrant Focus* (June). Available at http://www.migrants.org. Accessed August 15, 2006.

Mitchell, Ruth. 1981. Sick Filipina Faked Papers. *SCMP* 29 October.

Mo, Timothy. 1988. *Sour Sweet*. London: Faber and Faber.

"Mommie Jingco." 1991. Lowly Yet Fulfilling. *TF* (October):24.

Moore, Henrietta L. 1988. *Feminism and Anthropology*. Minneapolis: University of Minnesota Press.

Morgan, Joyce. 1987. Employers Are "More Likely to Break Contracts." *HKS* 28 April.

Nash, June. 1979. *We Eat the Mines and the Mines Eat Us: Dependency and Exploitation in Bolivian Tin Mines*. New York: Columbia University Press.

Newby, Howard. 1979. *The Deferential Worker*. Madison: University of Wisconsin Press.

Nicholas, Clair. 1992. The Eight Beatitudes of a Domestic Helper. *TF* (December) 24.

O'Neill, Mamie. 1993. Reports of Maid Abuse Rise Sharply. *HKS* 1 June.

Ong, Aihwa. 1987. *Spirits of Resistance and Capitalist Discipline: Factory Women in Malaysia*. New York: State University of New York Press.

——. 1991. The Gender and Labor Politics of Postmodernity. *Annual Review of Anthropology* 20:279–309.

Ong, Aihwa, and Michael Peletz, eds. 1995. *Bewitching Women, Pious Men: Gender and Body Politics in Southeast Asia*. Berkeley: University of California Press.

Ong, J. 1992. No Foreigner Can Stand above the Law. *SCMP* 15 December.

Ooi Keat Gin. 1992. The Black and White Amahs of Malaysia. *Journal of the Malaysian Branch of the Royal Asiatic Society* 65(2):69—84.

Ortner, Sherry B. 1995. Resistance and the Problem of Ethnographic Refusal. *Comparative Studies of Society and History* 34(l):173–93.

Padua, Jerome. 1991. Filipinos—Hong Kong's Evil Necessities or Environmental Nuisances? *TF* (December):65.

Palaghicon, Roselyn D. 1992. Angered by Car-Park Suggestion. *SCMP* 12 October.

Palmer, Phyllis. 1989. *Domesticity and Dirt: Housewives and Domestic Servants in the United States, 1920–1945*. Philadelphia: Temple University Press.

Palpal-Iatoc, Lou. 1995. HK Women Seek Work as Maids. *HKS* 24 July.

Parreñas, Rhacel Slazar. 2001. *Servants of Globalization: Women, Migration, and Domestic Work*. Stanford: Stanford University Press.

———. 2005. *Children of Global Migration: Transnational Migration and Gendered Woes*. Stanford: Stanford University Press.

Pascual, Clarence, and Cynthia Tellez. 1993. The Migrant Worker and the Law: Conflicts and Redress. Paper presented at the International Conference on Africa and Asia, Hong Kong, 24 August.

"Pelican." 1992. A DH for the Human Race. *TF* (July): 10.

Petersen, Carole, and Peggy Lee. 2006. Forced Labour and Debt Bondage in Hong Kong: A Study of Indonesian and Filipina Domestic Workers. Center for Comparative and Public Law, Occasional Papers, No. 16. June 2006. Available at http://www.hku.hk/ccpl/pub/occasionalpapers/index.html. Accessed August 22, 2006.

Philippine Statistical Yearbook. 1978. *Philippine Statistical Yearbook*. Manila: National Economic and Development Authority.

Piper, Nicola. 2005. Rights of Foreign Domestic Workers: Emergence of Transnational and Transregional Solidarity? *Asian and Pacific Migration Journal* 14(1–2):97–119.

Potter, Jack M. 1968. *Capitalism and the Chinese Peasant: Social and Economic Change in a Hong Kong Village*. Berkeley: University of California Press.

Powdermaker, Hortense. 1943. The Channeling of the Negro Aggression by the Cultural Process. *American Journal of Sociology* 48(6):750–58.

Power, Brian. 1988. Manila Bans Maids to HK. *HKS* 21 January.

Prakash, Gyan. 1990. *Bonded Histories: Genealogies of Labour Servitude in Colonial India*. Cambridge: Cambridge University Press.

———. 1991. Becoming a Bhuinya: Oral Traditions and Contested Domination in Eastern India. *Contesting Power: Resistance and Everyday Social Relations in South Asia*, ed. Douglas Haynes and Gyan Prakash, 145–74. Berkeley: University of California Press.

Pred, Allan. 1990. In Other Wor(l)ds: Fragmented and Integrated Observations on Gendered Languages, Gendered Spaces, and Local Transformation. *Antipode* 22(l):33–52.

Pruitt, Ida. 1979. *Old Madam Yin: A Memoir of Peking Life*. Stanford: Stanford University Press.

Pudjiastuti, Tri Nuke. 2003. The Changing Roles of NGOs in Relation to Indonesian Labour Migration. *Asian and Pacific Migration Journal* 9(4):429–57.

Quezon, Wilier B. 1991. Whichever Is Cheaper. *TF* (December):49.

Ragus, Evangeline C. 1992. Inheritor of the Glorious Past? *TF* (December):33.

Rahman, Noorashikin Abdul. 2005. Shaping the Migrant Institution: The Agency of Indonesian Domestic Workers in Singapore. *The Agency of Women in Asia*, ed. Lyn Parker, 182–216, Singapore: Marshall Cavendish Academic.

Rahman, Noor Abdul, Brenda S. A. Yeoh, and Shirlena Huang. 2005. "Dignity Overdue": Transnational Domestic Workers in Singapore. *Asian Women as Transnational Domestic Workers*, ed. Shirlena Huang, Brenda S. A. Yeoh, and Noor Abdul Rahman, 233–61, Singapore: Marshall Cavendish Academic.

Report. 1937. *Mui Tsai in Hong Kong and Malaya: Report of Commission*. Colonial Office, Colonial Report no. 125. London: HMSO (Her Majesty's Stationary Office).

Robinson, Kathryn. 2000. Gender, Islam and Nationality: Indonesian Domestic Servants in the Middle East. *Home and Hegemony: Domestic Service and Identity Politics in South and Southeast Asia*, ed. Kathleen Adams and Sara Dickey, 249–82. Ann Arbor: University of Michigan Press.

Rojas, Henry S. 1990. Filipino Labor Export: A Comprehensive Analysis. *Asian Labor: Migration from Poverty to Bondage*, app. 1:9–22. Hong Kong: Christian Conference of Asia, Urban Rural Mission.

Rollins, Judith. 1985. *Between Women: Domestics and Their Employers*. Philadelphia: Temple University Press.

——. 1990. Ideology and Servitude. *At Work in Homes: Household Workers in World Perspective*, ed. Roger Sanjek and Shellee Colen, 74–88. American Ethnological Society Monograph Series 3. Washington, D.C.: American Ethnological Society.

Romero, Mary. 1992. *Maid in the U.S.A.* New York: Routledge.

Rueda, Oly M. 1992. Some Food for Thought. *TF* (April):16.

Ruiz, Vicki. 1987. By the Day or Week: Mexican Domestic Workers in El Paso. *"Toil the Livelong Day": American Women at Work, 1780–1980*, ed. Carol Groneman and Mary Beth Norton, 269–83. Ithaca: Cornell University Press.

Salaff, Janet. 1974. Family Formation in Industrial Hong Kong: The Tension between Family and Individual Goals. Unpublished Paper.

——. 1981. Ci-li: From Domestic Servant to Government Service. *Working Daughters of Hong Kong: Filial Piety or Power in the Family*, 156–74. Cambridge: Cambridge University Press.

Salda, Elsie K. 1993. Enjoy Ma'am's Quiz. *TF* (June):48.

Salzinger, Leslie. 1991. A Maid by Any Other Name: The Transformation of "Dirty Work" by Central American Immigrants. *Ethnography Unbound: Power and Resistance in the Modern Metropolis*, ed. Michael Buraway et al., 139–60. Berkeley: University of California Press.

Sanchez, Maritess. 1993. 10 Simple Habits for Our Lives. *TF* (June):36.

Sanjek, Roger. 1990. Maid Servants and Market Women's Apprentices in Adabraka. *At Work in Homes: Household Workers in World Perspective*, ed. Roger Sanjek and Shellee Colen, 35–62. American Ethnological Society Monographs Series 3. Washington, D.C.: American Ethnological Society.

Sanjek, Roger, and Shellee Colen, eds. 1990a. *At Work in Homes: Household Workers in World Perspective*. American Ethnological Society Monographs Series 3. Washington, D.C.: American Ethnological Society.

——. 1990b. Household Workers in World Perspective. *At Work in Homes: Household Workers in World Perspective*, ed. Roger Sanjek and Shellee Colen, 189–201. American Ethnological Society Monographs Series 3. Washington, D.C.: American Ethnological Society.

Sankar, Andrea. 1978a. Female Domestic Service in Hong Kong. *Female Servants and Economic Development*, ed. Louise Tilly et al., 51–62. Michigan Occasional Papers in Women's Studies 1. Ann Arbor: University of Michigan, Women's Studies Program.

——. 1978b. *The Evolution of the Sisterhood in Traditional Chinese Society: From Village Girls' Houses to Chai Tangs in Hong Kong*. Ph.D. diss., University of Michigan.

——. 1984. Spinster Sisterhoods: Jing Yih Sifu, Spinster-Domestic-Nun. *Lives: Chinese Working Women*, ed. Mary Sheridan and J. W. Salaff, 51–70. Bloomington: Indiana University Press.

Sannad, June Lawagan. 1993. Some Disgusting Behavior. *TF* (September):5.

Saremo, Vivian E. 1993. Do You Easily Get Angry? *TF* (June):20.

Scott, James C. 1976. *The Moral Economy of the Peasant*. New Haven: Yale University Press.

——. 1985. *Weapons of the Weak: Everyday Forms of Peasant Resistance*. New Haven: Yale University Press.

——. 1990. *Domination and the Arts of Resistance: Hidden Transcripts*. New Haven: Yale University Press.

Sennett, Richard, and Jonathan Cobb. 1973. *The Hidden Injuries of Class*. New York: Vintage.

Silvestre, Susie Sapo. 1992. Optimism Is What We Need. *TF* (August):24.

Silvey, Rachel. 2006. Consuming the Transnational Family: Indonesian Migrant Domestic Workers to Saudi Arabia. *Global Networks* 6(1):23–40.

Sim, Amy. 2003. Organising Discontent: NGOs for Southeast Asian Migrant Workers in Hong Kong. *Asian Journal of Social Science* 31(3):478–510.

——. 2007. *Women in Transition: Indonesian Domestic Workers in Hong Kong*. Ph.D. diss., University of Hong Kong. Forthcoming.

Sinn, Elizabeth. 1994. Chinese Patriarchy and the Protection of Women in 19th-Century Hong Kong. *Women and Chinese Patriarchy: Submission, Servitude and Escape*, ed. Maria Jaschok and Suzanne Miers, 141–70. London: Zed Books.

Sinclair, Kevin. 1995. Case against the Filipinas. *SCMP* 12 July.

Smith, Carl T. 1982. The Chinese Church, Labour and Elites, and the Mui Tsai Question in the 1920s. *Journal of the Hong Kong Branch of the Royal Asiatic Society* 21:91–113.

Southam, Kate. 1986a. Domestic Dolls Degrade Us, Say Angry Filipinas. *SCMP* 18 May.

——. 1986b. Company Refuses to Change Dolls. *SCMP* 1 June.

South China Morning Post. 1986a. Filipino Maid Doll Insulting. *SCMP* 24 May.

——. 1986b. Home from Home in the Square. *SCMP* 6 October.

——. 1987a. Menace of the Agency Sharks. *SCMP* 26 May.

——. 1987b. Filipino Maid Loses Award over Dismissal. *SCMP* 17 October.

——. 1988. Maids Ban Cause for Concern. *SCMP* 29 January.

——. 1990. So Many Hawkers in Statue Square. *SCMP* 6 June.

——. 2001. Road to Justice. *SCMP* 21 July.

——. 2006. Streets Apart: Pride and Protest. *Sunday Morning Post* 2 July.

Star. 1979. Govt. Gets Tough on Filipina Maids. *Star* 18 September.

Stockard, Janice. 1989. *Daughters of the Canton Delta: Marriage Patterns and Economic Strategies in South China, 1860–1930*. Stanford: Stanford University Press.

Sutherland, David. 1981. *Americans and Their Servants from 1820 to 1920*. Baton Rouge: Louisiana State University Press.

Tagoylo, Julieta. 1991. Don'ts When Working Abroad. *TF* (August):12.

Tam, Bonny. 1992. Sunday Lure Proposed for Filipinas. *SCMP* 29 July.

Taussig, Michael. 1980. *The Devil and Commodity Fetishism in South America*. Chapel Hill: University of North Carolina Press.

Tellez, Eliseo, Jr. 1991. An Overview of Filipino Migrant Workers in Hong Kong. *Serving One Another: Report of the Consultation on the Mission and Ministry to Filipino Migrant Workers in Hong Kong*, app. 9:75–83. Hong Kong: Christian Conference of Asia, Urban Rural Mission.

Tenorio, Melba P. 1993. Persistence Is a Must. *TF* (April):20.

Thompson, E. P. 1963. *The Making of the English Working Class*. New York: Pantheon.

———. 1967. Time, Work-Discipline, and Industrial Capitalism. *Past and Present* 38: 56–97.

Tong, Simon. 1992. Complaints Heeded. *SCMP* 5 November.

Topley, Marjorie. 1975. Marriage Resistance in Kwangtung. *Women in Chinese Society*, ed. Margery Wolf and Roxane Witke, 67–88. Stanford: Stanford University Press.

Torrefranca, Sheila D. 1992. Criticisms Are Not That Bad. *TF* (July):28.

Trager, Lilian. 1984. Family Strategies and the Migration of Women: Migrants to Dagupan City, Philippines. *International Migration Review* 18(4): 1264–77.

Tucker, Susan. 1989. *Telling Memories among Southern Women: Domestic Workers and Their Employers in the Segregated South*. Baton Rouge: Louisiana State University Press.

Tyner, James. 1999. The Web-based Recruitment of Female Foreign Domestic Workers in Asia. *Singapore Journal of Tropical Geography* 20(2):193–209.

Tyrell, Paul. 1992. "Battle of Chater Road" Heats Up. *SCMP* 21 September.

United Filipinos in Hong Kong (UNIFIL). 1991. First Congress, UNIFIL-HK: Achieving Greater Unity for Overseas Filipinos, February. Hong Kong: UNIFIL.

———. 2007. Filipino OFWs in Hongkong Protest the New POEA Guidelines in Huge Rally. Press Release. January 28, 2007. Available at http://www.arkibongbayan.org/2007-01Jan28-Hkprotest/Hkjan28protest.htm. Accessed February 22, 2007.

United Nations Economic and Social Council (Commission on Human Rights). 2003. Specific Groups and Individuals: Migrant Workers. Available at http://www.unhchr.ch/Huridocda/Huridoca.nsf/(Symbol)/E.CN.4.2003.NGO.138.En?Opendocument. Accessed August 22, 2006.

"Vicky." 1992. Cook Yourself. *TF* (July):48.

Vincente, Marietta. 1991a. Statue Square University (part 1). *TF* (August):30.

———. 1991b. Statue Square University (part 2). *TF* (September): 10.

Von der Borch, Rosslyn. 2006. *Under One Roof: Migrant Domestic Workers and Expatriate Employers in Singapore*. Ph.D. diss.. Flinders University, Australia.

Wallis, Belinda. 1992a. Call for Campaign to Warn Maids. *SCMP* 4 June.

———. 1992b. Off-Duty Maids Spark Bid to Open Chater Road. *SCMP* 10 September.

———. 1992c. Proposal to Move Helpers to Car Park "Inhuman." *SCMP* 17 September.

———. 1992d. Maids Leave Six Tonnes of Litter. *SCMP* 18 September.

Wan, Mariana. 1992. HK Land under Fire for "Racist" Report. *SCMP* 13 September.

Watson, James L. 1975. *Emigration and the Chinese Lineage: The Mans in Hong Kong and London*. Berkeley: University of California Press.

———. 1976. Chattel Slavery in Chinese Peasant Society: A Comparative Analysis. *Ethnology* 15:361–75.

———. 1980a. Slavery as an Institution: Open and Closed Systems. *Asian and African Systems of Slavery*, ed. James L. Watson, 1–15. Oxford: Basil Blackwell.

——. 1980b. Transactions in People: The Chinese Market in Slaves, Servants, and Heirs. *Asian and African Systems of Slavery*, ed. James L. Watson, 223–50. Oxford: Basil Blackwell.

——. 1983. Rural Society: Hong Kong's New Territories. *China Quarterly* 95:480–90.

——. 1987. From the Common Pot: Feasting with Equals in Chinese Society. *Anthropos* 82:389–401.

Watson, Rubie S. 1985. *Inequality among Brothers: Class and Kinship in South China*. Cambridge: Cambridge University Press.

——. 1986. The Named and the Nameless: Gender and Person in Chinese Society. *American Ethnologist* 13:619–31.

—— 1991. Wives, Concubines, and Maids: Servitude and Kinship in the Hong Kong Region, 1900–1940. *Marriage and Inequality in Chinese Society*, ed. Rubie Watson and Patricia Buckley Ebrey, 231–55. Berkeley: University of California Press.

——. 1994. *Memory, History, and Opposition under State Socialism*. Santa Fe: School of American Research Press.

Wee, Vivienne, and Amy Sim. 2004. Transnational Labour Networks in Female Labour Migration: Mediating between Southeast Asian Women Workers and International Labour Markets. Working Paper Series No. 49. Hong Kong: Southeast Asia Research Centre, City University of Hong Kong.

——. 2005. Hong Kong as a Destination for Migrant Domestic Workers. *Asian Women as Transnational Domestic Workers*, ed. Shirlena Huang, Brenda S. A. Yeoh, and Noor Abdul Rahman, 175–209. Singapore: Marshall Cavendish Academic.

Williams, Hope Ng. 2002. Making It in Hong Kong. *Newsbreak* 13 May. Available at http://www.inq7.net/newsbrk/2002/may/13/nbk_7–1.htm. Accessed August 15, 2006.

Williams, Louise, and Brian Power. 1988. No Pact, No Maids. *HKS* 22 January.

Wing Suen. 1993. Market Procured Housework: The Demand for Domestic Servants and Female Labor Supply. Discussion Paper 144. School of Economics, University of Hong Kong.

Wolf, Eric. 1969. *Peasant Wars of the Twentieth Century*. New York: Harper and Row.

Wolf, Margery. 1968. *The House of Lim: A Study of a Chinese Farm Family*. Englewood Cliffs, N.J.: Prentice Hall.

——. 1972. *Women and the Family in Rural Taiwan*. Stanford: Stanford University Press.

Wong, Raymond. 1985. Charge Levy on All Filipina Contracts. *SCMP* 11 June.

Yamanaka, Keiko, and Nicola Piper. 2005. Feminized Migration in East and Southeast Asia: Policies, Actions and Empowerment. Occasional Paper 11. Geneva, Switzerland: United Nations Research Institute for Social Development.

Yeoh, Brenda S. A., and Shirlena Huang. 1998. Negotiating Public Space: Strategies and Styles of Migrant Female Domestic Workers in Singapore. *Urban Studies* 35(3):583–602.

——. 1999. Spaces at the Margins: Migrant Domestic Workers and the Development of Civil Society in Singapore. *Environment and Planning* 31(7):1149–67.

——. 2000. Home and Away: Foreign Domestic Workers and Negotiations of Diasporic Identity in Singapore. *Women's Studies International Forum* 23(4):413–29.

Yeung, Arthur Tso. 1992. Ridiculous Arrangement. *SCMP* 16 September.

Yeung, Ursula. 1991. Make Filipino Maids Pay for Amenities Idea. *HKS* 18 June.

Yuen, Mary C. Y. 1993. Letter. *SCMP* 23 July.

INDEX